At Home and Abroad in the Empire

At Home and Abroad in the Empire

British Women Write the 1930s

Edited by
Robin Hackett, Freda Hauser,
and Gay Wachman

DELAWARE
Newark: University of Delaware Press

Associated University Presses
2010 Eastpark Boulevard
Cranbury, NJ 08512

The paper used in this publication meets the requirements of the American National Standard for Permanence of Paper for Printed Library Materials
Z39.48-1984.

Library of Congress Cataloging-in-Publication Data

At home and abroad in the empire : British women write the 1930s / edited by Robin Hackett, Freda Hauser, and Gay Wachman.
p. cm.
Includes bibliographical references and index.
ISBN 978-0-87413-041-6 (alk. paper)
1. English literature—Women authors—History and criticism. 2. Women authors, English—20th century—Political and social views. 3. Imperialism in literature. 4. Race in literature. 5. War in literature. 6. Women and literature—Great Britian—History—20th century. 7. Politics and literature—Great Britian—History—20th century. 8. Great Britain—Social life and customs—1918–1945. 9. Nineteen thirties. 10. Modernism (Literature)—Great Britain. I. Hackett, Robin, 1963- II. Hauser, Freda, 1955- III. Wachman, Gay, 1943-

PR116.A82 2009
810.9'9287—dc22

2008024043

PRINTED IN THE UNITED STATES OF AMERICA

In memory of Lilian Robinson and Julia Briggs.

This collection represents the multi-generational endurance of feminism, which Lillian Robinson and Julia Briggs worked to advance throughout their lives and careers.

Contents

Acknowledgments

ON SEPTEMBER 15, 2000, CONFERENCE-GOERS FROM ALL OVER ENGLAND and the United States came to The Graduate School and University Center of the City University of New York for one day of sessions and conversation at "Inroads and Outposts: At Home and Abroad in the Empire, British Women in the Thirties," a feminist conference organized by Jane Marcus. That conference, one manifestation of Marcus's visionary work on British literature of the 1930s, inspired all the contributions to this volume. We thank Jane for this conference and the inspiration it provided, for the groundbreaking feminist literary criticism she has written over the course of her career, and for her kind, generous, and infinitely helpful mentoring. In addition, we thank the many individuals, departments, and organizations at The Graduate School and University Center of the City University of New York whose combined efforts enabled us to hold the conference. We thank President Frances Degen Horowitz, who supported the conference, as she supported feminist faculty, feminist students, and the Women's Studies program at CUNY during her tenure as president of the university. Also for their generous sponsorship of Inroads and Outposts: At Home and Abroad in the Empire, British Women in the Thirties, we thank the entire English Department and in particular Linda Sherwin and Joan Richardson, as well as Jill Dolan and The Center for Lesbian and Gay Studies. Special thanks go to Elizabeth Small, Patricia Clough, and the Women's Studies program for their support, and in particular for providing us with lunch and thus an extraordinary opportunity for an informal exchange of ideas among feminist literary and historical scholars at all stages of their careers. Special thanks go, too, to our most generous supporters, James de Jongh and Gloria Thomas at the Institute for Research on the African Diaspora in the Americas and the Caribbean-IRADAC-at The City College of New York.

Still more people and organizations contributed to this project as it developed as a collection. At the University of New Hampshire, Dean Marilyn Hoskin, and Jennifer Beard and Burt Feintuck at the Center for the

Humanities, provided material support for the editing of this collection. We would also like to thank our colleagues at the City College of New York, the State University of New York, Old Westbury, and the University of New Hampshire for their encouragement and for providing collegial places in which to work. Gratitude and thanks go to "cosoeurs," as Lillian Robinson calls her feminist and socialist colleagues in her essay in this volume, who generously contributed good humor, delicious pastries, and feedback on portions of this manuscript: Monica Chiu, Siobhan Senier, Eve Raimon, Lisa Botshon, Melinda Plastas, Alex Cornelius Diallo, and Rebecca Herzig. Thank you, too, to Tara Wade who took wonderful care of two toddlers Ruby and Dillen, allowing Robin to work on this volume. We also gratefully acknowledge Edinburgh University Press, who gave us permission to reprint Julia Briggs's essay " 'Almost Ashamed of England being so English': Woolf and Ideas of Englishness," which originally appeared in Briggs's *Reading Virginia Woolf* (Edinburgh University Press, 2006).

Finally, our heartfelt appreciation goes to the scholars who traveled to New York from far and near to share their work at Inroads and Outposts: At Home and Abroad in the Empire, British Women in the Thirties. Thank you, the editors: Robin Hackett, Freda Hauser, and Gay Wachman.

At Home and Abroad in the Empire

Introduction: Making the Private Public: Women Writers, Modernism, Empire, and War

ROBIN HACKETT AND GAY WACHMAN

THE LIVES AND WRITING OF WOMEN IN ENGLAND IN THE THIRTIES reflect the tremendous political upheavals of that decade: the approach and beginning of war; the tensions of the depression and appeasement years; the conflicts between Communism and Fascism in Spain and at home; the growing evidence of British anti-Semitism. Many women in the interwar period actively supported imperial ambitions, notwithstanding Virginia Woolf's often-cited assertion in *A Room of One's Own* that British women, by virtue of their lack of political power at home, bear no responsibility for the furtherance of empire (Woolf 1929, 112).[1] Many other British women in the interwar period also reflect in their writing English ambivalence about empire in the context of anti-imperialist unrest abroad. This engagement with difficult political questions is evident in the work of middlebrow writers such as Agatha Christie as well as high modernists such as Virginia Woolf. It is similarly evident in the work of activists such as Nancy Cunard and Sylvia Townsend Warner, and in the writing of the purported dilettante Edith Sitwell.

The degree to which women writers involved themselves with these political questions becomes increasingly apparent as literary critics support their claims for richer, more inclusive categories of "war literature" and "the literature of empire." Feminist social scientists such as Cynthia Enloe have shown the ways in which war and militarism shape the lives of women who are far from the front lines as well as those on the battle front (Enloe 2000). Literary scholars use parallel insights to argue that narratives about nursing, fatherless babies, or wrapping packages for soldiers, are all productively classed "war literature."[2] Similarly, literary scholars have built upon Edward Said's notion of the "cultural integrity of empire" to understand imperialism as a shaping force in literary works that seem remote from imperial concerns as well as those with more obviously imperial settings or themes.[3] The essays collected in *At Home and Abroad in the Empire: British Women Write the 1930s* focus on a set of aesthetically diverse 1930s texts by women writers and intellectuals with diverse politics and social positions. We discuss these works with attention to the ways in which they are involved with questions about war, empire, or imperial ideology, and we suggest that these are just a small portion of the works that might profitably be analyzed with such a focus. We hope that our explorations of British writing about empire in the 1930s will enrich current public debates about war, empire, patriotism, and dissent, and thus resonate with significance for readers in the early twenty-first century, a period in which war and empire, as well as terror and security, are part of the discourse of our everyday lives.

Current assessments of British literature of the thirties take place in several overlapping literary critical contexts. For twenty years, critics have written against the persistent myth that the decade was a literary failure in which polemics trumped artistry. Samuel Hynes created this orthodoxy about 1930s literary England when he characterized it as the "Auden generation." Hynes suggests that the literary efforts of Auden and his school friends—too young to have fought in World War I, but traumatized by the loss of fathers and brothers in that conflict—were largely failures because of their commitments to Left politics (1972). Hynes's characterization gathered authority from end-of-decade testimony by some 1930s writers themselves. Auden, for instance, describes the decade as "low and dishonest" in "September 1, 1939," a poem that some still consider "the decade's best epitaph" (Croft 1990, 16).

The myth of the thirties as a literary failure endures even against what has become a mass of critical work that exposes the aesthetic complexities of the writing and the diverse political interests of those working in the period. Valentine Cunningham began this revaluation with *British Writers of the Thirties* (1989), wrapping into his analysis an assertion that the separation between text and social contexts, which underlies Hynes's assessment, hobbles literary studies. Instead, he argues, texts and social contexts "collaps[e] purposefully into one another" (1). Many critics build on Cunningham's effort to revitalize thirties studies. Andy Croft (1990), Adrian Caesar (1991), and John Gindin (1992) discuss authors who were not in Auden's circle, including women and working-class writers. Keith Williams (1999, Williams and Matthews, 1997), Diana Wallace (1999), and Gillian Beer (1999), as well as Gindin, complicate the notion of the thirties as "the Auden generation" with their focus on prose instead of poetry. Essays in Anthony Shuttleworth's *And in our Time: Vision, Revision, and British Writing of the 1930s* (2003) emphasize the theoretical complexities that develop when thirties writers confront questions about politics, aesthetics, and instrumentality. Still other critics, such as Tony Davies (1984), Maroula Joannou (1999), and Elizabeth Maslen (1999), approach the negative valuation of thirties writing by discussing the formal qualities of realism, exposing its variety and its plasticity in the hands of various authors working out ways to convey commitment to ideas (Maslen 1999, 139). As Maroula Joannou puts it, the thirties are distinguished by a "well-chronicled shift to the left on the part of many British writers." But "modernism was not monolithic and was shaped differently in the hands of diverse men and women, and this is also true of Realism, which manifested itself in diverse ways and reflected diverse agendas" (1999, 3, 6).

Many critics of thirties literature focus on the distinctions of writing by women. Andy Croft (1990) and John Gindin (1992) include discussions of women writers in their early efforts to reevaluate British literature of the thirties, thus correcting the nearly exclusive focus on male writers that characterizes Hynes's and Cunningham's work. Studies by Jane Marcus (1987), Allison Light (1991), Maroula Joannou (1995), and Jane Dowson (1996) explore questions of gender, domestic themes and issues, and internal British politics in fiction and poetry by women. Marianne DeKoven (1991), Lisa Rado (1994), Rita Felski (1995), Janet Montefiore (1996), Erin Carlston (1998), Merry Pawlowski (2001), Phyllis Lassner (2003), and Jane Garrity (2003) elaborate the ways in which British women also wrote as public intellectuals about a broad array of the domestic and international political questions of their era. Ironically, once critics of thirties writing began to make headway against the notion that involvement in politics did not make literature a failure, critics of women's writing have had to "address the lingering misconception that women's poetry is of little significance in the field of thirties poetry because it is not political" (Dowson 1999, 46–47).

These efforts to resuscitate critical interest in thirties writing by women and men are wholly consistent with, but not always explicitly connected to, a broader effort to disrupt the tendency in Anglo-American modernist studies to define modernism by the formal experiments and aesthetics of the 1920s, and against the sociopolitical concerns more obviously a shaping force in the literature of the 1930s. Over the last twenty years, accounts of literary modernism have changed dramatically as a result of scholarship that fractures the notion of a monolithic modernism in favor of many modernisms with diverse aesthetics and grounded in divergent histories.[4] Houston Baker was among the first scholars to shift the boundaries of modernist studies with his 1987 *Modernism and the Harlem Renaissance.* Baker countered negative assessments of Harlem Renaissance literature as antimodern, and argued, instead, that Booker T. Washington's 1895 address at the International Exposition, and W. E. B DuBois's 1903 *The Souls of Black Folk* initiated an African-American modernism characterized by discursive maneuvers Baker calls "the mastery of form" and "the deformation of mastery" (1987, 15). Baker's work changed the content of the modernist canon, drawing in the works of many African-American writers. More significantly for this collection, though his work focused specifically on American writers, Baker initiated change that shifted the boundaries of the modernist canon more broadly by bringing attention to the distorting effect of historical accounts of modernism. "The very *histories*," he writes "that are assumed in the chronologies of British, Anglo-American, and Irish modernisms are radically opposed to any adequate and accurate account of the history of Afro American modernism" (1987, xvi). If conventional accounts of Anglo-American literary modernism are narrated largely in terms of the Great War, Baker argued that Washington's speech ushered in modernity for "a mass of black citizens who had struggled through the thirty years since emancipation buffeted on all sides by strategies, plans, hopes, and movements . . . without before 1895 having found an overriding pattern of *national* leadership or an approved plan of action that could guarantee at least the industrial education of a considerable sector of the black populace" (1987, 15). Baker's attention to history, and to the impact of historical accounts on our understanding of literary modernism, loosened modernism from its moorings in a way that has been continuously productive for modernist scholars with a broad range theoretical, national, and specific literary interests, including scholars whose primary focus is on 1930s writing by women.

Critics who use the phrase "late modernism" reflect both the shifting ground of Modernist studies and the ways in which critics of thirties literature are making modest headway against the commonplace of a failed decade. Tyrus Miller, in *Late Modernism: Politics, Fiction, and the Arts between the World Wars,* grounds his analyses of late modernist texts in social contexts of depression, geopolitical crisis, and collectivism (1999). He argues that late modernism is transitional and particular in ways not acknowledged by critics: it is a paradoxical mixture of backward-looking fatigue in the face of the "imperative to innovate" (1999, 209) and forward-looking anticipation of postmodern "reemergence of innovative writing after modernism" (1999, 7). Miller also takes as a given Cunningham's insistence that aesthetic qualities are inextricably linked to social and political contexts and thus represent progress against the commonplace of the decade as a failure because of its polemics. Jed Esty also uses the phrase "late Modernism" in his account of the relationship between declining British imperial power and English literature from 1930 to 1960 (2004). Esty argues that texts of the thirties represent imperial contraction in the form of an "anthropolitical turn" (2004, 2). If high modernists of the twenties produced primitivist art by looking outward with a sense of both vacant and, paradoxically, universal British culture, late modernists look inward as the empire contracts, particularizing English culture. Miller's and Esty's excellent books mark the ways in which studies of thirties literature and of modernism have recently been productively linked. However, Miller and Esty focus primarily on the thirties writing of some of the most celebrated high modernists—James Joyce, Virginia Woolf, T. S. Eliot—who were still writing and innovating in the thirties. Indeed, Esty argues that the anthropolitical turn he describes late modernists making is specific to those writers who were previously involved in high modernist formal experimentation: their "anthropological turn" is an "attempt to manage the transition between imperial universalism and national particularism." By contrast, "the minor-chord lament" of the generation known as thirties writers "stems in part from not having come of age artistically during the days of imperial centrality" (2004, 8). Thus Miller and Esty point to exceptions to the negative evaluation of the bulk of thirties literature without substantially dislodging the myth of thirties writing as formally (and monotonously) realist, politically committed, and dulled by the concerns of the period. Moreover, despite insights by Miller and Esty, among others, about the politics of high modernism, the myth of the failed thirties continues to shore up an equally narrow, if enthusiastic, myth of modernism as exclusively word centered, formally experimental, high art. Valentine Cunningham describes this pair of myths as a "traditional knee-jerk division between Modernism and the Thirties" (1997, 5). This myth, Jean Radford adds, "can be sustained only by caricatures of both (1999, 33). Cunningham and Joannou call for literary critical work that is specific and nuanced enough to replace these caricatures. In her introduction to *Women Writers of the 1930s: Gender, Politics and History*, Joannou writes that "it is with an understanding of how specific texts by women have constructed, mediated and represented aesthetic and other priorities and articulated various kinds of dissent in particular historical circumstances—not preconceived ideas about the inherent virtues of particular modes of writing—that we can begin to stake out a more flexible and accommodating understanding of both modernism and realism in the 30s" (1999, 6).

At Home and Abroad in the Empire builds on these critical reevaluations. Individual essays use gender, race, and empire as theoretical lenses through which to revise ideas about modernism in Great Britain. In addition, they offer detailed, specific explorations of ways in which politically active British women in the 1930s narrativize empire and war. Taken together, the essays urge readers to make more rather than less of discourses of race and empire in the 1930s. We take it as a given that in the 1930s, it is essential to emphasize the strong political commitments among writers whose work we hope to understand. In the 1930s, many writers thought their jobs as artists and intellectuals were no less than to change the world, and they wrote to meet the challenges they embraced. Writers and artists involved themselves intellectually and materially with the stark contrasts between poverty and privilege, with racism, fascism, and anti-Semitism at home, and with international struggles including the Spanish Civil War, the defense of Ethiopia against Italian invasion, and the Scottsboro trials in the United States. The essays in this collection trace the interweave of politics and aesthetics in individual texts of the 1930s, with attention to the heterogeneity of literature and ideologies of that decade. We do so with the expectation that such work simultaneously counters the myth of the failed thirties, expands critical views of modernism in general, and broadens critical understanding of the diversity of women writers' styles of engagement with aesthetic and political issues.

We wish to draw particular attention to the ways in which a sharp focus on questions of empire enhances understandings of British writing by women in the thirties. Edward Said initiated, with *Orientalism* (1979), the movement among literary scholars to consider British imperial history in accounts of modernism. This trend in literary scholarship gained momentum in the 1990s with Said's *Culture and Imperialism* (1994), Karen Lawrence's collection *Decolonizing Tradition: New Views of Twentieth Century "British" Literary Canon* (1992), and Kathy Phillips's *Virginia Woolf against Empire* (1994). Nigel Rigby notes that even before he and Howard Booth edited *Modernism and Empire* "the conceit of a modernism untouched by empire had begun to look increasingly unconvincing" (2000, 225). Booth and Rigby credit Jane Marcus and her work on

Virginia Woolf's novel *The Waves* for making it clear "that empire was simply a part of life in between-the-wars Britain, whatever one's social class, habits or politics, and that all writers were inevitably exposed to the wide range of imperial narrative being produced at the time" (2000, 225). In *Stepdaughters of England: British Women Modernists and the National Imaginary*, Jane Garrity erodes remaining critical reluctance to consider questions of empire in studies of modernism by addressing the "misperception that British imperial dominance had ended by 1914" (2003, 13). She writes that "territorial expansionism did not come to a halt with the Edwardian era: indeed, at its zenith in the 1920s, the British empire held territorial possessions . . . on all five continents, covering about one-quarter of the globe and comprising a population of some 400 million individuals" (2003, 14). British women of the interwar period are, thus, "inheritors of the legacy of colonial Englishness at a moment of transition: prior to the onset of decolonization but long after the apogee of imperial strength" (2003, 3). Moreover, interwar English literary discourse about empire warrants particular attention. As Janet Montefiore puts it in *Men and Women Writers of the 1930s: The Dangerous Flood of History*, "Great Britain's status as an imperialist world power mean[s] that its citizens' political commitments and debates in these years were never just storms in literary teacups" (1996, 6). Recent scholarship suggests tentative critical acceptance of the idea that questions of empire are profoundly important to scholarship in modernism and in the 1930s. Jed Esty's work on the anthropological turn in late modernism, for example, is built upon the assumption that the thirties is a period in which imperial strains and themes, whether or not they are explicit, are important.

The ways in which women writers, in particular, "identify with, repudiate and interrogate the legacy of empire," as Garrity puts it (2003, 13), are especially relevant because British interwar debates about empire were simultaneously debates about women, their sexual and marital behaviors in particular. Middle-class and white British women were burdened with the responsibility of preserving the strength, including the imperial strength, of England and the purity of Englishness as a race. For this reason, in the interwar period, spinsters were suspect; the behaviors of women deemed racially unfit were subject to increased regulation; and lesbianism was newly pathologized.[5] One manifestation of this inheritance, Garrity argues, is that experimental writing by women in the interwar period "bears directly on the question of national affiliation" and on those writers' efforts to negotiate such affiliation (2003, 5). For Garrity, this means that in experimental writing by Virginia Woolf and Sylvia Townsend Warner, among others, references to empire are thick with meanings and sentiment, often contradictory, about both national and international politics.

Following scholars who have focused simultaneously on questions of gender, empire, and modernism, we focus *At Home and Abroad in the Empire* on the ways in which British women writers of the 1930s manifest their inheritance of colonial Englishness. We argue that imperial discourse is as significant in work that is overtly about empire as in work that is not overtly about empire. The essays emphasize, in order to fully explore the significance of, discourses of race and empire in 1930s texts; they direct attention to the complications and ambivalence accumulating around the several meanings of Englishness; and they highlight the ways in which texts are shaped by their authors' public intellectual involvement rather than the ways in which those same texts might also be understood to chronicle personal psychological development. The essays discuss a diverse group of texts that might appear to have very little in common with one another; nevertheless, juxtaposed, these texts make it clear that a large selection of British women's literature of the 1930s is politically activist about questions of empire and war on a scale and in ways heretofore unacknowledged.

The essays that follow, with two exceptions, were originally presented at "Inroads and Outposts: At Home and Abroad in the Empire, British Women in the Thirties," a feminist conference held at the City University of New York, September 15, 2000, almost exactly one year before Mohammed Atta and collaborators flew airplanes into New York's world trade center and the pentagon. In 2000, our conference was motivated in part by debates about the survival of the public intellectual. In organizing the conference, we posed the questions "who was a British woman in the 1930s? What were her political concerns and how did she address them?" Post–September 11, 2001, in a political context in which dissent is often and powerfully equated with a dangerous lack of patriotism, we are even more committed to discussing the histories and accomplishments of outspoken public intellectuals and the communities in which they flourished. Also, in the context of the wars in oil-rich Iraq and Afghanistan, we are committed to examining the workings of empire, and to developing insight into the ways in which imperial matters can infuse conversations and literature that might seem to have very little to do with empire.

In this collection, essays by Phyllis Lassner, Linda Camarasana, and Freda Hauser illustrate the significance of seemingly casual choices about setting or references to world events. Agatha Christie's colonial mysteries, for instance, reference archaeology and foreignness in ways that constitute a substantial political commentary. Christie's readers, like her characters, are encouraged to follow Poirot's lead in looking for psychological motivations for murders. Such readings are satisfying, Lassner argues, but Christie's use of an outsider—Poirot—as investigator, her archaeological metaphors, and her regular citations of past events indicate that psychologizing may itself be a clue planted to distract readers from the real concerns of the novels: British insularism, imperial overconfidence, and reliance on orientalized stereotypes to shore up false dichotomies between a British self and a foreign other. If Christie's novels seem to assure readers that the murderer will always be captured, Lassner shows, they also suggest that such narrative assurances may compromise efforts to identify real, domestic villainy.

Similarly, settings in Jean Rhys's *Good Morning, Midnight* and Sylvia Townsend Warner's novella "The Salutation" are central to the anti-imperialism expressed in the fiction. Using illustrations of the 1937 World's Fair in Paris, Linda Camarasana shows that exhibits set up by European nations were designed to construct modern national identities predicated on the erasure of the specific histories of colonies and colonized people. Colonial exhibits perched on the outskirts of the fairgrounds are physical iterations of narrative efforts to erase colonial pasts from the European present. Rhys sets *Good Morning, Midnight* in the Paris of the World's Fair, Camarasana argues, to speak back to this effort to forget; to illustrate the unavoidable presence of a political and personal past. Sylvia Townsend Warner's choice of Argentina as a setting for her novella "The Salutation" is equally important to her narrative, though it is easy to dismiss the significance of the setting since Warner never visited South America. Nor was she ever in the South Pacific, the setting of the best-selling novel *Mr. Fortune's Maggot* in which the character, Mr. Fortune, first appears. In both places, Warner's English Mr. Fortune experiences self-revelation. This, Hauser reminds us, is an act of literary tourism whereby exoticized geography is coined as intellectual capital. On the other hand, setting her second story in Argentina allows Warner to explore imperialism's complicated and multinational history. Warner brings British imperialism, Spanish colonialism, church, state, and sugar—wealth produced by captive Africans—together into one scene to emphasize their collusion in capture, mutilation, and forced labor. Written in 1930, Hauser shows, "The Salutation" reveals not so much a picture of the 1930s as it does one woman's politicized thought as the 1930s began.

Essays by Julia Briggs, Claire Tylee, Geneviève Brassard, and Marianne Guénot-Hovnanian reveal the ways in which authors' political commitments show in the formal and linguistic qualities of their writing. In "'Almost Ashamed of England being so English': Woolf and Ideas of Englishness," Julia Briggs maintains that already in the nineteen-twenties and thirties, Virginia Woolf was aware that the "enchanted landscape recorded in a literary tradition" and, above all, in Shakespeare had been used as propaganda to inspire young men to enlist in the First World War by fostering an illusion of social harmony that had never existed. Briggs demonstrates Woolf's ambivalence about English landscape, literature, and history as reflected in two 1919 essays: her scathing satire of "the mood of national self-congratulation" in her review of the paintings on view at the Royal Academy's Summer Exhibition, and her lyrical meditation, unpublished during her lifetime, "Reading." Briggs's essay culminates in an analysis of *Between the Acts*, with its scenic old house and its pageant that simultaneously mocks and reproduces England's favorite narratives of itself.

Claire Tylee's essay about *Farewell Leicester Square* argues that Betty Miller manipulates conventions of both the *bildungsroman*, which frequently portrays a young man's conflict with society, and the Women's Novel, which foregrounds romance and/or domestic life, in order to critique British anti-Semitism during the 1930s. The novel follows Alec Berman, the protagonist, as he escapes from his petit-bourgeois Jewish family into the British film industry, where he becomes a successful director and marries a cultivated, upper middle-class, non-Jewish woman, Catherine Nicolls. But, Tylee shows, the domestic elements of the novel are as significant as the chronicle of Berman's development. Catherine's point of view dominates three of the novel's chapters. Moreover, Alec finally rejects the "cool, gracious, regulated emptiness of English bourgeois culture" and returns to his shop-keeping family and his self-denying, hardworking, and constantly loving mother. Tylee emphasizes as "racisms" both the "polite" British anti-Semitism that Alec fights within his marriage and that eventually causes his loss of both wife and son and the combination of Anglophilia and self-hatred (or, in Tylee's word, "Judaeophobia") that underlies both his ambition and his marriage.

Marianne Guénot and Geneviève Brassard provocatively extend a critical focus on imperial ideology to the study of translation in general, and to French translations of Virginia Woolf's 1931 novel, *The Waves*, in particular. The practices of translation, Guénot and Brassard show, reflect a society's understanding of the relationship between self and other: translations reveal how much of the foreign other the occidental self can take in, and what part the other plays in the constitution of an occidental subject. If, Guénot and Brassard suggest, a translation is to be a metaphor of the original, it must do what the text does. Marguerite Yourcenar's 1937 translation of Woolf's novel does not follow this mandate. Instead, the translation participates in the logic of imperialism on the level of syntax, reinscribing order and linearity into Woolf's text, thus reversing the politics of the original. Guénot and Brassard's argument builds on several decades of scholarship by Jane Marcus, who shows that Woolf was a public intellectual whose 1930s fiction is actively anti-imperialist and antifascist as well as feminist. The anti-imperialism of Woolf's novel, Guénot and Brassard show, finds expression not only in direct references to India, for instance, but also in her struggle as a novelist against narrative order and a reliance on visual plausibility. Yourcenar's translation, however, undercuts the anti-imperialist argument of Woolf's novel.

Essays about Nancy Cunard, Sylvia Pankhurst, and Rebecca West emphasize the self-consciousness with which these three writer/activists developed public and political selves in relation to questions of empire and race. Cunard's 1931 pamphlet *Black Man and White Ladyship* is part tirade against her mother, the prominent society host Lady Emerald Cunard, and part polemic against the racism of her mother's society. In "Nancy Cunard's *Black Man and White Ladyship* as Surrealist Tract," Tory Young confirms Cunard's significance as both political agitator in Britain and agent of the surrealist movement. The subjects of the pamphlet are hypocrisy among her mother's society friends—their attention to petty social taboos but willful ignorance of profound injustices—juxtaposed with accounts of the slave trade and lynching in America. But the manner in which these subjects are presented, Young shows, is surrealist. In the context of surrealism, Cunard's attack on her mother's values can be read as symbolic as well as personal, indicating the first step toward the destruction of social conventions surrealists hoped to achieve. Young's account of Cunard's pamphlet adjusts popular and reductive receptions of Cunard as outrageous personality of the 1920s and encourages an understanding of her work as fully involved in both aesthetic and political movements of the 1930s.

Similarly, Barbara Winslow writes to correct depictions of Sylvia Pankhurst's activism as primarily an emotional and generalized support for so-called underdogs. Instead, in "The First White Rastafarian: Sylvia Pankhurst, Haile Selassie, and Ethiopia," Winslow chronicles Pankhurst's intellectual and material involvement in struggles for women's suffrage,

Irish independence, international communism, and, as she described it herself, her most important antifascist campaign, the defense of Ethiopia. Winslow concedes that Pankhurst's loyalty to emperor Haile Selassie contradicts her lifelong commitment to socialist principles. But, Winslow argues, this loyalty also lent her credibility which enhanced her effectiveness in working for the cause of Ethiopian independence. In so arguing, Winslow affirms the antifascist political priorities in Pankhurst's work for women, the Irish, African-Americans, and Ethiopians.

Bonnie Kime Scott draws on her unique knowledge of Rebecca West's life and opinions, derived from editing *Selected Letters of Rebecca West* (2000), to argue that her construction of a public life was both deliberate and self-protective. Scott shows how West's essays in *The Strange Necessity* (1928) and *Ending in Earnest* (1931) demonstrate her important critique of modernism, challenging both the Joyce establishment's reception of *Ulysses* and T. S. Eliot's affiliation with the New Humanism's advocacy of classical moderation and restraint. It was during the 1930s, however, that West's fight against fascism established her as a public intellectual: letters seek help in saving individual Jews in Germany and other nations; she writes to Nancy Cunard in support of her pamphlet *Authors Take Sides on the Spanish Civil* War; and from 1936 to 1941 she writes detailed travel letters, on three British Council lecture tours to Yugoslavia, that anticipate her monumental work against the rise of fascism, *Black Lamb and Grey Falcon* (1942). Scott shows how West's affiliation during the Second World War with people in the British government depicts her increasingly conservative attitude to international politics; by the 1950s, she was writing regularly on treason, spies, and the dangers of communism. Scott provides a valuable narrative of a crucial decade in Rebecca West's complicated journey from her socialist/feminist articles before the First World War through the 1930s experiences that culminated in her literary/political masterpiece and in her becoming, during the 1950s, the unpredictable "conservative rebel" who supported McCarthyism and the FBI.

Jean Radford and Lillian S. Robinson underline the 1930s political commitments of Edith Sitwell and Dorothy Sayers by discussing Sitwell's *I Live Under a Black Sun* and Sayers's *Gaudy Night* in the context of other works, including better-known fiction of the thirties by Virginia Woolf and Djuna Barnes, as well as later twentieth-century philosophies. Radford argues that Sitwell's only novel, *I Live Under a Black Sun*, is at once a fictionalized biography of a twentieth-century Jonathan Swift, a meditation on mourning and melancholia, and a political allegory. The story of Swift's refusal of marriage and human sexuality foregrounds his will to power, which feeds on both hatred and love. The image of the black sun denotes not only hate and domination but also loss, melancholy, and madness. Radford elucidates the complexities of this extraordinary novel by reference to Julia Kristeva's *Black Sun: Depression and Melancholia* and Walter Benjamin's connection, in *The Origin of German Tragic Drama*, between melancholy and the "crisis of values" brought about by war and modernity. Radford further contextualizes *Black Sun* with Djuna Barnes's *Nightwood* and Virginia Woolf's *Three Guineas*. Like Barnes, Sitwell represents a "working through" of the failure of love and the bestialization of the human when love and knowledge are perverted into "power gone mad"; the structures of both Sitwell's and Barnes's novels depend on a juxtaposition of images rather than a sequence of narrative plot, and both are studies of melancholy which are also attempts to mourn. Like Woolf, Sitwell seeks to explain war in the connections between the military and the cultural, the public and the private, and the masculine and the feminine. Woolf and Sitwell respond to the impending war by breaking form: Sitwell, the poet, wrote an allegorical novel; Woolf, the novelist, wrote an antagonistic sociological essay.

Lillian Robinson analyzes the limited feminism of Sayers's novel *Gaudy Night* in order to also explore larger ethical questions about the notion that universities are apolitical, truth-seeking institutions. The novel is appealing to Robinson's feminist and socialist "cosoeurs," she argues, because it tells us that women do belong in the academy, and thus validates the principles by which academic women conduct our own searches for truth. But the novel is elitist. Where Woolf's 1930s work on education, *Three Guineas*, exhorts daughters of educated men to make common cause with the working classes and the dark-skinned victims of imperialism, Sayers is concerned with women as a class only insofar as she has to be in order to justify her own right to an education. Robinson's essay asks: Are contemporary feminists doing our work if we also affirm that the pure, disinterested search for truth is indeed what the university is about? And if we do solidify our own places in academia by appeals to truth-seeking, aren't we also "accepting the view that it is we, as feminist scholars, who are engaged in politicizing (and hence polluting) this pristine institution?" Without judging Sayers's politics by twenty-first-century values, Robinson uses the politics of *Gaudy Night* to get academic feminists to think about how we can acknowledge that we function within masculine university traditions and at the same time work to expose the elitist politics of those universities and work toward making them genuinely open places.

The essays in this volume describe the processes by which writers can be recast as activists who demonstrate how public life invades and politicizes the domestic sphere. Even the most removed, private, domestic-seeming narrative reflects memories of the First World War, or the hunger marches of the thirties, or the establishment of fascism in Germany, Italy, and Spain. The essayists write about how war invades the home, divides or decimates the family, and replaces private hopes with anxiety. At the end of Virginia Woolf's *Between the Acts*, the world loses stability: Mrs. Swithin escapes the news by reading about prehistory; Giles and Isa will fight and then make love "as the dogs fight with the vixen in the fields of night" (1941, 256). Sixty-five years later, in an increasingly weaponed and bitterly divided world, we need more than ever public and private debates about war, empire, patriotism, and constant, watchful dissent.

Notes

1. For discussions that refute Woolf's infamous claim about women's involvement with empire see Julia Bush 2000, *Edwardian Ladies and Imperial Power*; Antoinette Burton 1994, *Burdens of History: British Feminists, Indian Women, and Imperial Culture, 1865–1915*; Nupur Chaudhuri and Marget Strobel, eds. 1992, *Western Women and Imperialism: Complicity and Resistance.*

2. See Higonnet et al., eds. 1987, *Behind the Lines: Gender and the Two World Wars*, in which she points out that wars are fought by both men and women on many fronts. For other literary studies that have deepened the field of Great War literature to include home front and interwar, that is, peacetime writing by British women, see: Tylee 1990, *The Great War and Women's Consciousness: Images of Militarism and Womanhood in Women's Writing, 1914-1964* ; Light 1991, *Forever England: Femininity, Literature, and Conservativism between the Wars*; Goldman, ed. 1993, *Women and World War I: The Written Response*; Ouditt 1994, *Fighting Forces, Writing Women*; Raitt and Tate, eds. 1997, *Women's Fiction and the Great War*; Higonnet 1999, *Lines of Fire: Women Writers of World War I*; Gallagher 2000, *The World Wars and the Female Gaze*; Higonnet 2001, *Nurses at the Front: Writing the Wounds of the Great War;* and Cohen 2002, *Remapping the Home Front*, among others.

3. Said 1994, *Culture and Imperialism*. For a useful discussion of modernism as aesthetics produced by and producing British Empire and identity, see Lewis 2000, *Modernism, Nationalism, and the Novel.* Lewis, like Samuel Hynes, focuses exclusively on writers who were men, but otherwise his work usefully opens the field of modernism to a critique of imperialism and race. See also Booth and Rigby, eds. 2000 *Modernism and Empire*; and Barkan and Bush, eds. *Prehistories of the Future*. For discussions of women's writing on and of empire, see, for example, Marcus 1992, "Britannia Rules *The Waves*"; Wachman 2001, *Lesbian Empire: Radical Crosswriting in the Twenties*; Hackett 2002,

Sapphic Primitivism: Productions of Race, Class, and Sexuality in Key Works of Modern Fiction; and Marcus 2004, *Hearts of Darkness: White Women Write Race.*

4. See for example, Scott 1990, *The Gender of Modernism,* and 1995, *Refiguring Modernism*; DeKoven 1991, *Rich and Strange: Gender, History, Modernism*; Gilroy 1993, *The Black Atlantic: Modernity and Double Consciousness;* North 1994, *The Dialect of Modernism: Race, Language and Twentieth-Century Literature*; Rado 1994, *Rereading Modernism: New Directions in Feminist Criticism*; Felski 1995, *The Gender of Modernity;* Lemke 1998, *Primitivist Modernism: Black Culture and the Origins of Transatlantic Modernism*; Carlston 1998, *Thinking Fascism: Sapphic Modernism and Fascist Modernity.*

5. See Jane Garrity's *Stepdaughters of England: British Women Modernists and the National Imaginary* (2003), 155-57, and Lucy Bland's *Banishing the Beast: Sexuality and the Early Feminists* (1995).

Works Cited

Auden, W. H. 1939. "September 1, 1939." In *The Norton Anthology of English Literature.* Edited by Stephen Greenblatt, 2432–34, New York: W.W. Norton.

Baker, Houston A., Jr. 1987. *Modernism and the Harlem Renaissance.* Chicago: University of Chicago Press.

Barkan, Elazor, and Ronald Bush, eds. 1995. Prehistories of the Future: The Primitivist Project and the Culture of Modernism. Stanford, CA: Stanford University Press.

Beer, Gillian. 1999. "Sylvia Townsend Warner: 'The Centrifugal Kick.'" In Joannou 1999, 76–86.

Bland, Lucy. 1995. *Banishing the Beast: Sexuality and the Early Feminists.* New York: The New Press.

Booth, Howard J., and Nigel Rigby, eds. 2000. *Modernism and Empire.* Manchester, UK: Manchester University Press.

Burton, Antoinette. 1994. *Burdens of History: British Feminists, Indian Women, and Imperial Culture, 1865–1915.* Chapel Hill: University of North Carolina Press.

Bush, Julia. 2000. *Edwardian Ladies and Imperial Power.* London: Leicester University Press.

Caesar, Adrian. 1991. *Dividing Lines: Poetry, Class and Ideology in the 1930s.* Manchester, UK: Manchester University Press.

Carlston, Erin G. 1998. *Thinking Fascism: Sapphic Modernism and Fascist Modernity.* Stanford, CA: Stanford University Press.

Chaudhuri, Nupur, and Marget Strobel, eds. 1992. *Western Women and Imperialism: Complicity and Resistance.* Bloomington: Indiana University Press.

Cohen, Debra Rae. 2002. *Remapping the Home Front: Locating Citizenship in British Women's Great War Fiction.* Boston, MA: Northeastern University Press.

Croft, Andy. 1990. *Red Letter Days: British Literature in the 1930s.* London: Lawrence and Wishart.

Cunningham, Valentine. 1989. *British Writers of the Thirties.* Oxford: Oxford University Press.

———. 1997. "The Age of Anxiety and Influence; or Tradition and the Thirties Talents." In Williams and Matthews 1997, 5–22.

Davies, Tony. 1984. "Unfinished Business, Realism and Working-Class Writing." In Jeremy Hawthorn (ed.), *The British Working-Class Novel in the Twentieth Century*. Edited by Jeremy Hawthorn, 125–39. London: Edward Arnold.

DeKoven, Marianne. 1991. *Rich and Strange: Gender, History, Modernism*. Princeton, NJ: Princeton University Press.

Dowson, Jane, ed. 1996. *Women's Poetry of the 1930s: A Critical Anthology*. London: Routledge.

———. 1999. "Women Poets and the Political Voice." In Joannou 1999, 46–62.

Enloe, Cynthia. 2000. *Maneuvers: The International Politics of Militarizing Women's Lives*. Berkeley and Los Angeles: University of California Press.

Esty, Jed. 2004. *A Shrinking Island: Modernism and National Culture in England*. Princeton, NJ: Princeton University Press.

Felski, Rita. 1995. *The Gender of Modernity*. Cambridge, MA: Harvard University Press.

Gallagher, Jean. 2000. *The World Wars and the Female Gaze*. Carbondale: Southern Illinois University Press.

Garrity, Jane. 2003. *Stepdaughters of England: British Women Modernists and the National Imaginary*. Manchester: Manchester University Press.

Gilroy, Paul. 1993. *The Black Atlantic: Modernity and Double Consciousness*. Cambridge, MA: Harvard University Press.

Gindin, John. 1992. *British Fiction in the 1930s: The Dispiriting Decade*. New York: St. Martin's Press.

Goldman, Dorothy, ed. 1993. *Women and World War I: The Written Response*. New York: St. Martin's Press.

Hackett, Robin. 2002. *Sapphic Primitivism: Productions of Race, Class, and Sexuality in Key Works of Modern Fiction*. New Brunswick, NJ: Rutgers University Press.

Higonnet, Margaret R. 1999. *Lines of Fire: Women Writers of World War I*. New York: Plume.

———. 2001. *Nurses at the Front: Writing the Wounds of the Great War*. Boston: Northeastern University Press.

Higgonet, Margaret Randolph, Jane Jensen, Sonya Michel, and Margaret Weitz, eds. 1987. *Behind the Lines: Gender and the Two World Wars*. New Haven, CT: Yale University Press.

Hynes, Samuel. 1972. *The Auden Generation: Literature and Politics in England in the 1930s*. New York: Viking.

Joannou, Maroula. 1995. *"Ladies, Please don't Smash These Windows": Women's Writing, Feminist Consciousness and Social Change, 1918–38*. Oxford: Berg.

———, ed. 1999. *Women Writers of the 1930s: Gender, Politics, and History*. Edinburgh: Edinburgh University Press.

Lassner, Phyllis. 2003. " 'On the Point of a Journey': Storm Jameson, Phyllis Bottome, and the Novel of Women's Political Psychology." In Shuttleworth 2003, 115–32.

Lawrence, Karen, ed. 1992. *Decolonizing Tradition: New Views of Twentieth Century "British" Literary Canon*. Urbana: University of Illinois Press.

Lemke, Sieglinde. 1998. *Primitivist Modernism: Black Culture and the Origins of Transatlantic Modernism.* W. E. B. Du Bois Institute 3. Oxford: Oxford University Press.

Lewis, Pericles. 2000. *Modernism, Nationalism, and the Novel.* Cambridge: Cambridge University Press.

Light, Allison. 1991. *Forever England: Femininity, Literature, and Conservatism between the Wars.* London: Routledge.

Marcus, Jane. 1987. *Virginia Woolf and the Languages of the Patriarchy.* Bloomington: Indiana University Press.

———. 1992. "Britannia Rules *The Waves.*" In Lawrence 1992, 136–62.

———. 2004. *Hearts of Darkness: White Women Write Race.* New Brunswick, NJ: Rutgers University Press.

Maslen, Elizabeth. 1999. "Naomi Mitchison's Historical Fiction." In Joannou 1999, 138–50.

Miller, Tyrus. 1999. *Late Modernism: Politics, Fiction, and the Arts between the World Wars.* Berkeley and Los Angeles: University of California Press.

Montefiore, Janet. 1996. *Men and Women Writers of the 1930s: The Dangerous Flood of History.* London: Routledge.

North, Michael. 1994. *The Dialect of Modernism: Race, Language and Twentieth-Century Literature.* New York: Oxford University Press.

Ouditt, Sharon. 1994. *Fighting Forces, Writing Women.* London: Routledge.

Pawlowski, Merry, ed. 2001. *Virginia Woolf and Fascism: Resisting the Dictator's Seduction.* Houndmills, UK: Palgrave.

Phillips, Kathy. 1994. *Virginia Woolf against Empire.* Knoxville: University of Tennessee Press.

Radford, Jean. 1999. "Late Modernism and the Politics of History." In Joannou 1999, 33–45.

Rado, Lisa, ed. 1994. *Rereading Modernism: New Directions in Feminist Criticism.* New York: Garland.

Raitt, Suzanne, and Trudi Tate, eds. 1997. *Women's Fiction and the Great War.* Oxford: Clarendon Press.

Said, Edward W. 1979. *Orientalism.* New York: Random House.

———. 1994. *Culture and Imperialism.* New York: Random House.

Scott, Bonnie Kime, ed. 1990. *The Gender of Modernism: A Critical Anthology.* Bloomington: Indiana University Press.

———. 1995. *Refiguring Modernism. Vol. 1: The Women of 1928.* Bloomington: Indiana University Press.

Shuttleworth, Anthony, ed. 2003. *And in our Time: Vision, Revision, and British Writing of the 1930s.* Lewisburg, PA: Bucknell University Press.

Tylee, Claire. 1990. *The Great War and Women's Consciousness: Images of Militarism and Womanhood in Women's Writing, 1914–1964.* Iowa City: University of Iowa Press.

Wachman, Gay. 2001. *Lesbian Empire: Radical Crosswriting in the Twenties.* New Brunswick, NJ: Rutgers University Press.

Wallace, Diana. 1999. "Revising the Marriage Plot in Women's Fiction of the 1930s." In Joannou 1999, 63–75.

Williams, Keith. 1999. "Back from the Future: Katharine Burdekin and Science Fiction in the 1930s." In Joannou 1999, 151–64.

Williams, Keith, and Steven Matthews, eds. 1997. *Rewriting the Thirties: Modernism and After*. London: Longman.

Woolf, Virginia. 1957. *A Room of One's Own*. New York: Harcourt. 1929.

———. 1941. *Between the Acts*. San Diego, CA: Harcourt.

The Mysterious New Empire: Agatha Christie's Colonial Murders

PHYLLIS LASSNER

WHILE CRIME FICTION IS NOW A FAMILIAR PRESENCE IN LITERARY STUDY, Agatha Christie, who remains the best selling novelist of all time, has yet to win a secure place in the canons of modern fiction. Until recently, because literary critics were hard pressed to find any literary depth or cultural value in her stable of stereotypical characters, they turned their attention elsewhere. Trying to account for her popularity, Robert Barnard notes her playful involvement of the reader in "the investigative process," and claims that Christie writes "the *only* popular form whose appeal is primarily to the mind . . . rather than to the emotions" (Barnard 1980,126-27). And yet this evaluation, too, may be the source of the problem, especially since the ratiocinative process would inevitably expose the nastier side of Christie's caricatures, including her early anti-Semitic "Noseystein" in *The Secret of Chimneys* (1925), not to mention her homophobia, and closed, if not claustrophobic class system.[1] If this weren't damning enough, there is no escape from the stock plots that over the fifty years of Christie's writing life, can seem like an automated production line. According to Alison Light's reassessment, Christie mastered the art of "the crime puzzle" by the time she published her third novel, *The Murder of Roger Ackroyd*, in 1926, and then, until only death stopped the flow, turned out only more finely honed variations in her 67 novels and 117 short stories, the contours of which evenly matched the conventions that may have identified her as a doyenne of the Golden Age of women crime writers, but which also put off her critics while delighting her readers (Light 1991, 65).[2]

Light is one of the few scholars who study Christie outside of the genre of detective or crime fiction and instead align her with other interwar British women writers whose neglect, she argues, can be ascribed to their conservative outlook. Reversing Christie's position in this assessment, Light analyzes the forms of her novels as conservative, but also finds a redeeming "modernist spirit" in the author's deployment of popular fiction (1991, 61).[3] This is a turn that might very well enroll Christie as an appealing social critic, for her brand of modernism "aims to upset the Victorian image of home, sweet home" (1991, 67). With ironic glee, she deflates the "moral rectitude" of both the Sherlock Holmes-Dr. Watson partnership and Lord Peter Wimsey's snobbish disdain for the too ambitious middle classes (78).[4] But despite Christie's modern and laudable mockery of domestic quietude, Light's own analysis betrays her subject as incorrigibly conservative in not being able to cut loose from an English insularity.[5] What Light identifies as "a growing confidence about the rightness of [a] profoundly domesticated and more unashamedly inward-looking . . . middle-class" leads her to conclude that despite "the pleasures of travel which dominate her plots in the 1930s," Christie's fiction of this turbulent period is not about "adventure or conquest," but about "the domesticated and managed aspect of tourism. . . . Abroad was being imagined as a place for consumption and leisure, a home from home" (Light 1991, 86, 89, 90). So even as Christie's protagonists and antagonists journey far and wide to commit murder and be victimized, "By the end of the story they are revealed not just to share the characteristics of a household, cooped up together, but actually to be one. . . . Christie uses abroad as a more effective means of concentrating her plots and isolating her characters so that their local anxieties and indigenous behaviors are thrown into relief. Her characters take their domestic outlook with them, like so much bottled water, and murder simply works to reinforce the sense of privacy which has been invaded" (Light 1991, 90, 91).[6]

This emphasis on a homely village mentality is shared even by those critics who locate variously progressive permutations of gender analysis or even feminism in Christie's detective fiction.[7] This critical attachment to the homespun yarn may not be the whole story, however, especially as it ignores the persistent lessons of the peripatetic Hercule Poirot, our tour guide through most of Christie's travel mysteries. A foreigner himself, and as Susan Rowland notes, an affront to "English masculinity," the easily mocked but canny, egg-shaped little Belgian provides more than the road map through murderous minefields (2001, 63). His fastidious dress and habits, especially apparent when he travels, call attention to his own status as outsider and his fussy demeanor situates him as representing the necessity of keeping the loose gender boundaries of "abroad" at bay. And if the world of "abroad" is by its alien nature threatening to the masculinist and political image of Englishness as dominant, Poirot is always, "until the final and brief moment of his triumph," associated with the very "'alien' quality of murder" itself (Grossvogel 1983, 262). The necessity of employing an alien to solve a mystery that threatens the cohesiveness of British identity highlights a relationship deeply embedded in Christie's Oriental plots of the 1930s, that is, between Britain and all those Other nations that constitute its sphere of influence.

This spotlight on Poirot's alien persona serves as a clue to a plot running parallel to the novel's murder mystery. Poirot's own Otherness directs our attention to the cultural and political tensions created by a different kind of murderous clash, and this is the one resulting from seeing the fates of the English middle classes as implicated in global politics. As Lillian Robinson detects in the case of Dorothy Sayers (see Robinson's essay in this volume), what looks like "formula" engages a politics on "world-historic" sites "that have usually been assumed to be politically neutral." Thus, when Poirot points his finger at a guilty party, he is identifying a collective guilt, involving not only his individual suspects, but their group presence, whether they assemble in a plush carriage of the Orient Express or in a desert tent. As he typically circles a room and points to the probable guilt of each, he implicates the whole group as an alien tribe descending with murderous intentions on foreign soil that in turn resists their encroachment. Complicating the ironies that Light so astutely observes is Christie's equally wicked satire of readers who enjoy the Oriental setting as merely an exotic backdrop for a very English mystery. And while Rowland makes the salient point that crime fiction of this period typically projects "Englishness through an overtly Orientalizing psyche" that "destabiliz[es] and parod[ies] English stereotypes," this anxiety of identity once again exploits Otherness to foreground Englishness (2001, 68, see also 71). Given Christie's skill, however, especially at exploiting disguised identities, isn't it possible, as Poirot so often concludes about the murderer, that Christie sets a trap for us all and that we allow ourselves to be manipulated by noticing only her conventionally domestic plotting? Unlike the 1920s "literature of convalescence," that can be seen as a domestic healing from the Great War, the 1930s could be seen as producing a literature of menace in the light of fascism and other disturbing events (Light 1991, 70).[8] Indeed, if we take Poirot's lead and distrust our own domesticated judgments, we might find that Christie's drawing-room murders plot a political tale that extends beyond the overheated carriages of the Orient Express.[9]

I'd like to consider the possibility that four Poirot mysteries of the 1930s, easily labeled Colonial, may be designed to trip us up with the end result of making us the butt of a joke designed as an Orientalist tale of mystery. I take my first clue from Christie's intertextual references to murders that occurred in earlier novels. In *Appointment with Death*, the possibility of forgiving a family's revenge murder against its matriarchal despot is supported by "that affair of the Orient Express" (1986, 137). Poirot also tweaks us with conventional expectations that embed our stereotyping proclivities. As Sally Munt points out, Poirot "is a parody of the male myth; his name implies his satirical status: he is a shortened Hercules, and a *poirot*—a clown" (1994, 8; Munt's italics). Parodying the tendency of readers to position themselves in opposition to suspicious characters and to merge uncritically with Christie's narrative progression, Poirot notes his own story's self-critical exegesis. Again in *Appointment with Death*, he responds to a suspect's "very strong views as to the sanctity of human life" with the remark, "In a work of fiction you would be strongly suspected on that account" (1986, 199). The metafictional parameters of Poirot's statement suggest that our own suspicions are based on imagined, untested assumptions. Viewing *Appointment With Death* in relation to *Murder on the Orient Express* (1934), *Murder in Mesopotamia* (1936), and *Death on the Nile* (1938), we will see how Christie weaves a geopolitical mystery satire out of her Oriental mysteries and with the relationship she establishes teasingly with her readers.

Our first clue that gallows humor accompanies Christie's more obvious poisons and knives is the voice of a classic unreliable narrator in *Murder in Mesopotamia*, Amy Leatheran. Amy is a nurse hired by an American archaeologist to care for his neurasthenic wife, Louise Leidner, and Christie sets readers up to expect a straightforward if naive narration when Amy is introduced as the teller of the tale. The novel begins by luring readers into a frame that appears sturdy and reliable: a narration by the impeccably authoritative voice of a physician. In a foreword, Dr. Giles Reilly vouches for Amy's integrity by assuring us that her "highest . . . professional character" and lack of "previous connection" ensure the necessary impartiality to recount the murky murder mystery that will follow (*Mesopotamia*, 1965, 7). The novel's following short chapter, also labeled a foreword, continues the assured and dispassionate tone of Reilly's voice, conveying the sense of a seamless wisdom that glides directly into Amy's narration. As the novel progresses, moreover, we are constantly reassured of Amy's compassionate rationality, especially as the narrative contrasts it with Louise Leidner's "fancies" (15).

It's only when Poirot enters the scene that we are given any authoritative hint that Amy's narration provides much of the distorted vision that shapes the novel's mystery. The detective, whose outsider status is now doubled, by dint of being a Belgian among the English and an alien presence in Mesopotamia, is consequently endowed with a clarifying double vision. He can see through disguised Otherness and decode the narratives of disguise or false clues. Most pertinently, he deconstructs the foundational tale that underlies and forms the status of an Other. If we return to the foreword narrated by Dr. Reilly, we can see how this double weave of Otherness and encryption connects the novel's double foreword to the unfolding murder mystery. If Reilly's laudatory introduction to Amy doesn't put us off, consider his report of her assessment of Baghdad: "dirt and mess . . . not romantic at all like . . . the Arabian Nights" (*Mesopotamia*, 1965, 9). The setup of such heavy-handed Orientalism is only reinforced by Amy's view of Mrs. Mercado, another archaeologist's wife, who she sees as suffering from "a touch of the tar brush" (30).[10] If we grant Christie any skill as a mystery writer, we may admit that these bigoted comments were a tad too obvious, especially when read in tandem with Amy's assessment of the clay tablets found on the dig. While Amy sees their inscriptions as "queer heathenish-looking marks," Christie also has her convey their historical meaning and context, but these are derived from another source (43). This juxtaposed encryption already offers a glimpse into disjunctions between Amy's mindset and that of the overall narrative in which it is set. The subtle distinction between Amy's expressed judgment and her report of the tablet's significance may be, as Poirot is always telling us, a clue that has been planted, not just to trip him up, but also his author's complacent readers. That we are targeted as unreliable readers is confirmed by the novel also situating Amy as a reader, one who is mystified by the events unfolding around her but who eventually learns to mistrust her initial reactions: "To tell the story properly . . . I think I ought to try and recapture the point of view that I actually held–puzzled, uneasy, and increasingly conscious of *something wrong*" (50; Christie's italics). Likewise for readers of the novel, who must learn to trust their own intuitive distrust.

One clue that turns out to be an authentic heuristic is Amy's disclaimer that her narrative will pay scant attention to "local color" (*Mesopotamia*, 1965, 42). As in all of Christie's Oriental mysteries, the European, English, and American visitors are the narrative's defining presence. However exotically romantic the Middle East is imagined, from Egypt to Syria, it is the presence of the Westerner that makes that Other place significant. In effect, only Westerners make the Orient worthy of lending an exotic atmosphere to an Occidental melodrama. Thus, in *Mur-*

der in Mesopotamia, the contours of an old Arab house disappear into the archaeological compound built and therefore superimposed onto it. As for the locals, they're faceless and remain unknown.

In *Appointment with Death,* the murderess goes unnoticed because she has disguised herself as an unkempt workman, one of those "Arabs" who all "look alike" to the Western tourist (120). Typically, the Arabs are noticed only when they can be conveniently accused of sabotaging the American-European mission: "Truth as truth means nothing to them. They say what you want them to say as a mere matter of politeness" (75). Having been relegated to their one-dimensional stature, the Orientals turn out to be important only as decorative props that lend a mysterious air to an otherwise conventional tale of Occidental revenge. Among those standard issue props, we might recall from Christie's *Murder on the Orient Express* and other Orientalist thrillers, daggers encrusted with jewels later become adorned with the blood of victims while lurking in every shadow is either the vengeful Arab or some esoteric text that inscribes a will to violence. Recalling Amy Leatheran's reference to the Arabian Nights, it is as though the Orient is a fanciful concoction that contains the violence that originated beyond its pages. And here I mean contains in the combined sense of embedding and managing.

The exotic backdrop serves Christie's manipulation of her readers' response to an archaeological plot. Using the expertise she acquired on her forays to the Middle East, Christie glosses her novel with the trope of "the deep cut," an archaeological probe which, according to Amy, produces only "rubbishy broken pottery" from a layer of the dig, shards irrelevant to the goal of unearthing a much older and therefore much more significant civilization far beneath (*Mesopotamia*, 1965, 146).[11] That Amy's perspective is being mocked along with the myopic interests of the visiting experts becomes clear (note Leidner's satiric point of origin, the University of Pittstown) as the novel provides both false and careful readings of the past. The false reading involves isolating the text from context, as though, like a parody of New Criticism, the text will provide all clues to resolve all ambiguities by synthesizing them into a unified, stable meaning. With Poirot's double vision serving as guide, the narrative exposes the importance of context: an international presence in the volatile present of an ancient site. The archaeologists' goal, to discover only a very ancient civilization, extends to the design of Christie's murder mystery. For if the archaeologists assume that the meaning of the present is only revealed by digging up the distant past, what the solution of the mystery reveals is that both the ancient past and the present are deeply intertwined with each other through a continuous if disruptive history. And so the novel positions its archaeologists and readers to consider that the motivation behind Louise Leidner's murder lies in a historical relationship between present and past.

Like Amy, who as Wagoner observes, does not allow "setting [to] keep her from noticing basic psychological facts," Christie's readers have also been encouraged to ignore this historical context and relationship and instead to interpret her murder mysteries as psychologically motivated (1986, 57). The precedent is set by Poirot's own psychologizing, and despite Christie's mockery of psychiatrists, the search for latent or disguised motivation is confirmed as a model of analysis in other Christie novels by narrative respect for such psychological consultants as Dr. Gerard in *Appointment with Death*. Compounding this emphasis on psychological themes in *Murder in Mesopotamia* is the enigmatic character of Louise Leidner, which lends itself so easily to the perception that she is the victim of jealousy for her charismatic power.[12] In turn, the combination of individual character and generic motivation encourages a short interpretive step to the construction of a psychological Manichean allegory: "individuals attempting to exert unwholesome and dangerous power over others" (Wagoner 1986, 47). Such a universal theme not only provides an important heuristic unifying Christie's oeuvre, but also elevates the otherwise formulaic murder mystery into a "basic psychological" understanding of otherwise mystifying power.[13] Despite the deep satisfaction such readings afford, they are also transhistorical, and because of the novel's deep attention to past and present, they can also be seen as challenged by Christie herself, especially if we look at this psychologizing as another clue planted to distract us. The novel's intricate narrative voices and structure insist, instead, not only on a relationship between individual power and jealousy, but on power relationships between a timeless sense of the portable green and pleasant English village and the timeliness of British global interests.

In this light, we can review a rumor about the past that Christie plants as a canard but that turns out be a real clue to her present concerns in 1936.[14] And so we are led to see the present of *Murder in Mesopotamia* in the light of something that happened in the past: the possibility that Louise Leidner exposed her first husband as a German spy during World War I. Using Christie's archaeological trope enables us to read her 1936 *Murder in Mesopotamia* as deriving its tensions from that First World War, for one possible solution is that the younger brother of Louise Leidner's first husband had seen his brother not as a traitor, "but as a patriot, a martyr for his own country—Germany. In his eyes Mrs. Leidner is the traitor—the monster . . ." (1965, 104). The combination of the archaeological trope and Louise Leidner's persistent fears suggests a psychological reading where the pain of the present originates in the individual's past but also reflects a collective trauma. As Gill Plain argues, the novel's geopolitical context exposes not only "the trauma of loss" deriving from the First World War and continued fascination with "corporeal repulsion," but creates "a safe arena of fantasy" wherein confrontation with the past can lead to healing (2001, 40, 42). Though Plain doesn't mention the novel's exotic setting, we can certainly see how it would resonate not only with the threat of foreign destructiveness, but with the curative powers of fantasy. To read this setting as significant in itself, however, relates the trauma of the First World War to geopolitical anxieties that interfere with healing precisely because they expose a new threat, one that betrays none of the comforts of being able to recognize the familiar, haunting pain that derives from the past. And so a murder about individual rage assumes the importance of a world war, but the geopolitics this suggests in 1936 is not limited to the aftermath of World War I. The narrative interplay of past and present, England, Europe, and America, invites a reading that becomes more surprising than "the seemingly 'superficial' textual play of detective fiction," especially when the threat of political conflict is embedded in the Orient (Plain 2001, 43).

For just as Christie's surfaces often conceal passions seething beyond the drawing room, so the Middle East in the 1930s is the forgotten front and embroiled aftermath of World War I. As European rivalries and antagonisms escalated, this war spilled over, covered, and carved up the Middle East, leaving the layers of its history as shards. In this 1936 novel, as the ghost of World War I enters the scene, it suggests that despite the Allies' self-assurance, the victory of that First World War is not yet conclusive. Only four years earlier, when Iraq gained its independence from its European conception in World War I, it is invaded by another story of European violence—an English murder mystery. This invasion is so total, that as the title of the novel tells us, the name of the host nation, Iraq, has no recognition; it has completely disappeared—overrun by an Allied force interested only in its own origins and manifest destiny. Like Poirot himself, however, who never ceases to be a preposterous Other to those who won't take him seriously, Iraq reveals itself to be the source of a far more compelling mystery and source of knowledge than the Europeans can contrive. So while the American and European archaeologists are fervently digging to verify their own civilization as the fount of wisdom,

Christie pulls the Oriental rug out from under them and us. The novel's most interesting secret turns out to be covered by the debris of five millennia of conquest. Mesopotamia, after all, is none other than that cradle of civilization which produced the code of Hammurabi, progenitor of biblical law and justice. While the West is triumphantly claiming this as the source of their higher morality, they are being dramatized as killing each other off faster than they can dig up the graves of Others. The unreliable narration of that cautious nurse positions us as no more and no less self-deceived readers of the past than Christie's imperialist archaeologists.

To push Christie's archaeological satire further, I want to back up to 1934, the date of *Murder on the Orient Express.* This fictional journey from the Middle East to Europe highlights a narrative relationship between an English comedy of imperial murder and the global politics so difficult for Britain to unravel in the 1930s. Here, as the novel begins in Aleppo, World War I is again invoked as Poirot is welcomed by a French general for having "saved the honour of the Army," and returns the compliment by recalling that the general had saved his life in World War I (1960, 12). The train's departure from Aleppo can thus be seen as marking the triumphal return of the Allies who have rightfully defeated the barbarians, a victory parade that symbolizes and salvages the imperial energies of the Western powers. And so one tourist, the American Mrs. Hubbard, asserts, "We've got to apply our Western ideals and teach the East to recognize them" (1960, 32). But once the Orient Express embarks from Istanbul, just as the city bridges three continents, so the boundaries of villainy are blurred. As on the Mesopotamian dig, the manners of the fellow travelers on the train disguise the rage joining them in their murder of the villainous Mr. Cassetti.

Like Christie's archaeological compound, the stifling setting of the Orient Express contains its violence very comfortably. The setting is all artifice, but instead of resonating with the Orient, it seems to reject it. In both *Murder in Mesopotamia* and *Murder on the Orient Express*, the Orient as Other seems effaced by the British murder of manners. In its insulated and plush interior, the Express is transformed into a self-contained corner of Europe, carrying away an exotic Oriental souvenir but transforming it into a weapon all too familiar to readers of British murder mysteries. Indeed, the murder weapon is an ornate dagger—one could say, recalling Amy Leatheran's comment, right out of the Arabian Nights. Resonating with a text that is read by the English as romantic, the dagger is a sign of having tamed a political threat by translating it into an accessible English form. Any vestiges of a threatening Orient are then further transmogrified by being translated into a model for a conventional English melodrama of foreign intrigue. And so the Oriental dagger becomes the prototypical instrument of an exotic revenge tale which takes place in a snowdrift in the nearly Oriental Balkans, "cut off from all the normal routes of procedure" (1960, 191). But if we are lulled by this double translation into an Orientalist stupor, Christie jolts us awake with the surprise that the villainous victim is not an inscrutable Oriental, but an American power broker. And instead of being judged a barbaric act, the murder becomes an act of just retribution, an interpretive move that as Lillian Robinson argues in the case of Dorothy Sayers, pits absolute truth and principles against "human needs and relationships." In Christie's mystery, the focus on human loss cannot be relegated to the artificial conventions attributed to an Oriental dark ages, but originate in a neon-lit America. This revenge tale is based on the Lindburgh kidnapping; in the novel, a child related or close to all the killers was kidnapped and killed by Cassetti. Having escaped the American justice system, Cassetti is trapped by Christie's mocking satire of an Oriental murder.

When Poirot reconstructs the murder on the Orient Express, we are treated to another archaeological expedition. The Belgian outsider solves the mystery by unearthing a plot from the past. But instead of merely exposing the characters' stories as twists on the usual passions, he shows that the plot itself, a variation on the English drawing room melodrama, is an all too comforting anachronism. If readers expect a self-enclosed solution where the killer turns out to be an unassimilable interloper, they are in for a real surprise. The moving parlor on the Orient Express in 1934 can no longer be maintained as an insular and privileged space; instead, it is already implicated in a world of unstable boundaries and escalating violence. For example, we see the domestic boundaries of a family plot besieged by memories of an earlier threat to narrative and political stability as the train gets stuck in the Balkans where World War I began. As though the violent past both mocks and warns readers about their complacency and reliance on psychological models of explanation that speak to internalized trauma, the sheltered world of conventional melodrama is blown apart. The explosion, moreover, originates not only in an ongoing saga of European chaos, but in a very un-English, American story of violence.

As the American plot spreads its sphere of influence, the European travelers are exposed as also shaped by but disguising their American connections. The Hungarian countess Andrenyi is really the American younger sister of the woman whose child was murdered, while their mother, the actress Linda Arden, born Goldenberg, is among those "many nationalities [who] drift to America" (1960, 211). Their disguises, moreover, perform a fluid if anxious sense of identity, one that must form "a perfect mosaic, [with] each person playing his or her allotted part" in order to provide each other with credible alibis (1960, 249). While these performances are obviously related to the vendetta against Cassetti, their suggestiveness extends beyond the private tale. The interrelatedness of all the murderers and victims not only erases individual identity, but questions individuality as the ideology necessary to the formation of character, not to mention guilt and innocence in Western fiction. As the characters on the Orient Express perform as a collective power overtaking the individual face of an identifiable villain, they begin to reflect global politics in the thirties. In an era of increasing refugee flight, marked by assumed identities and fake passports, the passage of the Orient Express to the port of Calais, especially when it becomes mired down in a tense geopolitical corner, conjures up images of those who historically and in the present of the novel, apprehensively sought refuge three thousand miles from European turbulence—on the American stage. In turn, as a mass, these immigrants represent a threat to any cohesive American identity. As Poirot observes: "only in America" could there "be a household composed of such varied nationalities—an Italian chauffeur, an English governess, a Swedish nurse, a German lady's maid, and so on" (1960, 245). The novel's American connection shows that Otherness is not only Oriental and a minority presence, but forms a majority character as it has been enfolded into and constituted as another nation, the United States, which is composed of Others.

In fact, there is so much Otherness in America, the very character of that nation becomes the central mystery of the novel.[15] Like the Arab workman or the Belgian detective, the American can be caricatured, but unlike those Orientalized Others, whose fictional and stereotypical habits never change, the American has a power that lies in defying political or economic boundaries or the constraints of fiction and stereotype. If "Americans, as all the world knows, do not care what they pay," they possess an infinite wealth and capacity for consumption that absorbs definitive categories (*Orient Express*, 1960, 199). The infinitely fluid and therefore very confusing and mysterious character of America relates directly to the nature of the terror enacted in the novel. And this terror derives from the inability to withstand being enfolded into the American sphere. No matter how the characters on the Orient Express have redesigned and redirected their lives, they live in the shadow of an American plot. If in

Orientalist discourse, Western imperialism constructs the Other as irremediably different, distant, and inferior, Christie's Orientalist satire shows that the American imperial character is only too eager to take in difference, obliterate it, and by dint of its ability to support its global designs, be all the more superior for its assimilationist appetites. Christie, however, deflates any smugness or complacency that might accompany America's overpowering largesse—its expansiveness that suggests a different kind of colonialism. As part of the novel's archaeological work, digging up the past reveals that the American tragedy of the kidnapped and murdered child has its origins in a Wall Street fortune that was ultimately no protection against an equally boundless rage. Though Cassetti is established as an American, the foreignness of his name suggests a failure of America's lust for assimilation. His escape route on the Orient Express maps the global implications of the American tragedy as it is carried to and from the Middle East and Europe.

As the 1930s drew on, and the global power Britain had once relied on for its economic and cultural well-being was being threatened by fascism, Christie intensified the American role in her Oriental mysteries. In 1937, after Mussolini invaded Ethiopia and the United States entrenched its isolationism, Christie published *Death on the Nile*, in which an American heiress is murdered for her economic and charismatic power. Recalling Louise Leidner in *Murder in Mesopotamia*, both the victim in *Death on the Nile*, Linnet Ridgway, and her murderer, Jacqueline de Bellefort, are confident of their power to take what they want. And if Louise and Linnet are ugly Americans but innocent victims, their sins, like those of other Americans in Christie's Oriental mysteries, can only be brought to light and punished after being exposed by the unforgiving sun of the Middle East. We are told, for example, on several occasions in *Appointment with Death*, that the intolerable "wasn't so bad in America—but traveling brought it home to us so" that it was "on the journey to Petra [that] eyes were being opened" (1986, 142, 156). In *Death on the Nile*, Rosalie Otterbourne, the daughter of a romance novelist, Salome Otterbourne, discovers archaeological traces of latent desires in the setting of the ancient temple at Abu Simbel: "There's something about this country that makes me feel wicked. It brings to the surface all the things that are boiling inside one" (1986, 81). But instead of reveling in this romantic turbulence, Rosalie rebels against her mother's conventional outlook by also noticing that there may be a surprisingly disturbing ending: "Everything's so unfair, so unjust" (81). Ancient Egypt, like Mesopotamia and Petra, is not just the setting for the English *crime passionnel*, but the embodiment of dangerous mystery that is disguised by the performance of a personally motivated violent passion. Once again, Christie uses an archaeological trope to show that this exposure is a necessary danger in which the ancient site is exploited in order for the Westerners to "clear away the extraneous matter so that we can see . . . the naked shining truth" (254).

The "naked shining truth" behind the expression of passion is exposed by Poirot as having little to do with a sexually fraught Freudian romance of the sort Salome Otterbourne conventionally manages. Instead, Christie is tweaking her readers for expecting the murky plot turns and relationships that, in the conventional frameworks of romance thrillers, provide the origins of and solutions to the mysterious murder. As a corrective to this expectation, we learn from Poirot that the underlying motive behind Linnet's murder is really about her money. Linnet's murder is staged by Jacqueline and Simon (Linnet's husband and Jacqueline's lover and former fiancé) as a melodrama of love betrayed and avenged, but what they really crave is more venal. In fact, there can be no sexual romance without Linnet's money to support it, and Simon shows himself to be more interested in the pursuit of material comfort, sport, and gambling than in sexual passion. As Christie debunks expectations associated more with Salome Otterbourne's romances, she expands those of her readers by relating the mystery of Linnet's murder to mysteries of the ancient Near East and to modern global politics. Like the American tragedy in *Murder on the Orient Express*, the murder in *Death on the Nile* concerns the power of American money to produce and exacerbate global injustice. Linnet's money may have given her the confidence to seduce her best friend's fiancé, but her wealth is situated in contrast with the poverty of her "oldest friend" and murderess, Jacqueline, whose "mother lost all her money in the Wall Street crash" (*Death*, 1986, 7).

By extension, Linnet's money is implicated not only in a history of American slavery, but in the profit taking that marked some of the worst inequities of the American-born Great Depression. It is this ill-gotten wealth that allows her to stretch her power by buying a corner of aristocratic England.[16] Linnet's murder on a tour of ancient Egypt reveals a revenge plot against this representative of the economic power of the United States. Like Christie's concern with America's national character, this economic power breaks down boundaries without respect to traditional definitions of individual or sovereign rights. And so Linnet's purchase and transformation of a corner of English green totally disregards whatever integrity the village claims for itself. In all of Christie's characters who represent American wealth, we see its global power encroaching not only on Europe's own nationalism but on its expansionist politics. For not only does the United States absorb all of Europe in its immigrant population and extend its colonizing hand back to Europe to buy up its land, but this has led to a conflict in political security. In the interests of Europe and for Christie's colonial novels, the danger lies in the fluidity of American desire. What, after all, could be more suggestive of this fluidity than the languid but murderous cruise up the waters of the Nile? The very ideal on which the United States established its superiority, its belief in "absolute freedom," has granted legitimacy to the power to satisfy its insatiable desires (*Appointment* 1986, 31).

That this term, "absolute freedom," is an oxymoron, is dramatized in *Appointment With Death* by Mrs. Boynton, "a bloated . . . hulk of shapeless flesh," a former warden of an American prison who wields her inescapable economic power over her child and stepchildren, like "a story of black magic," with absolute tyranny (1986, 10, 48). In these terms Christie is once again debunking the romance of domestic serenity, as Alison Light observes, especially as the shapelessness of this matriarch suggests both an overpowering femininity and its dissolution. But in the extended power of an American woman prison warden, domesticity becomes insinuated in a more obviously craven public sphere where domestic nurturing of a civil society has failed. And if the failure is already there, as in Christie's village murders, the presence of an omnivorous American in a British imperial setting overwhelms any English penchant for violence as a weapon of power. This is especially the case as Mrs. Boynton appears as a demonized fantasied projection of perverted maternal largesse, both omnipotent and omniscient in character. With this figuration, one's associative and surely wickedly satiric temptations veer toward locating Mrs. Boynton's objective correlative in that American icon of maternal incorporation, the Statue of Liberty.

Mrs. Boynton's tyranny certainly extends beyond the tight family circle she has created. She also possesses an absolute memory that threatens her murderer, another woman. Turning the character of Mrs. Boynton inside out, the murderer is a woman who treasures her own power as she wields it, not within domestic insularity, but in the public sphere. Lady Westholme, progressive, feminist member of Parliament, becomes a new toy for Mrs. Boynton's lethal power games, replacing the latter's depressed children who can no longer satisfy their mother's drive for terror. Lady Westholme is enfolded into Mrs. Boynton's prison once again when the former warden cannily sees through the Parliamentarian's privileged guise and remembers her as one of her prisoners years earlier. Like Cassetti in

Murder on the Orient Express, Mrs. Boynton becomes the villainous American victim, but instead of representing an escape from naive American justice, her career as jailor, her uncanny memory, and boundless lust for domination cast a suspicious light on American justice. Mrs. Boynton, however, more than meets her match in Lady Westholme, for even as the former warden spreads her terror, the novel compounds it as it clashes with the character of her former prisoner. Although Mrs. Boynton's murder is motivated by her threatening recognition of Lady Westholme, the lack of information about the content of their conversations lends a mysterious aura to their confrontation. And while there is no reason to suspect that Lady Westholme had not fully served her past prison term, because the novel withholds verification and does not disclose the nature of her crime, it is her character alone that is impugned as dangerous. The lack of a contextual background creates the effect of leaving us with a sense of mystery that is all the more terrifying because the novel refuses to solve it. When the narrative divulges that Lady Westholme is also an American, the source of terror comes full circle to convey the sense that the construction of domestic peace at the novel's end may be another false clue. In this sense I read the conclusion differently than Rowland, who finds that the combined wisdom of the psychiatrist, Dr. Gerard, and the detective, Poirot, "contribute to the moral healing of a distressed community" (*Appointment*, 1986, 145). For while Dr. Gerard's diagnosis of Mrs. Boynton is certainly correct and the Boynton children are shown to have rebuilt their personal lives and found happiness, this attempt at domestic stability remains haunted by an unidentifiable American crime and the ghost of a nearly uncontained American menace.

What makes Christie's Oriental murders most modern is that the expansiveness of American productivity, in epistemological and material wealth, forms a new kind of colonialism, and like a grim joke on her readers, there are no clues, in ancient or exotic history, that can help unravel its motivations and meanings. Deeply embedded in a typical Christie plot of British manners, America is not an invisible presence, but indefinable in the terms of conventional romance mysteries. Its fictional presence parallels its unconventional history. Christie's multicultural American characters represent their nation taking in and spreading out, wishing no role, indeed, isolating itself from the political turmoil in the 1930s. In what may be her most malevolently gleeful gesture, Christie has the French psychologist, Dr. Gerard, analyze the ugly American, Mrs. Boynton, as a "human creature born with immense ambition, with a yearning to dominate and to impress her personality on other people. She neither sublimated that intense craving for power—nor did she seek to master it—no, *mesdames and messieurs—she fed it!* But in the *end*, what did it amount to? She was not a great power! She was not feared and hated over a wide area! *She was the petty tyrant of one isolated family!*" (*Appointment*, 1986, 203. Christie's italics). In Agatha Christie's Oriental mysteries, the new superpower is gleefully exposed and punished for exercising its political power in unanticipated ways. Though Christie's American characters are always part of an English group or community, sharing transparent social and cultural codes, they are also always different and ultimately unknowable. Neither the losses and lessons of past wars nor the shards and inscriptions of ancient empires provide models of foresight or explanation of America's threat to her British and European Allies. The emergence of a dominating American epistemology extends to the convention of crime fiction itself. If the detective story is "a game," as David Grossvogel argues, that "redefines mystery by . . . assuming [it] can be overcome," the American presence in Christie's colonial novels resituates it back in the murky realm "of the unknown" (1983, 253). Part of the reason this danger is unforeseen is illustrated and embodied by the character of Mrs. Boynton. Sitting in her cave at Petra, not only does her enormous body overshadow and therefore erase the ancient ruins and their story, but she shows absolutely no interest in them herself. It is as though the expansiveness of the American overtakes all models of meaning and incorporates them in such form as to make them inaccessible to anyone else.

The exposure of such grotesque power is not one-sided, however. On the very first page of *Death on the Nile,* two natives of the English village where Linnet has bought her estate agree that in addition to bringing "money into the town," Linnet will "wake us all up proper" (1986, 3). On the Orient Express, an American detective disguised as an iconic joke, the traveling salesman, tells Poirot: "You'd learn a few go-ahead methods over there [in America] . . . Europe needs waking up. She's half asleep" (*Mesopotamia*, 1965, 175). This sleazy American is warning Europe not to emulate the American naivete that allowed the arch-villain Cassetti to get away and that operates on the assumption that it can remake Others in its own invented image. At a time when British world power is being threatened inside and out by the rise of a militantly masculinist fascism, the place of the omnivorous feminine villain and the deconstructing feminized detective in these Oriental murders mocks our coupling of geopolitical anxiety and naivete. Despite Christie's assurance that in her scheme of things, the murderer will always be captured, she also raises the question of whether such narrative promises can serve as a model for identifying threatening power and stopping real villainy when our own vision is so clouded with conventional or stereotypical categories of identity. As the quintessential English colonel Carbury notes in *Appointment with Death*, "One doesn't want complications—or international unpleasantnesses," and as Poirot glosses, "Incredible! The English never grow up!" (1986, 90, 152). If it is Agatha Christie's "great strength that she never forgot that she was an entertainer" (Barnard 1980, 28), then her 1930s colonial mysteries can be assessed as brilliantly managing a set of serious political questions as literary and political satire. Combining the two, she satirizes the staying power of British manners and morals in places and plots that resist their efficacy.

Is she also, however, anticipating that American power may be needed to help Britain survive the coming threat? The audacious Poirot, veteran of World War I and canny political observer, mocks our comfortable reliance on stereotypical assumptions about the theoretical and political constructions of Self and Other. For as these Oriental mysteries show, Christie's construction of Other landscapes as inscrutable satirizes and therefore shows the weakness of those who tour its ancient sites searching for truths that will confirm their own power. The truth these sites reveal is the overweening imperial confidence that masks concerns about emerging imperial threats. Moving backward and forward in time and between the deployment of individual and collective tyranny, Christie's archaeological metaphor shows that what is inscrutable is not the Oriental landscape, but the lessons of history that remain opaque to her victims and villains alike. In these murders most modern, what archaeology uncovers is not just the individual will to power and the ebb and flow of empires but Christie's daring and prescient political vision.

Notes

1. Barnard shows that Christie's 1920s mysteries are replete with unembarrassed depictions of "foreigners of all kinds [who] are either comic or suspicious" (1980, 21). Gillian Gill, in *Agatha Christie: The Woman and Her Mysteries*, points out that in her early novels, Christie's Jewish characters are infected with a "kind of jingoistic, knee-jerk anti-Semitism" that depends on such insidious myths as planning an international financial takeover, and "as [Jews] being essentially and irremediably foreign" (1999, 89–90). Once her publishers started to worry about American readers, they began to edit out such slurs, but Christie herself saw their dangers only when confronted directly by what was considered socially acceptable anti-Semitism in 1932–1933. Her otherwise "gentle and considerate" host in Baghdad, German Antiquities Director Dr. Jordan, tells her

over tea, "You do not understand. Our Jews are perhaps different from yours. They are a danger. They should be exterminated. Nothing else will really do but that.' I stared at him unbelievingly. He meant it. It was the first time I had come across any hint of what was to come later from Germany" (Christie 1996, 539–40). Interestingly, in her 1938 novel *Appointment with Death*, set in Palestine and Petra, Jordan, the Arab tour guide is depicted as an "anti-Zionist" constantly railing against the Jews, while the British and American tourists are deeply chagrined by this (1986, 64).

2. Mary S.Wagoner notes that Christie's mastery of the "classic, or golden age, detective novel" submits "to the discipline of that rigorously patterned form," calling for "cerebral, rather than physical, action" (1986, 33). Other Golden Age writers include Margery Allingham, Ngaio March, Josephine Tey, Patricia Wentworth, and Dorothy L. Sayers. Gill agrees with Christie's own assertion that "she is not guilty of resorting to the least-likely-suspect technique to achieve a surprise ending" (1999, 136). Instead, Christie will always choose an insider to the scene, albeit one who is neither too obvious nor illogical to the plot. Earl F. Bargainnier argues that "classic British detective fiction" appeals "to the educated" because it "enables a reader to test his intelligence and perception," with "real intellectual activity" taking place between author and reader (1980, 30).

3. Bargainnier agrees with other assessments about the essential conservatism of detective fiction in its form of "disruption" and restoration of "community harmony" (1980, 10).

4. Barnard outlines the class identities of Christie's characters as only "a tiny part of the complex class structure of between-the-wars Britain . . . middle-middle to upper-middle" (1980, 13). As for Christie's "stereotypical class solidarity," Gill shows that her characters from the upper classes are as culpable as those from the lower orders (1999, 143–44). In fact, Christie mocks any romanticizing of any class in the character of Ferguson, the aristocratic socialist revolutionary in *Death on the Nile*, who accuses others of being "overcivilized" rather than looking "on death as the Oriental does. It's a mere incident-hardly noticeable" (1986, 226). Susan Rowland emphasizes the "use of self-conscious fictionality to criticize (as well as ultimately uphold) traditional class structures as they threaten to become outmoded and morally empty in modernity" (2001, 42).

5. Wagoner shows how from the very early *Murder of Roger Ackroyd* (1926), Christie created "a fundamentally comic English village world," using "an ironic narrator" (1986, 42). As regards Christie's own penchant for domestic comfort and stability, though she owned and lovingly decorated two country houses, she relished her extended forays with her second husband, Max Mallowan, to archaeological digs in the Middle East, where life was more itinerant and primitive. See her memoir of those excursions, *Come, Tell Me How You Live* (1985). Reporting on the "Agatha Christie and Archaeology" exhibition at the British Museum in 2001, Clare Griffiths notes that Christie worked at "sorting finds," photographing artifacts, "digs in progress, and made two cine films" (2001, :19).

6. Bargainnier concurs with this view by seeing "the exoticism of these [travel] works" as Christie's continuing creation of "closed societies, no matter what the country" (1980, 30). Barnard calls her settings "an eternal fairyland disguised as an English village" (1980, 14).

7. Rowland sees Christie's interwar fiction renegotiating women's traditional roles and validating women's "self-expression, but reestablishing "conventional social structures" (2001, 158), while Gill Plain finds subtle signs of gender critique (2001).

8. Gill Plain discusses Christie's attention to the interwar anxieties that combined haunting memories of World War I with the fears of a coming second world war.

9. In her study of Poirot, Anne Hart observes that in the "uncertain political times" of the 1930s, the compelling issues of the Great Depression, political unrest in China and India, and the forces of communism and fascism appear in the novels only as subjects of polite, drawing-room conversation "over cocktails and at tea" (1990, 46).

10. Wagoner insists that Amy's "matter-of-fact, unimpressed voice . . . serves both to make familiar the romantic setting and situation and to generate a comic mood" (1986, 57). Of course, the question remains as to who is meant to be laughing at what or at whom? Barnard dismisses Christie's comic talents to an occasional bon mot (1980, 14), but this ignores her broader satiric vision.

11. In her *Autobiography*, Christie notes that "the point of coming to Nineveh, for Max, was to dig down a deep pit through the mound of Nineveh. . . . In archaeology, prehistory had suddenly become the fashion. Nearly all excavations up to then had been of a historical nature, but now everyone was passionately interested in prehistoric civilization, about which as yet so little was known" (1996, 527).

12. Gill points out that the character of Louise Leidner is probably based on Katherine Woolley, doyenne and queen bee of digs led by her husband, renowned archaeologist, Leonard Woolley.

13. Barnard accounts for Christie's continuing popularity in her creation of "a timeless, changeless world" in which "right and truth will triumph over the evil and the obscure" (1980, 133).

14. Hart notes that the original Foreword to the novel states: "The events chronicled in this narrative took place some four years ago" (1990, 50). While this could account for the characters' unexpressed concern with global politics in 1932, the novel expresses Christie's own interest in historical relationships.

15. Kristi Vagstad shows how in *Murder on the Orient Express*, Christie satirizes British stereotypes of Americans and America as "an uncivilized and corrupt society" (1995, 85).

16. Susan Rowland aptly demonstrates the novel's concerns with colonialism and its relation to "consumer capitalism," but she also refers to "Western English or American identity," as though there is no difference between their colonial interests (2001, 73).

Works Cited

Bargainnier, Earl F. 1980. *The Gentle Art of Murder*. Bowling Green, OH: Popular Press.

Barnard, Robert. 1980. *A Talent to Deceive: An Appreciation of Agatha Christie*. London: Colllins.

Christie, Agatha. 1960. *Murder on the Orient Express* (1934).Pocket Books. New York:

———. 1965. *Murder in Mesopotamia* (1936).Dell. New York:

———. 1985. *Come Tell Me How You Live* (1946). New York: Bantam Books.

———. 1986. *Death on the Nile*. (1938). New York: Bantam Books.

———. 1986. *Appointment with Death* (1938). New York: Dodd, Mead.

———. 1996. *Autobiography* (1977). New York: G. P. Putnam's Sons.

Gill, Gillian. 1999. *Agatha Christie: The Woman and Her Mysteries*. London: Robson.

Griffiths, Clare. 2001. "Lured by the Past." *Times Literary Supplement,* (December 14, 19.

Grossvogel, David I. 1983. "Agatha Christie: Containment of the Unknown." In *The Poetics of Murder: Detective Fiction and Literary Theory*. Edited by Glenn W. Most and William W. Stowe, 252–65. New York: Harcourt, Brace, Jovanovich.

Hart, Anne. 1991. *The Life and Times of Hercule Poirot*. (1990) New York: G. P. Putnam's Sons.

Light, Alison. 1991. *Forever England: Femininity, Literature and Conservatism between the Wars*. London: Routledge.

Munt, Sally R. 1994. *Murder By the Book? Feminism and the Crime Novel.* New York: Routledge.

Plain, Gill. 2001. *Twentieth-Century Crime Fiction: Gender, Sexuality and the Body*. Edinburgh: Edinburgh University Press.

Rowland, Susan. 2001. *From Agatha Christie to Ruth Rendell: British Women Writers in Detective and Crime Fiction*. Basingstoke, UK: Palgrave.

Vagstad, Kristi. 1995. "Yankees on the Orient Express." *The Armchair Detective* (Winter): 82–90.

Wagoner, Mary S. 1986. *Agatha Christie.* Boston: Twayne Publishers.

Exhibitions and Repetitions: Jean Rhys's *Good Morning, Midnight* and the World of Paris, 1937

LINDA CAMARASANA

NEAR THE END OF JEAN RHYS'S *GOOD MORNING, MIDNIGHT*, SASHA Jansen, the protagonist, along with her companion for the evening, a gigolo named René, visits the *Exposition Internationale des Arts et des Techniques Appliqués à la Vie Moderne* which was held in Paris in 1937. In keeping with the elliptical style of Rhys's experimental, modernist narrative, the only part of the Exhibition Sasha and René comment on is the Star of Peace, a monumental structure intended to symbolize international harmony the Exhibition was to have promoted. From the characters' vantage point by the Trocadéro entrance to the Exhibition grounds, however, the monument to peace would have been behind them. Before them lay the main site of the Exhibition, a grand vista displaying most prominently the pavilions of European nations. Figure 1 shows a view from the Trocadéro entrance. Aside from the Eiffel Tower, the buildings which dominated this view were the Nazi German pavilion, pictured here on the far left, and the Soviet Union pavilion, which is not in this picture but was located directly opposite, to the right of the Eiffel Tower. To the south, along the Left Bank, were located the pavilions of the regions of France. Further still, segregated from the rest of the fairgrounds and beyond the purview of visitors from the main entrance, were the pavilions of the French colonies in Asia, Africa, and the Caribbean.

The world, as an Exhibition promoter proclaimed, *had* come to Paris the summer and fall of 1937, though the display of monuments, material objects, and people both exceeded and undermined the planners' intentions. The world Sasha inhabits is a representation of the international modern world. In Rhys's novel her characters, tellingly, have their backs to

Trocadero Fountains, German Pavilion in background. *Exposition Internationale des Arts et des Techniques Appliqués à la Vie Moderne, Paris 1937: Album officiel (Paris: La Photolith, 1937).*

the Peace Monument; the Exhibition display before them is a sight Sasha has tried to avoid since the beginning of the novel. And the novel, likewise, averts its gaze from the Exhibition, focusing instead on characters who struggle to survive economically and emotionally in a world of deracinated people whose stories reveal the racial and sexual exclusions inherent in nation.

Until recently much criticism of the novel has read it as a character study of Sasha, a typical "Jean Rhys woman"—more pathetic than sympathetic, a singular figure of failure, defeated by her life and unable to get past her past—and has paid scant attention to the significance of setting the novel in 1937 in Paris. Ignoring the setting prevents readers from taking Rhys seriously as much more than a stylist in the modernist canon, a writer narrowly preoccupied with "women's emotional life" who lacked "an enlarged vision of the contemporary world" (Staley 1979, 84). Like other modernist women writers, Rhys contextualizes her characters' sufferings historically—if somewhat indirectly. This reading builds on more recent criticism which considers the significance of the setting[1]—Paris during the Exhibition, and the Exhibition during a time of escalating European national conflict.

Sasha's journey to the Exhibition in the penultimate scene completes a nightmare she has at the beginning of the novel. In that nightmare Rhys's protagonist is trapped in a London tube station and is looking for a way out. Instead of the way out, she is confronted by signs pointing to the Exhibition. The novel itself begins with oblique references to disturbing events from the main character's past, and the novel unfolds as Sasha navigates her way through Paris over a period of ten days, fruitlessly trying to avoid places that are "saturated with the past" life she led in Paris several years prior (Rhys 1969, 91). The connection Rhys makes between literal space and inner conflict is made apparent from the beginning of Sasha's stay in Paris when she takes a room on a street called an impasse. That Sasha will fail to negotiate her way around the city and her pain is apparent by her lack of sense of direction: "north, south, east, west—they have no meaning for me" (1969, 26). As she wanders about the city, Sasha desires not progress, but stasis. Her past is painful and her future inconceivable. She remains in motion, however; not quite the flâneur of Walter Benjamin's boulevards, Sasha's goal is to avoid the memories triggered by her surroundings. With careful "avoidance of certain cafés, of certain streets, of certain spots" (1969, 14), Sasha hopes to avoid the nightmare that haunts her.

The difficulty of coming to terms with a troubled past, while specific to Sasha's story, takes on greater meaning when we consider Rhys's West Indian origins and the place of the Caribbean, historically, in the shaping of the modern world. As Eric Hobsbawm writes, modern history, synonymous with Western history—especially for the British who came to dominate the capitalist world they helped produce—depends upon the erasure of the histories of other peoples.[2] The diasporic, colonial world is also the past confronted. It is this world the Exposition planners literally pushed to the margin of the fairgrounds and that Rhys's plot recuperates. Although some critics might describe Rhys's historical frame as "after Victoria, before Hitler" (D'Acosta 1986, 390), this demarcation doesn't capture Rhys's perspective properly. As Hobsbawm notes, the nineteenth century continued to have its imperial effects well into the twentieth, and the British Empire was at its height just following World War I (Booth and Rigby 2000, 2). Historical references that would more closely capture the precarious nature of the "peace" between the wars might note instead

Soviet Union pavilion at the Exposition, 1937. *Exposition Internationale des Arts et des Techniques Appliqués à la Vie Moderne, Paris 1937: Album officiel (Paris: La Photolith, 1937).*

that the novel is set in the year that Guernica was destroyed; that Rhys was writing while the Nuremberg laws were in effect; that the novel was published four months after *kristallnacht*. Hitler's presence was felt in Europe in the 1930s well before the outbreak of war, and *Good Morning, Midnight*'s sympathetic portrayal of displaced Russian Jewish characters is evidence of Rhys's awareness of the personal results of political disruptions Europe experienced with the coming of Stalin and the rise of Hitler.[3] Instead, the novel, with its circuitous narrative pattern, its modernist emphasis on repetition and memory, illustrates the unavoidable—and sometimes horrifying, but always interconnected—presence of a political and personal past.

Representing the Nation

Paris in 1937 was teeming with people from around the world, as both spectators of and participants in the Exhibition. During the six months it was open, 3.4 million visitors attended the sixth, last, and largest of the Paris World Fairs (Allwood 1977, 184). Obvious in retrospect is the Exhibition's display of the competitive nationalism of European empires: "Even though the organizers attempted to imbue the site with an optimistic modernism, the Exposition was saturated with an abrasive nationalism which served only to confirm the irreconcilability of major European states. It was the cultural equivalent of the military engagement shortly to follow" (Greenhalgh 1988, 130). The prescience of the Exhibition, however, was not lost on some contemporary observers. Located prominently in the lobby of the Spanish pavilion was the first showing of Picasso's *Guernica,* which prompted Michel Leiris to write, "Picasso is sending us our death announcement: everything we love is about to die" (qtd in Peer 1998, 47). The pending inter-European conflict was suggestively staged in architectural confrontations, especially, as has been most frequently commented on, by the location of the Nazi German pavilion (as seen in Figure 1) and the Soviet Union pavilion (Figure 2) directly facing each other.

Although the Soviet pavilion planners tried to increase the height of their building by using it as a pedestal for Vera Murkhina's statue, *Worker and Collective Farm Woman,* the German building, designed by Albert Speer and topped by a National Socialist eagle perched on a swastika, dominates the view from the main entrance. Inside, the pavilion offered screenings of Leni Riefenstahl's already controversial *Triumph of the Will.* A promo-

Deutsche Reichsbahn **(German railways) brochure cover.** ***Exposition Internationale des Arts et des Techniques Appliqués à la Vie Moderne, Paris 1937: Album officiel (Paris: La Photolith, 1937).***

tional brochure for the Nazi pavilion proudly asserts Germany's role in modern technological progress: "Nobody can leave the Exposition without having the feeling that in Germany, and particularly on the railroads of the Reich, all the assets of modern technology are used to achieve the greatest possible safety" *(Deutsche Reichsbahn* 1937, 6). The front and back cover (Figure 3) with its border illustrations of trains chillingly complements the text in its celebration of recent industrial advances in rail travel, which a few years later would be utilized for mass transport to concentration camps.

Besides displaying cultural and technological products, an important part of the Paris Exhibition was the display of the nation itself, and how France in particular conceived of the role of the colonies in representations of *Grande France*. While other European nations housed their colonial exhibitions within their national buildings—except, of course, Germany, which had to surrender its colonial possessions per the Treaty of Versailles—as host nation, France exhibited its colonies in separate build-

French colonial pavilions at the Exposition, 1937. *Exposition Internationale des Arts et des Techniques Appliqués à la Vie Moderne, Paris 1937: Album officiel (Paris: La Photolith, 1937).*

ings. The Hobsbawm quote cited earlier calls attention to a defining aspect of Western modernity: like the Creoles, hybrids, and diasporic communities it produces, modernity is based on an internal split. It is an historical narrative that produces an historical erasure, even while the evidence of that erasure, such as the segregated colonies that constituted the French pavilion, are blatantly evident.

The official welcome to the 1931 *Exposition Coloniale Internationale à Paris* acknowledged that "the colonies will . . . become the new battlefield in works of peace and progress" (qtd in Lebovics 1992, 52). If, as Walter Benjamin concludes, the world fairs were "summary smothering acts of imposed historical interpretation" (Hinsley 1996, 120), the 1937 Exhibition amply demonstrated the place of the colony in the political and cultural economy of empire. In an effort to sell the idea of a Greater France,[4] an extensive French colonial section was located west of the Champs de Mars in pavilions built on huge pontoons floating on the Seine (see Figure 4). There were separate buildings for Morocco, Tunisia, Guadeloupe, Indochina, Martinique, Madagascar, Algeria, Réunion, and Corsica. Segregated from the main site, with no claim to be on terra firma, natives imported from the colonies labored for the profit of the Exhibition. Confined to the reconstructed "colony," "native artisans lived and worked in the display pavilions, and were not allowed to leave these areas without special permission from exhibition authorities" (Ezra 1995, 34). The French colonial natives were under constant surveillance of the steady stream of visitors and policed by organizers who made sure the profit from the products they produced while on display went to the Exhibition.[5] Rather than presenting an image of a unified nation, the presence of the natives in the metropole emphasized the distinction between colonizer and colonized.

Bodies and Commodities

The role of labor is among the myriad ironies of the Paris Exhibition. The original scheduled May Day opening had to be postponed due to a labor strike in Paris during construction of the Exhibition. Popular Front Prime Minister Léon Blum and General Commissioner of the Exposition Edmond Labbé colluded to subordinate all other concerns to the "national interest" of completing the construction, in spite of the fact that the labor struggles surrounding the Exposition "mirrored the class struggle outside the fairgrounds which was rapidly undermining the Popular Front" itself (August 1980, 47–48).

By emphasizing the role of economic necessity in her characters' present geographic location and their individual struggles, Rhys writes a counternarrative to the triumphant and purportedly inclusive nationalism that is on display in the Exhibition. Three of the male characters—Sasha's former husband, Enno; the gigolo, René; and Nicolas Delmar—served in foreign armies, Enno for the French Foreign Legion during the First World War; René also purportedly fought for the French Foreign Legion, in Morocco, which he has just deserted by making his way through Franco's Spain. References to the Foreign Legion are indicative of France's imperial incursions into North Africa. The image suggested is of imperial Europe at war, producing not just exiles and emigrés but mercenaries, too, as national wars were fought by displaced people desperate and struggling to survive.[6] René in particular is in a precarious position. Without papers, he is in need of a fake passport to escape France for England, where he hopes to make his living selling his body to English women. The former Legionnaire, having deserted the battlefield for the bed, engages in erotic rather than heroic maneuvers now.

If the men in the novel are revealed to be defenders of nations to which they don't belong, the depictions of women emphasize a different type of economic struggle. For Sasha, economic existence is dependent on appearance, on the exchange value of the female body, and several of the jobs she's described having held—as a hostess in a women's clothing shop, as a mannequin—emphasize the display of female bodies. Throughout the novel Sasha is preoccupied with being looked at. She perceives disdain in looks aimed her way, because she is getting old, because she is assumed to be English, because she is alien. In response to a malicious comment directed her way, Sasha concludes: "*Qu'est-ce qu'elle fout ici, la vieille?* What the devil (translating it politely) is she doing here, that old woman? What is she doing here, the stranger, the alien, the old one? . . . I quite agree, too, quite. I have seen that in people's eyes all my life. I am asking myself all the time what the devil I am doing here. All the time" (Rhys, 1969, 46, ellipses in original). As the city of consumption, Paris (per Benjamin) offers Sasha the promise of making herself anew. The appeal of the commodity, particularly as presented in a world's fair, is that it provides workers a way to "submit to being manipulated while enjoying their alienation from themselves and others" (Benjamin 1978, 152), making them participant in rather than passive observer of the modern world. The one certain aspect of Sasha's identity is that she doesn't fit in: "Please, please, *monsieur et madame*, mister, missis and miss, I am trying so hard to be like you. I know I don't succeed, but look how hard I try. Three hours to choose a hat; every morning an hour and a half trying to make myself look like everybody else. Every word I say has chains around its ankles; every thought I think is weighted with heavy weights" (1969, 88).

Repeatedly, Sasha tries to recuperate from her personal failures and painful encounters by consuming. Among the activities that bring pleasure are buying a dress and then a hat and having her hair dyed. To achieve the dye color she wants she is told all her original color must be removed first before the *cendre* is applied. As Rhys depicts it, Sasha's self-fashioning is not just a display of self, but a mask, an obliteration instead. Sasha as consumer of self-image fits thematically with the novel's direct (and the Exposition's unintended) revelation that outward displays attempt to obliterate origins and history. If she is to be perceived as a spectacle, the proper appearance will shield her from her spectators' critical eyes. On one of her excursions about the city, on a street that houses "at least ten milliners" (1969, 58), Sasha sympathizes with a bald woman making an "extraordinary ritual" (59) of trying on hats. Like the woman who needs a hat to hide the truth of her baldness, Sasha is obsessed with clothing because she is acutely aware of the necessity of hiding the truth of the effects of age and drink on her body.

The World of Not Belonging

While the Exhibition site foregrounds the modern, progressive ideology of nation, and ironically illustrates the competition between, hierarchies within, and exclusions from European nationalism, Rhys's novel refuses to make clearly legible the nationality of its characters. The characters Sasha encounters are all displaced souls who migrate across borders of various sorts, and the text is filled with people from around the world, all of whom are mediated through the protagonist's perceptions. In spite of the thematic importance of place and nation, Sasha declares: "I have . . . no country. I don't belong anywhere" (1969, 38). Sasha's assertion that she has no home is the credo of the colonial Creole that articulates the position of all of the outcasts in this novel. As Mary Lou Emery notes, the alienation and estrangement that are such important themes in modernism take on a different nuance when read not just as the crisis of a universalized Western subject, but when this condition is recognized to be a product of the modern world. In Rhys's novels the dilemmas her main characters face emanate from "an absence rather than loss of identity and the homelessness of one who never had a home" (Emery 1990, 14).

Originally named Sophia, Rhys's protagonist re-names herself Sasha. Her new name, along with the astrakhan coat and Cossack hat she took to wear when she departed London for Paris, obliterate her identity. Besides adopting a new first name, Sasha's last name, being that of the Dutch husband who abandoned her, further obscures her national origin. Like the *cendre* dye, marriage bleaches away origin. Sasha seems to attract, and is attracted to, people whose national identity is complicated by migration. The novel is concerned with not just revealing the diversity of Paris in the thirties but in depicting characters who are preoccupied with identifying people they encounter, often resulting in misidentifications. Sasha habitually takes notice of the nationality of other patrons at the restaurants and cafés she frequents. She notes the cuisine, too, which is international and becoming more so. A restaurant that "used to be a place where you could only get hot dogs, choucroute, Vienna steak, Welsh rabbit and things like that. Now, it's more ambitious. 'Spécialités Javanaises'" (1969, 38).

All the characters Sasha interacts with in her brief visit are from disputed or colonized territories, and the disjunction between what Sasha assumes upon first sight and what the characters claim as their homeland simultaneously foregrounds the importance and destabilizes the notion of national origins. At the Jardin Marco Polo, where she first notices the Russians, Nicolas Delmar and his companion, Sasha assumes they are German or perhaps Scandinavian. The three "stop under a lamp-post to guess nationalities" (1969, 39). Delmar is from the Ukraine, which, following a brief period of independence post–World War I, was under the control of the Soviet Union; 1937 is the year the hammer and sickle were added to the Ukrainian flag, as well as a time of one of Stalin's Great Purges in that region. She thinks René is Spanish or Spanish-American, but he insists he is French-Canadian, an ethnic and linguistic minority of the British Commonwealth. In the Exhibition the Canadian pavilion was literally annexed to that of Great Britain. Sasha speculates that the artist Serge Rubin is Russian, but we never learn for certain his national origin, nor, as Maren Linett (2002) notes, do we really know if his first name should be pronounced with a soft g (as if he were French) or a hard g (as if he were Russian). And although Sasha, much to her chagrin, is repeatedly perceived as English, as critics have generally noted, there are several important clues that she is from the West Indies.

Besides emphasizing the importance of national identity, the novel also illustrates how nationality is secured through sexual relations. As an unmarried woman, Sasha's national identity, and thus her very subsistence and existence, is precarious. The most painful of Sasha's memories are the death of her son and subsequent abandonment by her Dutch husband, Enno Jansen, resulting in a life of poverty and destitution exacerbated by the economic depression Europe experienced in the 1930s. Her brief, if impoverished, romance and marriage with Enno occurred in the post–World War I years. Sasha reflected at that time: "The war is over. No more war—never, never, never. Après la guerre, there'll be a good time everywhere" (1969, 96). But instead of a "good time" in the interval of "peace" between the wars, Enno, as his name, phonetically spelled "n-o,"[7] seems to portend, will not provide the way out for Sasha. Chief among Sasha's many failures, and the one that precipitates the departure of her husband, is that she fails to produce a child. Hard up to earn a living during their few years together, the Jansens fail at both economic production and biological reproduction. After the birth of her son Sasha is virtually mummified. The midwife bandages Sasha's abdomen in order to prevent stretch marks, a process that, though intended to preserve her appearance and thus her viability as a sexual commodity, effaces Sasha's role as procreator, and, coupled with the death of the newborn, erases the evidence of her labor. Besides her unmarried state, Sasha is thus also marked as a sexual outsider because she is literally unable to reproduce.

In contrast to the Paris Exhibition, which propounded faith in material progress, in the machine age, Sasha cannot put her faith in historical narratives of progress. Sasha's pain isn't simply the suffering of a mother who survives a dead child or a spouse dealing with abandonment. The ideology of nationalism—a narrative that also excludes Sasha—is another progress narrative that proceeds by exclusion. The others with whom Sasha connects are likewise outside the bourgeois heterosexual economy. Sasha's identifications are with the outcast, the injured, the impoverished, those whose place in the world, and thus their identities, have literally been disrupted: the dishwasher "who does all the dirty work, and gets paid very little for it" (1969, 87); the girl with strong legs and hands, hands that "sing the Marseillaise. And when the revolution comes, won't those be the hands to be kissed? Well, so Monsieur Rimbaud says, doesn't he? I hope he's right. I wonder, though, I wonder, I wonder. . . ." (1969, 88; ellipses in original); the Hindu clerk who insists Sasha, who intends to buy a "calm book about people with large incomes," buy instead a book of "lurid stories of the white slave-traffic" (1969, 111). As Sasha climbs the stairs to the room she and Enno share she thinks, "I get back to the hotel and climb upstairs to my room. This is a hard thing to do. Has anybody ever had to do this before? Of course, lots of people—poor people. Oh, I see, of course, poor people" (1969, 49). She watches an old woman trying on hats and fears, "Watching her, am I watching myself as I shall become? In five years' time, in six years' time, shall I be like that?" (1969, 58). Moreover, besides noting the outcasts that surround her in Paris, Sasha is acutely aware how they, like she, are held up for ridicule. When asked by Enno if she would like to "go in and have a look" at café patrons who have paid to be able to sleep rather than drink, she notes his suggestion sounds "as if he were exhibiting a lot of monkeys" (1969, 35).

Sasha's encounter with the Jewish artist Serge Rubin occurs in the middle of the novel and deserves special attention. As Sasha's sympathies cross borders of cultural difference and national identity, so do those of Serge. Two of the episodes from their meeting, Serge's story of his London encounter with a mulatto from Martinique and his production of African art objects, connect the Jewish character with a diaspora not directly his own. My reading here diverges from critics who have read these scenes as evidence of Serge's own racism and his willingness to engage in primitivist appropriation of another culture, or who read the encounter between Serge and Sasha solely in terms of what it reveals about her, rather than how it fits in with how the novel as a whole reveals the borders and exclusions inherent in European nationalism.

While visiting Serge in his artist's studio, Sasha breaks down in tears. Her despair reminds Serge of an episode in London when he met a mulatto woman from the Caribbean who was "at the end of everything" (1969, 80). Defeated by the racist hatred in the eyes of Londoners and the other inhabitants of her boarding house, she remains in London and in an abusive relationship with a white man because she has no place else to go. Serge tries to comfort her, but he also assumes she wants sex from him, to which he fails to respond: "I knew all the time that what she wanted was that I should make love to her and that it was the only thing that would do her any good. But alas, I couldn't" (1969, 81). She becomes insulted by his rejection: "When I passed her on the stairs next day I said good morning, but she didn't answer me" (1969, 81). Serge's presumption that she wanted sex and his refusal to offer it have been read as indicative of his own racism (Thomas 1999, 126–27). His presumption seems to signal a racist stereotype since "in Paris during the 1930s blacks represented sexual expression untrammeled by the repressive conventions of European society" (Gilman 1985, 120). However, what critics have not yet considered is that if his aversion to female sexuality is just that, an aversion to female sexuality, then as such it should be read as evidence of Serge's homosexuality.[8] Since male Jews in this period were read as effeminate or homosexual (Gilman 1985, 119; Boyarin 2000, 72), Serge's story of the encounter is more complex than has thus far been suggested. He says further of the episode: "There were two other women in the house. . . . I must say I never heard them speaking to the Martiniquais, but they had cruel eyes, both of them. . . . I didn't much like the way they looked at me, either . . ." (1969, 81). The novel thematically stresses the importance of exhibitions and appearances, of looking and displaying, of belonging and excluding. Sasha is constantly anxious and aware of being seen as an outsider, a foreigner, an old woman, a rich woman. In the scene above, it's narratively unclear what the other boarders see when they look at Serge—A Jew? A homosexual? Both? What is clear is that like Sasha and like the Martiniquan he knows he's being defined and excluded. The other boarders look at him, too; he, too, is one to whom "it is safe to be cruel" (1969, 81).

Trying to read Serge leads us into the confused, but politically potent, racist rhetorics of difference that construct (and often conflate) Jews and blacks in Europe in the 1920s and 1930s. A common construction was to elide difference and see the two groups as interchangeable (Gilman 1985, 31; Gilroy 1993, 211–12). Georges Montandon, chair of ethnology of the *Ecole d'Anthropologie,* employs this racist conflation when he refers to Léon Blum, France's first Jewish Prime Minister, as a "Nigger of the Nile" (Lebovics 1992, 42). Further complicating representations, both anti-black and anti-Semitic stereotypes are constructed through sexual categories that are mutually exclusive. While Serge perhaps could be read as a "white Negro" in certain contexts, he cannot be white in relation to other characters. When he tells Sasha that when he was in London he "looked quite an Englishman from the neck down" (1969, 79), he marks the limits performing whiteness can take him. Sasha herself, in her first description of Serge, immediately stereotypes his unmistakable Jewishness: "He has that mocking look of the Jew, the look that can be so hateful, that can be so attractive, that can be so sad" (1969, 76).

When Serge attempts to lift Sasha's spirits he plays Caribbean music, a West Indian folksong, *Maladie d'amour,* and dances for her while he dons one of the "West African" masks he has made. Serge's display takes on multiple levels of significance. Being a displaced Jew, his performance indicates not so much Western appropriation of African culture, but cultural reference to commonality. The sympathetic bond shared by Jew and African is repeated in the painting that Sasha buys depicting "an old Jew with a red nose, playing a banjo" (1969, 83).[9] This picture is significant to the novel not just because it reflects Sasha's own "marginalized state" (Sternlicht 1997, 91), but because it is culturally syncretic; it depicts one diasporic culture using the instrument of another to express itself.

The most frequently quoted line of the novel is Sasha's assertion: "I have no pride—no pride, no name, no face, no country. I don't belong anywhere" (1969, 38). In response to the question of what binds diasporic Africans, Ralph Ellison refers to what he calls "an identity of passions . . . a share[d] . . . hatred for the alienation forced upon us by Europeans during the process of colonization and empire." He concludes, "We are bound by our common suffering more than by our pigmentation" (1964, 255). More recently Brent Edwards has asserted the usefulness of Ellison's concept because "it forces us to take up whatever 'diaspora' might mean in a context shaped by European imperialism and racist exploitation. It also forces us to take up the issue in a frame of what Earl Lewis calls 'overlapping diasporas'—reminding us that peoples of African descent are not the only peoples who have been scattered by those forces" (1999, 796).

In contrast to the world that Sasha experiences walking around Paris, one full of hateful stares and hurtful gossip, or the world of the Exhibition, which Sasha spends the whole novel avoiding, what the world of Serge's studio offers is a culturally syncretic diasporic world; exiled Jew and white Caribbean who don't have a home in the metropole can cry and dance together. Besides being the only friendship she forms while in Paris, the episode with Serge affords Sasha her only peaceful reverie—a memory that stands out from the rest because it's the only one in the novel that does not bring pain. While Serge plays Martinique béguine music on his gramophone, Sasha recalls "lying in a hammock" in a place located between hills and the sea. As a number of critics have noted, the music identifies Sasha as a Creole with a past, if not an origin, in the Caribbean (e.g., Sternlicht 1997, 91; Savory 1998, 117).

Furthermore, I want to consider reading Serge's imitation of native African art as destabilizing claims to authenticity. The discourse of native and authentic—a discourse on abundant display in the colonial pavilions where imported "native" artisans crafted objects sold for the profit of the Exposition—is often used to undergird essentialist notions of identity, notions that in contexts more invidious than Exposition souvenir shops or museum vitrines would be used to identify, isolate, and, in violence more material than epistemic, obliterate difference. Discourses on race simultaneously resorted to essentialist constructions while linking outcast and degenerate categories. By claiming to create "authentic African art" Serge invalidates the "myth of black difference" (Gilman 1985, 125) that underlies much of modernist primitivism.

The numerous songs that punctuate the novel and articulate Sasha's thoughts are in contrast to the cold, inhuman mechanical production promised by the futuristic Exhibition. Instead of providing a means of self-expression, the world promised by the Exhibition makes Sasha "feel like an automaton." In contrast, when Serge shakes her hand, she notes: "The touch of the human hand. . . . I'd forgotten what it was like, the touch of the human hand. . . . Then he gives my hand a long hard shake and says 'Amis.' When he shakes my hand like that and says 'Amis' I feel very happy" (1969, 84; first set of ellipses in original). This is the only acknowledgment of friendship in the novel and one of the few times the troubled protagonist claims to feel happy. Serge's simple handshake is also in sharp contrast to other mentions of hands and limbs in the novel, the artificial limbs Sasha sees in a London shop, and especially the mechanical hand in her nightmare that points her to the Exhibition.

Conclusion: No Way Out

Setting her novel against the backdrop of the Paris 1937 *Exposition Internationale des Arts et des Techniques Appliqués à la Vie Moderne* enables Rhys to draw attention to the complex cultural conflicts that the Exhibition staged. As art historians have noted, the emphatic nationalism of that exhibit, in spite of its attempt at forecasting a hopeful future, calls attention instead to an impending repetition of a recent violent past. Reading the repetitions, and the myriad meanings embedded in them, helps explain the fatalistic logic behind *Good Morning, Midnight*'s final linguistic paradox: Sasha's yeses.

Although the encounter with Serge provides Sasha a respite from the world outside his studio, it is with René that Sasha finally attends the Exhibition and it is he who leads Sasha to confront the nightmare she's been avoiding. The novel's conclusion refers back to the beginning, and structurally the plot doesn't just move Sasha forward in time as she has her various encounters, but leads her, and the novel's readers, to confront her past. As the title—good morning, midnight—indicates, greeting the future often entails facing darkness. Rhys structures the plot in such a way as to make history itself an important theme of the novel. As Jean Radford notes, "One of the ways in which history is written into [1930s modernist] texts is by refusing to totalise, by posing the narrativisation of the past as a problem, so that the reader, like the participant in history, must piece together his or her own fragmentary and contradictory grasp of events. . . . [T]he characters' struggles to make sense of their memories stage questions of history and historicism as urgently, if differently, as any realist novel of the period" (2000, 36).

After visiting the Exhibition, René and Sasha end up in her room, where she allows herself to be seduced by him. She changes her mind, resists, and, after a violent struggle, René leaves. The scene that ends the novel has led critics to propose remarkably divergent interpretations of Sasha's final actions. Wanting René to return to her, Sasha opens her door slightly, undresses, and hopes for his return. Instead of René, the man in the room next to hers, having overheard the aborted encounter between René and Sasha, enters. The novel ends as Sasha, realizing that the man in her room is the traveling salesman—the *commis voyageur*—whom she has studiously and fearfully avoided and who gives her a "nightmare feeling" (1939, 31), says "yes—yes—yes" to his advances (159).

Various critics have noted the allusion to *Ulysses* in Rhys's ending (e.g., Savory 1998, 131), but while the echoes of Molly Bloom do ring through the concluding words of the novel, Sasha's affirmation is not the orgasmic and life-affirming cry of the autoerotic and decidedly un-chaste Penelope. Desiring stasis from the start, Sasha has discovered that she can neither stop time nor avoid her past. Like Walter Benjamin's Angel of History, Sasha is swept forward while facing an inescapable past. Overwhelmed by the accretion of that past, her surrender to the *commis voyageur* is a futile attempt to prevent herself from being swept along any further in a plot not of her making. By the end of her narrative Sasha can no longer distinguish temporal differences: "You are walking along a road peacefully. You trip. You fall into blackness. That's the past—or perhaps the future. And you know that there is no past, no future, there is only this blackness, changing faintly, slowly, but always the same" (1969, 144). Anticipating sex with René, Sasha thinks she has managed to be in a place outside of time, to achieve the stasis she's wanted from the beginning of the novel: "No past to make us sentimental, no future to embarrass us" (1969, 149). She engages in pre-sexual rituals "as slowly as possible." Wanting René to be patient, Sasha's interior monologue is inundated with repetition and delay : "Time, time, give me time—wait a minute, wait a minute, not yet . . ." (1969, 149; ellipses in original). But in spite of her efforts, the scene moves forward. The clock, as Sasha notes several times, "keeps ticking." Sasha wants to get René back because of the brief hope the encounter offered for stopping time. As she herself imagines chasing after him, she thinks, "It isn't too late, it isn't too late. For the last time, for the last time" (1969, 157).

With René gone, "all that is left in the world is an enormous machine, made of white steel. It has innumerable flexible arms, made of white steel. Long, thin arms" (1969, 156). This vision recalls the nightmare from the beginning of the novel which Sasha had upon first arriving in Paris. In that nightmare a man with a hand "made out of steel" (1969, 12) points her to the Exhibition instead of the way out she desires. Choosing to attend the Exhibition with René, Sasha, whose painful memories have all been dredged up by this point, acknowledges that there is no way to avoid the past. As a way to avoid the future, Sasha surrenders to the *commis*. As the novel's final, futile repetition, Sasha succumbs in a last effort to "despise another poor devil of a human being for the last time. For the last time . . ." (1969, 159; ellipses in original).

Notes

1. See Judith Raiskin (1996); Mary Lou Emery (1990); Veronica Gregg (1995); and Elaine Savory (1998).

2. "It is still difficult, if not impossible, to look back dispassionately on that century which created world history because it created the modern capitalist world economy. For Europeans it carried a particular charge of emotion, because, more than any other, it was the European era in the world's history, and for the British among them it is unique because, and not only economically speaking, Britain was at its core. . . . For the rest of the world's peoples it was the era when all the past history, however long and distinguished, came to a necessary halt" writes Eric Hobsbawm in *The Age of Empire, 1875–1914* (1987, 338).

3. While there are scant references to political events in Rhys's letters, the entries that do mention politics are indicative of her sensitivity to the effect events of the thirties had on people's lives and well-being. In 1933 while on holiday near Brighton she wrote: "I came down here crazy with depression. . . . Berlin fell through. [Hitler was elected chancellor] Leslie's friend who is a Jew has packed up and gone to America or is going. There was so little money that I chose a month here instead of a week in Holland. So you see— I'm so horribly sorry things are rotten in America too. Sorry for myself too. For everybody. But it can't go on. It's impossible and incredible" (Rhys 1985, 22).

4. For a full analysis of the development of the twentieth-century idea of an imperial *Grande France* to rival Great Britain and the collusion of museum and Exposition exhibits in fostering cultural change see Lebovics 1992, 64–83.

5. The artisans were paid a salary; their earnings, however, "amounted to 1/5 the monthly salary of the French cashier who worked in the shops that sold their products" (Ezra 1995, 36).

6. For more on colonial natives and their participation in and sacrifice to World War I see Lebovics, "Nearly one million natives of the colonies and external regions of France fought in World War I; 205,000 died for France" (1992, 62).

7. I am indebted to Jane Marcus for this observation.

8. In that regard, this scene echoes Sasha's recollection of the last tutoring session she had with another Russian, who wants to read all the works of Oscar Wilde, frowns "when he says the word 'femme'" (1969, 115), and seems to fear that Sasha wants him sexually.

9. Carole Angier claims that Serge is modeled on the Belarus-born painter Simon Segal, whom Rhys met in Paris. She bought a painting from him entitled "Old Man with a Banjo," which she ripped up in a fit of drunken despair over writing the conclusion of the novel (Angier 1990, 365–68).

Works Cited

Allwood, John. 1977. *The Great Exhibitions*. London: Studio Vista.

Angier, Carole. 1990. *Jean Rhys: Life and Work*. Boston: Little, Brown.

August, Thomas G. 1980. "Paris 1937: The Apotheosis of the Popular Front." *Contemporary French Civilization* 5.1: 43–60.

Benjamin, Walter. 1978. "Paris, Capital of the Nineteenth Century." In *Reflections: Essays, Aphorisms, Autobiographical Writings*, Edited by Peter Demetz. 146–162.Trans. Edmund Jephcott. New York: Harcourt Brace Jovanovich.

Booth, Howard J., and Nigel Rigby. 2000. Introduction to *Modernism and Empire*. Edited by Howard J. Booth and Nigel Rigby, 1–12. New York: Manchester University Press.

Boyarin, Daniel. 2000. "Outing Freud's Zionism, or, the Bitextuality of the Diaspora Jew." In *Queer Diasporas*. Edited by Cindy Patton and Benigno Sánchez-Eppler. 71–104. Durham, NC: Duke University Press.

D'Acosta, Jean. 1986. "Jean Rhys." In *Fifty Caribbean Writers: A Bio-Bibliographical Critical Sourcebook*. Edited by Daryl Cumber Dance, 390–401.New York: Greenwood.

La Deutsche Reichsbahn à l'Exposition Internationale. 1937. N.P. Édité par la Deutsche Reichsbahn.

Edwards, Brent Hayes. 1999. Interview with Charles H. Rowell. *Callaloo* 22.4: 784–97.

Ellison, Ralph. 1964. "Some Questions and Some Answers." In *Shadow and Act*, 253–63. 1953. New York: New American Library.

Emery, Mary Lou. 1990. *Jean Rhys at World's End: Novels of Colonial and Sexual Exile*. Austin: University of Texas Press.

Ezra, Elizabeth Rose. 1995. "The Colonial Look: Exhibiting Empire in the 1930s." *Contemporary French Civilization* 19.1: 33–49.

Gilman, Sander. 1985. *Difference and Pathology: Stereotypes of Sexuality, Race, and Madness*. Ithaca: Cornell University Press.

Gilroy, Paul. 1993. *The Black Atlantic: Modernity and Double Consciousness*. Cambridge, MA: Harvard University Press.

Greenhalgh, Paul. 1988. *Ephemeral Vistas: The Expositions Universelles, Great Exhibitions and World's Fairs, 1851–1939*. Manchester, UK: Manchester University Press.

Gregg, Veronica. 1995. *Jean Rhys's Historical Imagination: Reading and Writing the Creole*. Chapel Hill, NC: University of North Carolina Press.

Hinsley, Curtis M. 1996. "Strolling through the Colonies." *Walter Benjamin and the Demands of History*. Edited by Michael P. Steinberg, 119–140. Ithaca: Cornell University Press.

Hobsbawm, Eric. 1987. *The Age of Empire, 1875–1914*. London: Abacus.

Howells, Coral Ann. 1991. *Jean Rhys*. New York: St. Martin's Press.

Lebovics, Herman. 1992. *True France: The Wars over Cultural Identity, 1900–1945*. Ithaca, NY: Cornell University Press.

Linett, Maren. 2002. "The 'No time region': Trauma and Jewishness in Jean Rhys's Fiction." Unpublished manuscript.

Peer, Shanny L. 1998. *France on Display: Peasants, Provincials, and Folklore in the 1937 World's Fair*. Albany: State University of New York Press.

Radford, Jean. 2000. "Late Modernism and the Politics of History." In *Women Writers of the 1930s: Gender, Politics and History*. Edited by Maroula Joannou, 33–45. Edinburgh: Edinburgh University Press.

Rhys, Jean. 1969. *Good Morning, Midnight*. 1939. Harmondsworth, UK: Penguin.

———. 1985. *Letters 1931–1966*. Edited by Francis Wyndham and Diana Melly. London: Penguin.

Raiskin, Judith L. 1996. *Snow on the Canefields: Women's Writing and Creole Subjectivity.* Minneapolis: University of Minnesota Press.

Savory, Elaine. 1998. *Jean Rhys.* Cambridge, UK: Cambridge University Press.

Staley, Thomas F. 1979. *Jean Rhys: A Critical Study.* Austin: University of Texas Press.

Sternlicht, Sanford. 1997. *Jean Rhys.* New York: Twayne Publishers.

Thomas, Sue. 1999. *The Worlding of Jean Rhys.* Westport, CT: Greenwood Press.

Worldly Chickens in a Homely Empire: Accounts of Colonialism in Sylvia Townsend Warner's *The Salutation*

FREDA S. HAUSER

AN "ALARMING WOMAN WITH A CLEAR [AND] MINATORY VOICE, DARK, dripping with tassels—like a black and slender Barb . . . ," as her friend David Garnett described her,[1] Warner was a familiar figure among British intelligentsia, and her novels and short stories a familiar presence on household bookshelves around the globe by the 1930s. Consequently, the thirties were an exciting decade for Warner personally, politically, and professionally. A musician whose training as pianist and composer was interrupted by the Great War, Warner began her literary career with a wartime article on her experience as a munitions worker, but supported herself as a musicologist, editing an authoritative encyclopedia on Tudor church music. In the 1920s, she also began publishing poems and novels; her first novel, *Lolly Willowes* (1926), became the first Book-of-the-Month Club selection. In the early thirties, during the time she was writing *The Salutation*, Warner bought a cottage in Dorset, fell in love with Valentine Ackland, her lifetime partner, and became a local activist against domestic labor abuse. Afterward, in the late thirties, Warner joined the Communist Party and traveled to Spain in support of the Republican Army. During this time, she began to write novels in a more historic and less fantastic vein. Remarkably, considering her politics, the *New Yorker* began to publish her work then as well, distributing the first of the more than one hundred short stories and poems that appeared in its pages until her death in 1978. Thus, although Sylvia Townsend Warner is relatively unknown today, she was both locally and internationally famous by and throughout the 1930s—a figure essential to any survey of British women writers, and particularly, as my reading of *The Salutation* describes, those writing about empire between the wars.

The Salutation is the sequel to the novel that critics most often read for its anti-imperialism, *Mr. Fortune's Maggot* (1927). In *Mr. Fortune's Maggot*, a mild mannered, former bank clerk, Timothy Fortune, travels as a missionary to the South Sea island of Fanua. His way of making sure he feels at home is to bring the machinery of the "civilized" world with him. His selection includes a measuring tape and a medicine spoon as well as a harmonium and most importantly his watch: all tools with which to measure (and make a measured place of) the "primitive."[2] His mission is not a success. The only islander he thought he had converted to Christianity, Lueli, has secretly kept his pagan faith, and worse still, Timothy finds that he loves and desires Lueli despite, or because of Lueli's spiritual integrity. Moreover, he begins to realize the extent to which his mission contributes to Fanua's occupation by other Englishmen, and his realization leads him to decide to leave Fanua. Thus, Warner's satiric critique of Timothy Fortune as an English colonialist who "means well" ends when he gives up his life as a missionary and sails off toward the horizon at the start of the Great War.

But whereas *Mr. Fortune* represents Warner's lighthearted critique of the British Empire, I suggest that her novella-length sequel represents Warner's more somber misgivings, and the misgivings of thirties leftists in general, about the insidious inheritance the empire left in its wake. In many ways that are the subject of my essay, Warner's *The Salutation* (1932) represents the British Empire from the unique perspective of a thirties leftist in the process of developing her political philosophy as well as her writing style. As *The Salutation* demonstrates, Warner's critique of colonialism did not end with *Mr. Fortune's Maggot*: her sequel makes clear that although an Englishman gives away most of his possessions along with his mission, he finds it impossible to leave his profession as an accountant (whether of cash or souls). When the story of *The Salutation* opens, the Englishman has spent the war drifting from one job to another on Pacific ships. Numb with grief, he seems fated to coast forever until he glimpses the Andes from a Chilean streetcar and feels compelled to visit the vast plains that (so he has heard) lie on their eastern side. His journey is long, requiring more stints on ships around the southern coast and a long trek north through exotic cities and rugged countryside. By the time Timothy Fortune reaches the House of the Salutation, he is ill with sunstroke and sorrow, but he must again face the role he has played and still plays, however unwittingly, as an agent of the British Empire.

Looking back, Sylvia Townsend Warner would call *The Salutation* "the purest, the least time-serving story that I ever wrote, and . . . one of my best" (Harman 1989, 124).[3] Warner's choice of words illuminates her criteria in composing—and so suggests my way of reading—*The Salutation*. Warner's use of the terms "pure" and "least time-serving" would have had a particular technical meaning to her as a musician and poet: "pure" refers to a musical piece played in tune, while "least time-serving" may refer to a rhythm that does not follow the conventions of Western music. To Warner as a woman writer and so, by her own definition, a writer with an "obstinate and sly" sense of humor,[4] the phrase "least time-serving" could also refer to a story whose plot and politics alike do not follow the conventions of Western progress narratives and the imperialism they engender. In calling *The Salutation* her "least time-serving story," I suggest therefore that Warner conceivably meant to point out her mockery of bourgeois domestic schedules, capitalist time clocks, and even perhaps Mussolini's reputedly timely trains. Her estimation implies that *The Salutation* eludes the discipline (the simultaneously formal, ideological, and physical demands) of metronomes and timetables alike, and by extension also implies that fascism is the natural heir of imperialist politics and aesthetics. This essay begins with Warner's reflection in order to describe *The Salutation* in this vein: as a sly act of thirties leftist literary activism against the "time-serving" narrative poetics so useful to old and new authoritarian regimes.

Because she was a citizen and resident of the British Empire, Warner could compose her narratives of imperialism abroad from relicts she found at home. Unlike the hero of her Mr. Fortune stories, Warner never traveled to either the South Seas or South America. Rather, as she was fond of explaining, she drew the details of these exotic locales from local sources, some literary and some not.[5] For example, Warner explained that her first story about Timothy Fortune, *Mr. Fortune's Maggot,* had its origins in a volume of letters written by a woman missionary in Polynesia. Her memory of these letters, borrowed from the Paddington Public Library years before, along with "the influence of Duncan [Grant]'s painting" and "Bea Howe's childish recognition of the Valparaiso earthquake" (Warner 1982, 10–11), contributed to a dream Warner had about a missionary, which she turned into the novel's opening scene. Once she began writing, Warner culled memories from her experiences of English libraries, drawing rooms, cottage shelves, and gardens to describe the daily life of an English missionary on a tropical island. As she explained in a letter to fellow writer Garnett: "there is nothing original about [*Mr. Fortune's Maggot*], for it takes place on a Pacific island (like Defoe and H. de Vere Stacpoole), and the hero is a clergyman (like Mrs. Humphrey Ward and Oliver Goldsmith), and it is written in alternate layers of Powys and Garnett, both imitated to the life" (Warner 1994, 26–27). A friend's "bulldog who spent the night killing the neighbor's ducks parented my pigs," she wrote to her editor, and "the parrot [who appeared in Fanua] lived next door to the cottage at Wayford in Somerset," on the shelves of which stood an idol brought home from the empire's outreaches (1982, 11). Similarly, when she published *The Salutation* Warner confessed in a letter to Garnett, "It takes place in the Argentine. . . . I have killed a rhea for local colouring, and put in some hens. They are invaluable animals because they can be studied at home, and transplanted almost anywhere" (1982, 21).[6] Consequently, whether he contemplates his middle-aged life on a tropical island or mourns his Pacific past on the Argentinean pampas, Mr. Timothy Fortune travels through landscapes composed from explorer's tales, exotic artifacts, domestic devices, and domesticated animals, all of which Warner observed from home.

The copious details of *The Salutation*'s homely empire confirm that empires, like chickens, "can be studied at home and transplanted almost anywhere." If Warner did not need to see foreign landscapes for herself in order to convincingly describe their geography or politics, neither did she need to travel to see their effects on her Englishman, Mr. Fortune. As his hostess, Angustias, reflects, "the English have a way of being more or less at home anywhere" (*TS*178).[7] And the narrative arc from novel to sequel demonstrates that an Englishman is "more or less at home anywhere" because his compatriots and their colonialist cohorts have settled there already. The continuing story of Mr. Fortune's adventures begins when he arrives, travel-worn and feverish, at the House of the Salutation. Fortunately the hacienda's mistress takes him in, nurses him back to health, and offers him a job as her general factotum. Here in Angustias's house on the Argentinean pampas, the Englishman finds an "abundance" of things like broken clocks and tattered deeds—but no inventory. The story turns upon the House's abundance of material goods, for it is through the Englishman's contemplation of these things and his subsequent return to accounting that he finds a temporary home.

For if Warner's Englishman feels at home in the House of the Salutation, it is because he finds there the same material goods he—or Warner—might as easily have found at home. Most of all, like home, any "cupboard, boxroom, and storehouse" of the hacienda yields a remarkable number of documents, all artifacts of the print cultures (of Spain and England, specifically) that have built the House of the Salutation on South American soil. He finds that: "The remains of two races and two civilizations were mingled here, lying pell-mell . . . old books of devotion, advertisements from hardware manufacturers. . . . Stuffed into the crannies of the great desks and domed travelling trunks were packets of old letters, deeds, invoices, crumpled fiddle-music, daguerrotypes, astronomical charts, pedigrees of horses and dogs" (*TS* 197–98). This list of printed materials suggests the larger apparatus that has contributed to South America's colonization by two imperial powers, since as it turns out, both Spain and England have built the House. To the extent they are "mingled" together, the hacienda's books, letters, and charts represent their commonality as contributors to its history. The deeds and invoices represent the means by which the Spanish and English claimed and occupied colonial territory; the "books of devotion" and fiddle-music the vehicles with which they "civilized" its indigenous peoples; and the astronomical charts and pedigrees the way they maintained sovereignty over its landscape. Moreover, the texts' juxtaposition—the sacred "mingled" with the commercial and the scientific with the artistic—reveals not only their commonality but also Warner's ironic comment on the collusion between state, church, and capitalism in pursuing imperialism abroad. Warner's irony in this passage draws further attention to the ways in which her story mimics and revises, as well as simply represents, the authoritative apparatus necessary to colonial powers.

The "least time-serving" narrative form of *The Salutation* supports literary critic Gillian Beer's observation that Warner's "experiments are narratological rather than verbal" (Beer 1999, 77), and so leads to my further argument that *The Salutation*'s narrative form mimics and mocks the kinds of documents its protagonist finds. Accordingly my essay traces Warner's narrative strategy from her opening mimicry of master narrative's formal conventions to her montagelike narration of the accountant's South American experience, and finally her concluding aesthetic rebellion against the same conventions she mimics at the story's start. My first section describes the composition of the opening scene's narration as it includes the discourse of postcolonial novels, domestic manuals, and other progress narratives. In this way *The Salutation*'s opening sequence, as Gay Wachman observes of Warner's writing in general, "crosses cultural boundaries by mixing literary genres" (2001, 43). As I add, the story avoids reifying these literary genres' conventions as they justify conquest. I then turn to the middle section of *The Salutation*, which expresses Warner's more explicit critique of colonialism through the critical perspective of an English accountant who is both reluctant and yet compelled to feel national pride and practice his trade. Warner's protagonist is more than just an Englishman; he is an English accountant who has worked as a Lloyd's Bank clerk and a South Sea missionary and subsequently repented of saving either cash or souls. As he wanders upon the pampas, the accountant's ambivalence causes him to question the similarities between his household inventory and a conqueror's map, and here Warner's narration both represents his state of mind and resists the form of such imperial accounts. And lastly, in the story's final section, the accountant dreams, and his dream takes yet another form than those of the story's earlier scenes. Like much of Warner's writing, the Englishman's dream "combines the irresponsibility of fantasy with a meticulously accurate adherence to the minutiae of history" (Wachman 2001, 43), and thereby allows Warner to complete her critique of colonialism's accounts by eschewing their narrative norms. Together, I argue that the three sections of *The Salutation* perform as radical alternatives to the forms necessary to colonialist practices and consequently suggest the ways in which storytelling contributed to 1930s leftist activism.

The opening scene of *The Salutation* recapitulates that of master narrative by presenting the South American landscape as if spread before the imperial gaze. Though the rest of the narrative is told from the perspective of the House's mistress, Angustias Bailey, or of Mr. Fortune, the initial view of the pampas comes through an omniscient narrator describing the panorama. Like Plutarch's Caesar who came, saw, and conquered, the narrator surveys the scene without interruption. The view is open to the implied reader's possession because the residents are conspicuously absent. They are unnecessary because the narrator is an informed expert who possesses knowledge of indigenous habits, here passed on to the reader. The pampas appear unpeopled (as yet "undiscovered") because it is "the hour of the siesta, for a while yet nothing would move but the sun and the shadows. All round the house, for miles and miles and miles, though there was no ear to hear it, a continuous small sound existed—the crackle of the ripened sunflower seeds breaking from their envelopes" (*TS* 157). Though removed from the scene, the reader may still assess (and sensually possess) the landscape's plentitude, even while the natives who live for miles around are asleep and cannot hear the seeds crackle. The ripening sunflowers and the grazing cattle, the sleeping pups and yellow bitch, the abundant pumpkins—and the chickens basking in the dust—all lie available to the imperial eye of master narrative. Only the knowing narrator comes between the property and the reader by interpreting the House's history manifested by the multilayered roof line, the rusty shutters, the ornate arbor complete with empty bird cage and "put up long ago, in the taste of mid-nineteenth century Europe, sentimentally eclectic" (*TS*, 158). But even this commentary, couched as it is in the discourse of a travel guide that encourages the tourist to know and hence possess the scene, allows the reader's eye to peruse the hacienda and its rancho without interference.

Yet it is clear that this is no ordinary imperialist tale, for as soon as the mistress of the House of the Salutation begins to awaken from her siesta, her point of view dominates that of the omniscient narrator. This narrative disruption both violates the conventions of progress narratives, as stories told by an authoritative narrator, and emphasizes Angustias's role as the narrator of this section of the story, which is, not coincidentally, the part that establishes the Englishman's identity. The widow's accounts of "the stranger" would make of him an Englishman were he from England or not. It is Angustias (not nature or Warner speaking through her) who iterates the stranger's qualities as a "well-conditioned" (we might now say "naturalized") Englishman (*TS* 166). As the omniscient narrator introduces her, Angustias is an expert on English manners because she is the relic of "Harry" Bailey, an English settler, and by extension, presumably, because all Englishmen are alike. Even half-asleep, she can identify the nationality of the dry cough outside her window. Only the English cough in such a peculiarly restrained way. Arising, she finds his appearance confirms her identification because only the English wear braces, canes, and hats like the stranger's, though he is lacking the usual gloves, which should be lying "methodically face to face like a pair of kippers" beside him (161). Moreover, he has a watch, the Englishman's lodestone (and the English habit an Englishwoman such as Warner could count on him carrying anywhere). Angustias knows him even though he does not speak English for quite a while, instead "employ[ing] a tongue like no language of the Christian world": "bad and rather slangy Spanish" (164). In fact, her reiteration of his national identity is so powerful that it seems to dominate the entire story, since the Englishman's name is never mentioned; he is "the stranger" or "the Englishman," and only recognizable as Timothy Fortune of *Mr. Fortune's Maggot* because of his tattoo and intricately recalled experiences (the second only revealed when his free indirect discourse manages to overtake that of Angustias).[8] Hence, the meeting between Angustias and the wandering stranger reprises and mocks another feature of imperial tales: nationalism determined by common "race" (rather than by culture, for example), or, in other words, by what Benedict Anderson calls "imagined community." National identity, in Warner's story, is both arbitrary and coercive, a product of small sounds like coughs and props, like suspenders and gloves, that despite their pettiness engender their subject.

Her recognition causes Angustias to stir her household into frenzy, and here Warner mockingly reiterates the importance of schedules and other schemas for ordering imperial time and space. The stranger himself asks for nothing. But although he languishes sadly in bed long after his fever has passed and is indifferent to his surroundings, Angustias insists that the house be made worthy of his English need for order:

> At his third cough she had opened her eyes and looked round on her domain as sharply as a stranger. This was wrong, that was lacking, Soul of God, what outrageous cobwebs! All this would never do before an Englishman. For they liked to have things just so, well-ordered, well-conditioned —that extraordinary race who added to their reckless and incalculable fantasies the crowning fantastic touch of being neat; who would pick up a length of twine and twist it into a circle during an earthquake, who would run mad punctually. (*TS* 166)

Angustias identifies English desire and strategy: to make the world "orderly" by using "manly implement[s]" such as hammers (175). She then seeks to revive the stranger's Englishness by bringing him string to wind and clocks to fix. Actually, Timothy is really more housewifely than "manly" and more concerned with souls and sorrow than cobwebs and dirty dogs.[9] Nor would the Englishman in question remain calm and orderly during an earthquake: the Fanuan eruption of his earlier story sent Mr. Fortune into a frenzied, ineffectual tizzy. But Angustias's convictions persevere. According to Angustias, an Englishman's presence calls for a particular routine involving certain rituals: hygienic applications of hot water, domestic schedules run according to the rhythm of well-wound clocks and swishing black taffeta, and the periodic consumption of "*Tea*!" (161–62). As well, the English require a more precise allotment of space. Her daughter Rosa, housekeeper Quita, gardener Gregorio, and manservant Pepe must tackle chores from mending fences to unearthing the pastry cutter, all in the name of Englishness. Or, in other words, Englishness is a formula, possibly of the absurd (though neither Quita nor Gregorio feels its whimsy), since Angustias's "manuscript book of recipes" suggests to her that appropriate remedies for an Englishman's recovery from sunstroke include "a great many tisanes" along with a ham soufflé served by a maid wearing a light-blue straw hat (164). Being English, Warner implies, means nothing more than a recipe for a soufflé, so long as one creates the airy concoction in the proper order and proportions.

But if Englishness is merely a matter of the right orders, empire is not, as a recipe with grimmer implications attests when Angustias engages the Englishman in making apricot brandy. The apricot brandy recipe is a recipe for colonialism, and doubly significant because it produces the narrative turn from Angustias's to the Englishman's point of view. This turn from the Spanish widow to the Englishman as narrative agent replicates their nation's histories in Argentina: the Spanish occupied the territory in the seventeenth century, while the English later invested heavily in its infrastructure. Fittingly, the recipe from Angustias's domestic manual involves their cooperation in laying equal layers of apricots and sugar, products of Spanish occupation, in jars. The Englishman adds the finishing touch of dipping the jars in wax. Their first moment of accord happens when, "speaking almost simultaneously," they agree that the jars "ought to be sealed with a seal," and Angustias "ran it to earth in the deed-box—the old rusty seal of the House of the Salutation, which had once been used for branding slaves, printing into their flesh the small sharp outlines of the two cloaked and haloed holy women, Mary and Elizabeth," they decide that "it was exactly what they needed" (*TS* 176). More for aesthetic than practical reasons, they matter-of-factly print into wax the same signifier once burned into indigenous or African captives' skin. Ironically, the House's seal bears an image that recalls both Catholic saints and British or Spanish queens. Lying side by side with the land grant from a Spanish monarch or the deed from a slave dealer, the household seal represents the multinational collusion in brutality that has established and maintained the House of the Salutation. In addition, the provenance of the slave brand suggests closer attention to the other ingredients of the recipe it seals. The apricots would have come from trees whose stock was originally transplanted from China to the Mediterranean (possibly, legend hints, by Alexander the Great, an expert imperialist) and thence to the New World (usually by Spanish missionaries). Brought to Argentina by marauding imperialists and evangelical Christians, the apricots were planted in orchards cleared of native plants and people. In turn, the Spanish missionaries helped clear the way for the Spanish plantation systems worked by captive labor. The "clear brown sugar like lumps of quartz" that the Englishman pounds, "freeing it from its fibres of string" (175), ironically evokes the history of sugar production. The apricot brandy sealed with the household seal implicates British imperialism and Spanish colonialism, church and state as they have accounted for the capture, mutilation, and forced labor of innumerable people.[10]

The scene in which the Englishman and the Spanish widow prepare apricot brandy together calls particular attention to *The Salutation* as a political allegory in which Fortune, as the allegorical Englishman abroad, finds the same colonialism he has found at home and elsewhere abroad as the products and producers of Anguish. As Angustias has already explained, her name is translatable into English: "It means Anguish," she tells the Englishman (*TS* 171). Fortune discovers his fate in the house of Anguish as served by Quita (a form of the verb *quitar*, meaning "to remove"). Englishmen have lived with anguish in the House of the Salutation before now. Because Anguish is a landowner and established colonist, she is in a position to reify the English and their routines. She gives the Englishman shelter with her salutation, by recognizing and honoring him (in more than one sense). Ominously and significantly, however, Fortune has no name in anguish's house. Through the ministrations of Anguish and Quita, the Englishman forgets his name is Fortune and so regains the strength with which to collude once more in colonialism. Angustias has already reminded her guest of his heritage as an Englishman, though he would rather forget it; now she teaches him to preserve the fruits of slavery's history.

Thus far, *The Salutation* follows Angustias's perspective and the plot conventions of imperialist master plot from opening gambit to occupation to exploitation. But once Angustias and the Englishman collude over brandy, the narrative shifts to his perspective, which becomes the vehicle for Warner's most explicit critique of empire. For example, the Englishman is in an ideal position to understand how other bookkeepers such as geologists or geneticists contribute to the idea that the world is a possession that can be conquered by classifying and naming its features. And in this third section of Warner's story, Mr. Fortune can therefore satirize the role he is supposed to play historically as an Englishman. Soon after canning the apricot brandy, he pictures his sorrow as a souvenir from Fanua. "It's a wonder," he thinks, "that I didn't present it to a museum with all the other things I brought from the island. *Example of a sorrow, full length. Made by an Englishman in the Southern Hemisphere. Presented by, etc.* The lettering would be calm and neat, a lettering equally applicable to gold-bearing nuggets and marsupials" (*TS* 190–91). The Englishman's whimsical caption criticizes the Henry Stanleys, David Livingstones, and Charles Darwins whose science serves as a first inroad for imperialists and capitalists. His ironic comparison between deep emotion and gold nuggets or exotic kangaroos points to the cheap estimation of human lives in establishing claims over territory, whether on the American or the Australian continent. The imperial explorer, Warner implies, disciplines his newfound territory through science, via numbers and descriptions, as well as through guns.

The South American landscape under the Englishman's regard also puts the accounts of explorers, surveyors, cartographers, and settlers in perspective. For, rather than being inspired by territory below his potentially imperial gaze (as is the narrator in the story's opening scene), the Englishman feels desire stir only when he gazes up at the Andes from a Chilean streetcar far below their peaks. Furthermore, even his "authentic excitement and acknowledgment" in response to their unconquerable vastness does not give him the urge to possess them. Rather, he scorns such ambitions. He contemplates the enormous difference in scale between the lofty mountains and men's petty concerns:

> Absently his mind fingered their names like a string of bright beads. Man, armed with intelligence like a housewife with a feather whisk, runs through the world, hasty and tidy, dabbing at this or that with an exploration, with a name. Whether a summit be called Chimborazo or Mount Brown is but a dab with the whisk; for the existence of being a mountain there is no name and no exploration; mysteriously emerging and subsiding, the mountains heave along the land in a secrecy as unassailable as that of the waves wandering along the ocean. It is for fear that man has snatched up the feather whisk. This Tom, Dick, and Harrying of Chimborazo and Mount Brown is the familiarity, rather vulgar, of the parvenu. So, in the war—he had heard—people would call one death or another Minnie or Bertha. Yet these accredited, licensed fears . . . are man's expedient against a vaster terror. We hire the fear of death to protect us against the fear of life. Man sets the unscalable Himalayas as a guard between him and a blade of grass. (*TS* 187)

His musing has both metaphysical and political import. The "parvenu" who "dabs" at mountains avoids thinking about the violent effects of the artillery he calls "Big Bertha" or the mortar "Moaning Minnie," and he trivializes them so he can return fire more easily, without remembering the corpses they produce.[11] In addition, his thoughts imply that if bombs are feminized and thereby trivialized, so is territory when it is mapped. The surveyor who claims geographical features by mapping them engages in as silly, yet dangerous an act as a cross-dressing house-husband with a feather duster trying to dust a mountain. And here Warner turns the trivializing sexist process upside down and presents it in the context of empire. Explorer's accounts, along with bombs named after women, are equally ridiculous and even dangerous euphemisms for "a vaster terror" such as imagining the infinity represented by "the existence of being a mountain" or the arguably vaster terror of the death caused by imperialist wars. War, like the mountains, exceeds the limits of maps, clocks, and names.

As the above scene hints, *The Salutation*'s story, like that of *Mr. Fortune's Maggot*, turns upon the accountant's ambivalent and simultaneous desire for the eternal and the measurable. The Englishman remembers his desire for the mountains and rejection of imperialism as he paces upon the pampas on their other side, but he has been seduced into accounting again, this time by Harry Bailey's collection of clocks. Ironically, his fascination with time fuels his ambivalent desire for both mountains and clocks. Himself a "parvenu," a vulgarly recent arrival comparable to the nouveau riche, the Englishman is hypnotized by the antiquity of the mountains. He projects his desire for the postchronological upon the Andes (which, like Argentina, Warner does not name): "And then, without in any way changing, they put on their true being, and rose up out of a continent, with time wandering across their slopes like a slight cloud, and ships and cities scattered at their base no weightier than cobwebs" (*TS* 187). The mountains exceed human occupation, industry, and history. The Englishman's realization—that the time it has taken for the mountains to "r[i]se up out of a continent" infinitely exceeds the measure of "time" or power found in cities—gives him a dizzying new perspective. Their sublime fascination draws him around a continent and from the Pacific to the Atlantic. Yet in arriving at the House of the Salutation, he returns to his trade, assessing the House's "alarm clocks, travelling clocks, chiming clocks, clocks combined with barometers or showing the phases of the moon . . . clocks with one hand only, clocks with painted dials, and a clock whose weights had been founded out of a church bell possessed by the devil." Angustias's husband once used these clocks in "enforcing his punctuality upon a continent of *mañana*" (197). In other words, Harry Bailey's clocks were meant to coerce lazy "natives" into becoming laborers ruled by the clock. Their abundance first compels the Englishman to offer his service as a bookkeeper, even though he once regarded the trade as "deceitful" (*MFM* 11). In his continuing reverie, the Englishman contrasts the Andes with clocks and finds mountains infinitely more worthy, but he desires both. In Warner's critique, the imperial subject can be as disciplined by clocks and schedules as by stories, maps, recipes, or even brands or guns, even when he is self-aware.

Yet all this is not to say that *The Salutation* demonstrates unproblematic anti-imperialist politics from the point of view of the early twenty-first century. As Jane Garrity observes, "*Mr. Fortune's Maggot* geographically displaces the homoerotic on to a foreign locale," where "Polynesia . . . functions as a liberating Other" (2003, 147), and in its sequel, Mr. Fortune similarly projects his desires onto the South American landscape. In contrast to the world of billboards and "Berthas" that he rejects, the Englishman idealizes the Argentine as he once did Fanua. And in this same vein one might add that in setting *The Salutation* in a "foreign locale" that she never even visited, making of its mysterious landscape a site of English revelation, Warner coined an exoticized land as intellectual capital. In her story, South America functions as a potentially liberating dreamscape in which the Englishman—or an Englishwoman, presumably—may search for salvation. The mountains become the locale of enlightenment about "man." And the plains become psyche and thence the possible site of self-realization: "The different aspects of the unvarying landscape melted into each other like thoughts merging, colliding, returning, sliding off for ever, conditioned and unforeseen" (*TS* 183). The "flat and blank" pampas "release [him] into indirection . . . like the comfort of sleep without its cheating" (184). The blank affect that the Englishman finds in both the South American landscape and himself has the disturbingly solipsistic, self-indulgent, almost decadent flavor found in Byronic heroes (and aptly, Angustias thinks she might remind herself of what Englishmen are like by rereading "Byron, Surtees, and the prize volumes of the Badminton library" [167]). His conception of the pampas as a location whose sole purpose is his satiation connects Mr. Fortune to a lineage stretching back through jaded Romantic poets on their Grand Tours to the character of Robinson Crusoe.

If *The Salutation* were only a straightforward tale about an Englishman's personal journey, this judgment of Warner and her hero as imperial tourists might summarize its story. However, as Jane Marcus observes, "Warner was always turning fictional plots upside down" (1990, 534), and this story is no exception. Mysteriously, and unlike the narrator in the opening scene of *The Salutation*, the accountant cannot find a vantage point from which to survey the pampas. The prototypical experience of the imperial explorer eludes him. Unlike Julius Caesar or Robinson Crusoe, Mr. Fortune cannot climb to the top of a hill and survey his new territory. Instead, he tramps on "leisurely paths that curled over the waste with no appreciable scheme, a map as baffling and traditional as though it had been traced out by hares" (*TS* 183). Unable to see any farther ahead than a rabbit, he cannot distinguish between the landscape's features. Even when he finds a view, it is generic rather than scenic: "There seemed to be little or no cover in this flattened landscape, yet a few minutes of following one of these paths would dandle one on the edge of a prospect apparently unknown. A clump of gaunt thistles reared against the sky might look familiar, but was it the same or different as the clump he had seen before?"And even when he comes upon the signs of human occupation, "a tarred hut, a zinc water-trough, a rubbish heap," they are so similar that they are "insignificant" landmarks (184). Given such a landscape, navigation is impossible. The pampas give this Englishman "no appreciable scheme" through which to map, or to possess them.

In this scene, Warner also turns her own plot "upside down" by rewriting the story's opening scene, for here the pampas cannot be romanticized as a wild landscape spread before the gaze of the imperial view for more than one reason. They not only elude mapping, they are also littered with the debris of human occupation. Furthermore, at least one of those humans resists and even returns the imperial gaze. The first sign of resistance comes when, like the "English" cough that woke Angustias from her siesta, a Scotsman's clean laundry interrupts the Englishman's daydream: "And then, breaking in upon it like the tones of speech, one of those hovels would rise up, and perhaps a troop of children would run acclaiming from the doorway or McGregor's shirt hang airing upon the line" (*TS* 183). McGregor's shirt—the sole distinguishing feature of the pampas—is an earthier version of the cane, hat, and suspenders that prompt Angustias to "recognize" the Englishman in the story's opening. The shirt means that this is where the only other (arguably) British denizen of the pampas lives, a Scotsman originally christened McGregor in Greenock but now locally known as Gregorio. Long ago Harry Bailey discovered McGregor drunk and penniless and gave him the job of gardener, and now McGregor is the Englishman's reflection through a looking glass similar to Alice's in its reversals. If the housewifely accountant imposes order on the domestic scene, for example, the hypermasculine McGregor disseminates chaos and children into the wild. McGregor a.k.a. Gregorio has forgotten most of his English and been assimilated, somewhat literally, into local life by virtue of having "strew[n] the neighborhood with bastards" (183). McGregor is also noteworthy as Warner's play upon another McGregor: the ogrelike gardener who chases Peter Rabbit and his siblings from the garden in Beatrix Potter's tales.[12] In both Potter's and Warner's stories, McGregor is a taciturn man given to occasional bad-tempered fits of passion. In *The Salutation*, his Scots name, trade, and gruff character are identical to Potter's character, except that in Warner's version the gardener breeds like a rabbit and eventually stirs the Englishman's political self-awareness. In Warner's story, McGregor is the larger-than-life expatriate "gone native" of *Peter Rabbit* and postcolonial literature in general, as well as the local storyteller of native fables who later illuminates the Englishman as his own worst nightmare: a hobgoblin colonialist.

The South American dreamscape initiates *The Salutation*'s narrative turn into the long dream the Englishman has after his walk on the pampas, a dream that culminates in the final realization of Warner's story as a radical "narratological experiment" with master narrative. As in the story's waking scenes, the dream scenes critique—while its narration escapes and reshapes—the conventions of maps, schedules, and progress narratives. The dream's erratic plotting follows an idiosyncratic rather causal logic that depends on the Englishman's desires and fears, and so consequently eludes the conventions of those narratives about the British Empire that would have been as familiar to Warner as her neighbor's chickens.

The Englishman's dream follows the convention established by fantasy novels such as *Alice in Wonderland*, in that it begins unannounced and only slowly reveals, through a series of increasingly fantastic scenes, its genre. The dream's more explicit critique of imperialist acts begins with a tableau that represents the history of colonialism in miniature (with some pathos). It begins with a gun shot by the young heir to the hacienda, Alfredo, when he kills a rhea in front of the Englishman. The rhea is a true native of the pampas, a bird that has the two-legged, six-foot-tall stature of a dead man even when lying in the dust, as the Englishman uneasily notices. Alfredo pauses proudly on his horse: "Slender, fiercely erect, racked with youth and pride, the boy with a gun stood there in a trance of hatred, defying a world of rheas, a world of harmlessness, dowdiness, ungainliness. There could be no mistaking his intent. Apollo could not have bent his bow with a more divine single-mindedness to destroy. . . . One might as well have blamed a flash of lightning" (*TS* 202). Hovering above the corpse of the native and his "Grandmother's Englishman," Alfredo defiantly challenges the interloper and establishes his own authority as Angustias's (anguish's) heir. The shot and the following brief, but shocking tableau do not seem like a dream, but they are soon revealed as part of an unconventionally plotted exposé of the Englishman's waking preoccupation with the imperial mission in which the world is property to be claimed with guns.

In his dream, as when awake, the Englishman finds he can only understand his surroundings by comparing them with what he knows, and so the first hint he is dreaming comes when he again finds the pampas haunted by his memories. In his dream, these "memories" penetrate and even temporarily replace the pampas. Alfredo rides off, and as the lone mourner over the rhea's corpse, the Englishman finds the landscape around him permeated by nostalgia. For the first time in years "the desire to go home to tea, to tea in England" ravages him. The pampas around him give way to his desire, and in a series of brief verbal snapshots, he is suddenly in England in November, first approaching a muffin man offering his wares on the street, then sitting before a fireplace filled with glowing coals. The experience seems real, since he not only sees the "sober, emptied streets" but also hears and feels "the light rattle of tea cups, the noise of the canister opened, the blurred breathing of the kettle. . . ." His memory brings longing for a muffin and a cup of tea. Yet his "memory," as he realizes a moment later, is of a memory forged from cliché; he thinks, "as a matter of fact I always preferred a current bun, toasted" to muffins. The Englishman has been caught up in "a fancy . . . an imagination" (*TS* 203–4), and his false nostalgia calls into question his perceptions in general, as well as his ability as an accurate accountant. Furthermore, the brief verbal snapshots that represent the Englishman's false nostalgia for his lost origins make up a narrative palimpsest that implies that all maps are similarly pieced together, fictional constructs based on comparisons between places and times and therefore predicated upon the (necessarily faulty) perceptions of their cartographer. The dream questions the expatriate's authority as either an historian of "home" or a geographer of elsewhere. How many other historians (however well meaning) inscribe their desire into their texts? How many other surveyors inscribe the ghosts of England's healthy heart/hearth into their reports and maps?[13]

In direct contrast to his experience on the pampas, where the scheduled English ritual of teatime overlays the wild and rebellious South American countryside, the Englishman finds chaos and revolution threatening the English practice (as exhibited by not only the Englishman but also Angustias's husband before him) of "keeping time" and thereby possessing private, interior domestic space as well as the wider public space laid out in maps. If the dream plot makes the accuracy of maps suspect, so too that of calendars and clocks: if cartography cannot chart the wild neither can chronography tame the domestic. When the Englishman returns to the house, household routine and narrative sequence fall apart. The clocks strike the time, but Quita scrubs the floors at bedtime, since "she had long ago outgrown the fences of law and order, and did the whim move her to bake at midnight, wash the dog at dinner-time, no one said her nay" (*TS* 210). In the dream world, rather than the master "enforcing his will upon a continent of *mañana*," the servant determines the domestic schedule (197). More ominously, while she scrubs at odd hours, Quita conspires with the young Alfredo against the Englishman, and they whisper furiously outside the Englishman's bedroom doors. Her conspiring whisper suggests a revolution, and the sound of her brush and the whispering fittingly invoke a second slippage between times and places. The English practice of keeping time has become meaningless.

As Quita's (or in allegorical terms, quitting) time overtakes the bourgeois schedule, and the dissatisfied domestic worker collaborates with the jingoist heir (who has his own reasons for wanting an uprising), the Englishman is overwhelmed. He retires to bed and dreams a dream within his dream. The embedded dream's narration performs as a prose montage of his life that challenges the hierarchies by which the Englishman has lived, and reminds him of the similarities between artifacts of empire and so-called primitive artifacts. Scraps of scenes represent the places he has lived and people he has known mingling as if in a strange, hallucinatory ritual conducted with both "primitive" and "civilized" artifacts. He is in Fanua, where Quita appears as a wooden idol before which Alfredo plays the flute, while an earthquake shakes them all (*TS* 211). The idol becomes flesh and sinks into the earth, crying out, "Remember Endor" (211). As the dream continues, so does the chronological chaos that juxtaposes not only reality and dream but also day and night, pampas and Pacific, the Bible and Defoe, wood and body, and, perhaps most important, as in his frame dream, master and servant. Through its form and content, the embedded dream exposes the conventions and authority of master narrative as convenient fictions. Composed of other texts as much as original material, randomly interrupted and concluded, the embedded dream has no discernible causal sequence, but it does have a moral. Its chaos spills over: when the Englishman awakens from his dream within a dream, he finds the household in an uproar; furious at Quita's rebellion, Angustias fires all the servants and enters the kitchen herself. Christianity and the happiness of servants are myths, the mistress can do housework, if need be, but the master cannot really ever "keep time."

In building to its climax, the Englishman's dream embeds not only a dream within a dream but also an anticolonialist folk tale with a moral when Alfredo repeats a fable told him by McGregor. Retold, McGregor's fable characterizes the Englishman as a "Brown," a variety of friendly, but insidious hobgoblin. Browns never labor themselves. Instead, they find hosts and follow them wherever they go, always eager for more. They seem harmless when they arrive on one's doorstep, but they quickly show their true nature. They make themselves at home by consuming all the contents of the household's larder and garden without a thought for others or for the future (*TS* 220). The moral of McGregor's tale, especially as told with especial emphasis by Alfredo (and, ironically, while they are driving through colonized territory), is that progress for the colonialist means devastation for the colonized people and their landscape, even when the colonialist has every good, but unthinking, intention. The moral particularly resonates for the Englishman because the fable was told to Alfredo by McGregor (maybe about him) and before that to others about other Englishmen. The Englishman sadly thinks that he has again become an accountant. He recognizes the similarity between himself and the "Brown": he too has arrived unexpectedly and lived from others' labor while contributing no more than the printed pages of his inventory. And with this recognition, the Englishman also realizes—for a fleeting moment—the extent to which his accounting has contributed to the work of empire, despite his own good intentions.

But the revelation the Englishman experiences in his dream is fleeting, and as a result Warner's *Salutation* again interrupts progress. That Warner's dream revises master narrative along with maps and timetables (and thereby conquest and class oppression) becomes particularly apparent when the Englishman's dream ends, for the accountant's and the narrative's progress alike are subject to his disastrous clumsiness when he accidentally overturns the vehicle of his advancement. Speeding from the hacienda to the town inside Alfredo's sleek automobile, the Englishman sits between the elderly Spanish widow and her heir. Angustias and Alfredo debate his presence between them. Alfredo views him with rancor, considering him an interloper whose "race" and work have given him too high a place in Angustias's esteem. At this moment, the Englishman fully realizes that his motives are, and always will be suspect, and for good reason—but no conventional narrative pause follows his epiphany. Instead, the Englishman's sad realization is interrupted by first a radical metamorphosis and then a literal revolution, for the "infallible machine" around him seems to become a "prowling beast" as fireworks, set off as part of some religious festival, explode in the sky before them (*TS* 221). In his confusion, he lurches against the doorhandle, letting in "a thrust of icy air . . . through the wound of the opened door, pinning the car to a standstill, toppling it over," and waking him (224–25). As an ending to a dream, this sudden, violent conclusion violates expectation.

Warner's use of dream as prophecy is not unusual, of course, since the dream plot can be traced back beyond the Old Testament to Homer, but Warner's dream plot is unique in that her dreamer, shaken awake by his dream's violent ending before he could absorb its moral, forgets both dream and moral. Just as Angustias reads a letter from her grandson announcing his impending arrival, just as the Englishman begins to think he should "cry out a warning, against what threatened her and himself, and this other one, already aimed towards them," his memory of his dream "snapped like a bubble" (227). The dream's sudden end cuts off any resolution that might otherwise come from further conversation with Alfredo. And doubling the shock, the Englishman's forgetting cuts off any progress he might otherwise make as a character. The frailty of the Englishman's dream is particularly remarkable because it calls the meaning of the entire story into question. When the Englishman forgets his dream, he forgets his realizations about himself and must learn the same lesson again. His loss of memory is the last of many ways in which Timothy Fortune avoids the heroic mold. Following the abrupt interruption of his epiphany, the abrupt break in the dreamer's memory after he wakes emphasizes that this dream plot, and by extension the entire story, eschews any usual ending.

But before the Englishman forgets his dream, he speculates about its origins in a way remarkably similar to that of Warner divulging the inspiration for her stories. As he slowly emerges from his dream, the accountant thinks: "Our dreams should remind us of ourselves, . . . for they, more obviously than ourselves, are at the mercy of chance. A nothing deflects them" (*TS* 225). Like Warner, her protagonist traces his dream back to homely artifacts—a dog's bark and a shepherd's story: "The end of my dream, that seemed so terrible and yet so full of dark consolations, may well have been spun from a draught out of the window, the bark of the old bitch in her kennel. . . . Gregorio the shepherd had spoken of shooting a rhea. There was the seed from which, wafted hither and thither in its growth by accidents of body and mind, untraceable, the dream had sprung" (225–26). The Englishman's speculation parallels Warner's disclosure, intimating that Warner "transplanted" her dilemmas as a British leftist in the 1930s, along with her memories of chickens, to the House of the Salutation.

And this leads to my final question: if "dreams should remind us of ourselves," what does this story reveal about its author? Warner traced her story back to relics of the British Empire brought home, and her desire to write the story to a dream, but what other dreams and artifacts inspired *The Salutation*? Significantly, Warner's choice of setting represents not just any homely empire "transplanted almost anywhere" but rather one specific location of English investment in Spanish empire. By the time of the story's setting, the Spanish had long since taken over Argentina, enslaving, murdering, and uprooting its indigenous peoples. In the late nineteenth and early twentieth centuries, the English invested heavily in its infrastructure. Hence, in *The Salutation,* the representatives of two imperialist powers meet in a country they have both colonized. That Angustias is the Spanish widow of an Englishman suggests her husband's role as a British investor in the colonies, as do the newer bricks of the farm buildings (*TS* 157). The phrase "rich as an Argentinean" became standard coinage around the world—until the year in which Warner began writing *The Salutation.* In 1930 Argentina appeared in British headlines as the Great Depression reached Argentina's banks and a coup d'état established a military right-wing government. The rustiness of the hacienda's ornaments and guns hint at the recently failing economy of what was once one of the wealthiest agricultural nations in the world, and Alfredo's appearance calls to mind Argentina's newly installed right-wing government. Under Anguish's tutelage, the Englishman's catalog of "the remains" of the House of the Salutation explores postdepression Argentina's complicated place in the global history of imperialism and the transatlantic spread of fascism in the 1930s.

The Salutation's setting, and Warner's later support of the Spanish Republican Army, suggests a source for the story she never mentioned: newspaper reports of the growing fascist movement in Europe, and especially Spain. From its opening gunshot to its concluding upheaval, the Englishman's dream represents fascism as the natural successor to imperialism. The suddenness of his shot and the Englishman's subsequent equation of the rhea's death with murder ("as portentous as a man's") suggests a coup d'état. When he meets the Englishman in the House of the Salutation, Alfredo's posture is militant. In a telling scene, the young master-to-be throws open the ordinarily latched gun cupboards, "their glass panels waking unaccustomed flashes of light in the unvisited dark corner." The flashes of light illuminate the gun collection at the masculine center of the House which is Harry Bailey's smoking-room. Alfredo takes charge of the guns, complaining of their rustiness and polishing one barrel after another (*TS* 206). Until now, even when he was completing his inventory of the House, the Englishman had not known enough about the guns to assess them in the House's books (207). Hence Alfredo's posturing as the heir effectively challenges the Englishman's "ripening . . . authority as a power for order," suggesting that his time, and that of the British Empire, is almost over. And although many young people can be similarly surly, this young man is not only hostile but also obsessed with order. Alfredo's automobile with "a slender arrogant shape, steel-coloured, contoured like an orchid" evokes the technological fetishism of Italian Futurism (205). His automobile is an "infallible machine" (221), and his future estate must run as smoothly, which means putting elderly women and middle-aged Englishmen in their place. Alfredo objects to the Englishman because he sullies Angustias's honor by appearing to be her "gigolo" (223). Alfredo persists in his paternalism, implying that his grandmother (an older woman with a known weakness for Englishmen) has no inherent honor of her own, though Angustias repeatedly and with great dignity objects to his autocracy. Alfredo also objects to inheriting the financial burden of supporting an aging and incompetent accountant (223): the accounts of the House of the Salutation must be streamlined. The future and natural heir to the colonial household, Warner suggests, could be a right-wing general, appearing suddenly, heralded by bullets, and eager to establish a new order.

If dreams should remind us of ourselves, it's fair to add that *The Salutation* hints at the political environment in which Warner lived during the early 1930s. Her character of McGregor, for example, draws upon an archetype common to colonized people's fables and political cartoons alike: the gigantic colonialist terrorizing indigenous peoples who depend upon the land. McGregor's fable (though ironically retold by a colonist for his own purposes) is class conscious: the "Brown" is the Englishman who does nothing, that is, the aristocrat who expects service as his due. Likewise, Warner's characterization of Alfredo as a young militant man with his gleaming guns and hostile attitude must surely have called to mind, for Warner's contemporaries, journalists' photographs of uniformed young fascists in Spain, Italy, and Germany. The Englishman's fleeting realization at the end of his dream is that he must leave the House of the Salutation or again (as in Fanua) prove himself a parasitic colonialist, though on South American rather than Polynesian soil. By extension, one might even suggest that the Englishman represents Warner's growing awareness of the connection between imperialism and fascism so convincingly described not long afterward by Virginia Woolf in *Three Guineas*, a connection supported by their common totalitarianism, patriarchy, and jingoist, racist nationalism. And, arguably, *The Salutation*'s story of the relationship between an Englishman and a Spanish woman reflects the newspaper reports of the Spanish fascist movement which Warner must have read as she wrote *The Salutation*, and anticipates the Englishwoman's trip to Spain not many years afterward.

Warner wrote of the Englishman's dream: "there was the seed from which, wafted hither and thither in its growth by accidents of body and mind, untraceable, the dream had sprung" (*TS* 226). Here she suggests that all stories be discussed within a longer, wider context. The political problems raised by *The Salutation* and its "narratological experiments" derived from, and contributed to a much larger conversation, a conversation in which Warner and other writers represented by this volume participated. In making this assertion, I follow Marcus's early work on Warner, in which the feminist scholar compares Warner's feminist fantasy novels with Rebecca West's, concluding that both construct a woman's "wilderness of one's own, away from family control of domestic space and male control of public space" (Marcus 1984, 136). Marcus's comparison leads me to compare Warner's construction of herself through her novella with West's construction of herself as a public intellectual through her letters. (See Scott's essay in this volume.) I follow as well Wachman, who locates Warner's writing within the context of "the work of a diverse group of writers who used fantasy as a means of escaping, reshaping, and critiquing a world fragmented by loss and pain" between the world wars (Wachman 2001, 2). At their core, writes Wachman, these writers "castigated without fear the dominant culture to which they appeared to belong, all were sexual outlaws, discerning in their ability to live full lives and think for themselves without the tutelage of men" (2001, 182). This assessment, in turn, calls my attention to Linda Camarasana's essay in this volume: I compare Jean Rhys's sexual and national "outlaw" to Timothy Fortune, and Rhys's narratological resistance to official maps and other documents to Warner's. *The Salutation* bears comparison with Virginia Woolf's writing as read by Briggs in this volume as well: Warner's novella illuminates the workings of Englishness and the British Empire. I also follow Hackett's comparison of Warner's writing to Virginia Woolf's, among others, when Hackett traces the discourse and appearance of such British artifacts as legal documents, court proceedings, and comparative ethnography in Warner's and Woolf's novels (Hackett 2004). I leave it to my reader to draw further conclusions about the many other "seeds" from which Warner's writing has sprung.

Perhaps most arguably, *The Salutation* bears out Warner's later claim: "Women as writers are obstinate and sly," meaning that because of the stringent demands on their time and constrictions on their movements, they must be stubborn and artful about how they express themselves (Warner 1990, 539). From the story's opening scene to the Englishman's dream Warner obstinately critiques imperial conquest as it depends on appraisals by imperial explorers and anthropologists, housewives and slavers, scientists and museum curators, cartographers and horologists, linguists and—not incidentally—bookkeepers. In addition, and as if in response, *The Salutation* performs as literary activism by "escaping, reshaping, and critiquing" the 1930s. In writing her "purest" and "least time-serving story," Warner slyly set her reshaping of the colonized world against the "pure" notes of a flock of chickens. Accordingly, she composed *The Salutation* of familiar scenes: "it was here, in the soft earth, that the fowl scratched themselves in. When the pumping fans began to clank, Quita would come and shoo them away; and the morrow they would sleep there again" (*TS* 158). But against this homely routine, Warner wrote a counterpoint that refers to, but eludes the master narrative's progression from imperial gaze to conquest with bibles and bombs to the commodification of territories and bodies for profit and power. And showing her foresight, *The Salutation* expresses both Warner's "obstinate" protest as a leftist feminist against colonialism and her "sly" warning that empires have spawned not only colonialism but also the fascists who wait to claim their accounts.

Notes

As with any writing, this essay stems from many conversations, and here I must gratefully thank feminist scholars Robin Hackett, Gay Wachman, Emily Hinnov, and Jane Marcus in particular.

1. See Garnett's reprinted letter to Warner from 11 Nov. 1924 (*PNReview*, 1981, 41).

2. The relationship between the British Empire, primitivism, and time in *Mr. Fortune's Maggot* is a key topic of Warner scholarship. See discussions by Wachman (2001), Hackett (2004), and Hinnov (2006). These critics agree that *Mr. Fortune's Maggot* satirizes a British missionary's desire for a life ordered by clocks rather than "the primitive," but they diverge in their various interpretations of those clocks' failure in Fanua.

3. In her 1989 biography of Warner, Harman usefully cites this and other passages from Warner's brief notes on her early books, which notes are presently maintained by the Dorset County Museum in Dorchester, England.

4. See Warner's lecture, Women as Writers (1959), in which she observes that "it is well known that a woman can be in two places at once; at her desk and at her washing machine." Women's consequent "bi-location" means that "women as writers are obstinate and sly" (Warner 1959, 540).

5. My description of Warner's sources draws from her letters as reprinted in *Letters* (1982) and *Sylvia and David* (1995) as well as from an account she wrote for her editor, William Maxwell, who published it in *Letters* (10–11); Warner also gives a version of this account in her preface to *Mr. Fortune's Maggot, and The Salutation* (2001, 8).

6. Warner never specifically names the country in which *The Salutation* takes place, perhaps preferring to evoke its unique geography (by referring simply to "the pampas")

rather than its national identity. This lack of a proper name has led to readerly confusion. According to Warner's biographer, Claire Harman, the story is set in Chile (1989, 125), whereas Adam Mars-Jones, the editor of its 2001 republication, claims its setting is Brazil. (This may be why, at the time of this writing in 2007, the U.S. Library of Congress mistakenly lists *The Salutation* under the key word "Brazil.") However, Warner's specificity confirms my identification: the pampas (home to the rhea) are an ecosystem that extends mostly throughout Argentina and part of Uruguay. Moreover, Timothy's final landfall before reaching the House of the Salutation is in "San Diego" (*The Salutation,* 192), presumably referring to the port at the tip of the Argentine. Most persuasively for my case, Warner's letter to Garnett, along with the note that William Maxwell, her editor and literary executor, attached to it when he published Warner's letters, explicitly verifies that *The Salutation* is set in Argentina (*Letters*, 1982, 21, fn. 2)

7. In further discussion, parenthetical references to pages in *Mr. Fortune's Maggot* (*MFM*) and *The Salutation* (*TS*) refer to the 2001 edition of *Mr. Fortune's Maggot, and The Salutation.*

8. In *The Salutation,* Warner explores the possibilities of free indirect discourse in a particularly intriguing way by using it in a bilingual situation: free indirect discourse becomes the means by which a native Spanish speaker, Angustias, enters English narrative discourse, with the result that she appears as an articulate thinker rather than as the simple native she might otherwise seem if represented by dialect. Warner's appreciation for Jane Austen (often credited as the mother of free indirect discourse) later led her to write a monograph on Austen in 1961 for the British Council and National Book League.

9. Presumably only a man could be lucky enough to play the part of "Fortune" in the 1920s and 1930s, but Warner did her best to be gender inclusive (or so I like to think) by making him as womanly a man as possible for a character who could travel the world alone. For further discussion of Warner's representation of Mr. Fortune's gender as well as sexuality see Wachman (2001), Garrity (2003), Hackett (2004), or Hinnov (2006).

10. In my discussion of the slave brand I am inspired by Robin Hackett's reading of Warner's exposé of the British slave trade in *Summer Will Show* (1936), which reveals the history of Caribbean slavery and consequent British profit represented by sacks of sugar and jars of guava jelly (Hackett, 2004, 112–114; see *Summer Will Show*, pp. 34–35). In *Summer*, as Hackett points out, Warner "critiques Britain's economic dependence on money made through imperialist exploitation and the slave trade by showing that Sophia's and Frederick's wealth comes from the Caribbean" (2004, 113). Hackett's reading leads me to a similar observation regarding Warner's *The Salutation* as a critique of British and Spanish imperialism represented by the artifacts of slavery the protagonists use to do their domestic work.

11. "Big Bertha" refers to the German 42-cm. siege gun produced by an arms manufacturing company owned by Bertha Krupp von Bohlen and used to attack the Belgian forts at Liege when the war began. Allied soldiers quickly began to use the name for any large German artillery, also coining the term "moaning Minnie" to describe German mortars because of their sound in flight.

12. *The Tale of Peter Rabbit* was first published in 1902 and quickly became a canonical children's book on both sides of the Atlantic. In developing my reading of this passage and the direction of my essay in general, I am deeply indebted to Gay Wachman for

a personal conversation in which she pointed out Warner's reference to Beatrix Potter's Farmer McGregor and observed that Warner's use of the child's tale, and particularly her playfulness with *Peter Rabbit*'s political commentary, is typical of Warner's writing.

13. A contemporary review of *The Salutation* published by R. H. Mottram in the *Bookman* (1932) claims that the effect of Warner's stories depends upon "possession . . . nearly always a benign spiritual seizure which . . . drives these perfectly credible, if never commonplace men, women, and beasts just over the border of their ordinary existence into a dimension or plane of being which is not ordinary" (qouted in Harman 1989, 125). My essay agrees with Mottram in characterizing "The Salutation" as the story of an Englishman "possessed" by his past through his own and others' material possessions, which compel first his physical and then his spiritual, imaginative journey.

Works Cited

Beer, Gillian. 1999. "Sylvia Townsend Warner: 'The Centrifugal Kick.'" In *Women Writers of the 1930s*. Edited by Maroula Joannou, 76–86. Edinburgh: Edinburgh University Press.

Garnett, David. (1981). "Letters between Sylvia Townsend Warner and David Garnett." *PN Review* 8.3: 41–43.

Garrity, Jane. 2003. *Step-daughters of England: British Women Modernists and the National Imaginary*. Manchester, UK: Manchester University Press.

Hackett, Robin. 2004. *Sapphic Primitivism: Productions of Race, Class, and Sexuality in Key Works of Modern Fiction*. New Brunswick, NJ: Rutgers University Press.

Harman, Claire. 1989. *Sylvia Townsend Warner: A Biography*. London: Chatto and Windus.

Hinnov, Emily. 2006. "A Counter-reading to Conquest: Primitivism and Utopian Longing in Sylvia Townsend Warner's *Mr. Fortune's Maggot*." In *Critical Essays on Sylvia Townsend Warner: English Novelist, 1893–1978*. Edited by David Malcolm, John Simons, and Gill Davies, 83–102. Lewiston, NY: Edwin Mellen Press.

Marcus, Jane. 1984. "A Wilderness of One's Own: Feminist Fantasy Novels of the Twenties: Sylvia Townsend Warner and Rebecca West." In *Women Writers and the City: Essays in Feminist Literary Criticism* Edited by Susan Merrill Squier, 134–60. Knoxville: University of Tennessee Press.

———. 1990. "Sylvia Townsend Warner (1893–1978)." *The Gender of Modernism: A Critical Anthology*. Edited by Bonnie Kime Scott, 531–38. Bloomington: Indiana University Press.

Mars-Jones, Adam, ed. 2001. Introduction to *Mr. Fortune's Maggot, and The Salutation*, by Sylvia Townsend Warner, vii–xiii. New York: New York Review of Books.

Wachman, Gay. 2001. *Lesbian Empire: Radical Crosswriting in the Twenties*. New Brunswick, NJ: Rutgers University Press.

Warner, Sylvia Townsend. 1926. *Lolly Willowes, or the Loving Huntsman*. New York: Viking.

———. 1982. *Letters by Sylvia Townsend Warner.* Edited by William Maxwell. New York: Viking.

———. 1987. *Summer Will Show*. 1936. Reprint, London: Virago.

———. 1990. Women as Writers. Peter Le Neve Foster Lecture to the Royal Society of Arts, February 11. In *The Gender of Modernism: A Critical Anthology*. Edited by Bonnie Kime Scott, 538–546. Bloomington: Indiana University Press.

———. 1995. *Sylvia and David: The Townsend Warner/Garnett Letters*. Edited by Richard Garnett. London: Sinclair-Stevenson.

———. (2001). *Mr. Fortune's Maggot, and The Salutation*. 1927, 1932. Introduction by Adam Mars-Jones. New York: New York Review of Books.

"Almost Ashamed of England being so English": Woolf and Ideas of Englishness

JULIA BRIGGS

IN THE SIXTY YEARS SINCE HER DEATH, VIRGINIA WOOLF'S ENGLAND HAS disappeared. Many English country houses and homes, both large and small—Knole and Sissinghurst, Charleston Farmhouse and Monk's House—have been adopted by societies committed to preserving them for the heritage industry, and they have been redesigned for the enjoyment of visitors, a process of democratization that has altered their identity forever. The fabric of English society has also radically changed. We have become a multiracial, multicultural society, for whom the concept of 'Englishness' is at best an empty myth, the invention of an imaginary past, and at worst an occasion for prejudice and political reaction. It has become a potential embarrassment, almost a dirty word. As Raphael Samuel observes, "British history makes 'Englishness' problematical and invites us to see it as one amongst a number of competing ethnicities"; as for English literature, its teaching is now "associated with the missionary position in sexuality, parochialism in high politics and tea-shop gentility in the world of letters" (1994, 24, 49). This outworn concept of "Englishness," tied as it has been to ideals of continuity and community, evolved partly as a reaction to the speed of change, resisting the process even as it responded to it. Yet the conflicts that accumulated around the various meanings of "Englishness" had begun well before Woolf's death, and her responses to them are among the most provocative, subtle, and acute.

In April 1926, Virginia and Leonard Woolf spent five days at Iwerne Minster, a village in Dorset close to Cranborne Chase. There they found the woods carpeted with anemones, bluebells, and violets and echoing with the call of the cuckoo, herald of the spring. "We stole off and were divinely happy . . . in a country, at a moment, which really made one almost ashamed of England being so English," she confessed to Raymond Mortimer, "and carpeting the woods, and putting cuckoos on trees, and doing exactly what Shakespeare says" (1989, 207). She was remembering the spring song at the end of *Love's Labours Lost*: "When daisies pied and violets blue . . ." Part of the pleasure of the woods was that they had been there so long, they had been recorded by Shakespeare. In an old country, poetry, like landscape, provides a link with an imagined past.

Shakespeare, as the national poet, is also a poet of the English landscape; for Richard Jefferies, he "carries, as it were, armfuls of violets and scatters roses and golden wheat across his pages, which are simply fields written with human life" (quoted in Looker 1937, 256). During the First World War, Shakespeare had been invoked as a source of patriotic inspiration by, among others, Sir Walter Raleigh.[1] "When the guns fired in August 1914 no one saluted them more rapturously than the Professor of English Literature at Oxford," Woolf wrote, in a review of Raleigh's *Letters* for *Vogue*, early in May 1926 (1986–1994, *Essays* 4: 346). She had been reading them while on holiday in Dorset. Earlier in the same letter to Raymond Mortimer, she had complained of "that beast Walter Raleigh [who] fills my soul with loathing" (1989, 206). She had already registered the appropriation of Shakespeare as part of the campaign to attract young men into the army: in *Mrs Dalloway* (1925), Septimus Smith "was one of the first to volunteer. He went to France to serve an England which consisted almost entirely of Shakespeare's plays and Miss Isabel Pole in a green dress walking in a square" (1992, 94).

So Woolf's pleasure at inheriting an enchanted landscape recorded in a literary tradition was modified by her recognition that the carpeted woods and the cuckoo had become clichés open to exploitation as propaganda. She indicated her awareness of this danger by treating them as a joke—a joke that reveals, as jokes are inclined to do, an underlying tension and self-division.

The concept of "Englishness" has its own history. It is usually thought to have come into being (like Woolf herself, born in 1882) in the last quarter of the nineteenth century.[2] It grew out of changing economic and social conditions: as British industry lost ground to Germany and the United States in world markets and wealth began to migrate from north to south, an ideal of the past was generated that bypassed factories and cities to dwell upon the countryside, and, in particular, the "South country"—of downland, manor house, thatched cottage, church spire, and village green. As an ideal, this landscape depended on assumptions of a social harmony that had never really existed.[3] Class and gender warfare, increasingly visible on contemporary city streets, were usually excluded from the rural picture, and foreign commerce was regarded as a potential threat. Alongside more formal expressions of national pride—such as the *New English Dictionary* (1884–1928) and the *Dictionary of National Biography* (1885–1900), first edited by Woolf's father, Leslie Stephen—myths of a distinctive national identity came into being, although these were to alter substantially under the impact of two world wars.[4] As the countryside was increasingly invaded by tarmac roads and suburban estates, the preservation of "the sweet especial rural scene" became an urgent issue. E. M. Forster's fiction, for example, is always preoccupied with what it might mean to be English, whether at home, in Italy, or even in India. In his novel *Howard's End* (1910), representatives of different social groups struggle for possession of the Surrey farmhouse whose significance lies in its continuity with the past, both communal and personal, as well as in its symbolic links with "the whole island . . . lying as a jewel in a silver sea" (1941, 133) a conscious echo of John of Gaunt's speech from *Richard II*—a locus classicus for patriotic sentiment, in which England becomes "This precious stone set in a silver sea," at once loved and at risk (II.i.46).

Both Forster and Woolf celebrated those aspects of "Englishness" that were linked with a sense of the past, even while deploring the more sinister sides of nationalism. In *To the Lighthouse* (1927), Woolf evokes English seaside holidays, family games of cricket in the garden, walks on the sands, and the long summer twilight. In *Mrs Dalloway*, Clarissa and her friends look back to life in the English country house at Bourton, with its terraces, park, lake, and kitchen garden. On a far grander scale, *Orlando* evokes the long and literary history of Knole, the ancestral home of her beloved friend Vita Sackville-West. As a woman, Vita was debarred from inheriting it when her father died, so in her novel, Woolf re-created for her its hundreds of bedchambers, whispering galleries and ancient hall, its rolling grounds and ancient oak trees. In *The Waves*, a lady writes at a table between two long windows at Elvedon, while the gardeners sweep the lawn. The view from Pointz Hall, in *Between the Acts*, takes in "the spire of Bolney Minster, Rough Norton woods and on an eminence rather to the left, Hogben's folly" (1992, 34). It has survived unchanged for a hundred years. Mrs. Swithin is saddened by the thought that the view will still be there when they are all dead, but her nephew Giles burns with the knowledge that war is coming, and bombs could destroy the view in minutes. In their various ways, each of these landscapes is either already lost to the past, or else under threat.

The English landscape was, for Woolf, inextricably bound up with English literature—"the woods do exactly what Shakespeare said"—while literature, and the discussion of literature, were constant sources of pleasure and passion to her. During her lifetime, the teaching of English language and literature came to be established as a distinct discipline, taught and researched in schools and universities.[5] In general, she had little time for academe, but through her reviewing for the *Times Literary Supplement* and writing the two volumes of *The Common Reader*, she put together her own less conventional canon of English literature, whose idiosyncrasies she teasingly linked with those of the climate: "In England the atmosphere is naturally aqueous, and as if there weren't enough outside, we drench ourselves with tea and coffee four times a day. It's atmosphere that makes English literature unlike any other—clouds, sunsets, fogs, exhalations, miasmas" (1986–1994, *Essays* 3: 181).[6] Fifteen years after her death, Nikolaus Pevsner, in his Reith lectures on *The Englishness of English Art* (1956), linked the monosyllabic language and the damp climate as possible influences on the character of English art—changeable features, yet constant in their changeability (1997, 16–19). Both of them were partly echoing the views of Roger Fry, who, according to Woolf's biography, had pointed out that "the light was full of vapour. Nothing was clear. There was no structure in the hills, no meaning in the lines of the landscape; all was smug, pretty and small" (1995, 131).

Woolf often exulted in the delights of the English language: "those of English birth," she observed in *Night and Day* (1919), were "brought up from childhood . . . to disport themselves now in the Saxon plainness, now in the Latin splendour of the tongue, . . . stored with memories . . . of old poets exuberating in an infinity of vocables" (1992, 258). The earliest version of *The Years* had paid tribute to Joseph Wright, author of *The English Dialect Dictionary*, not only for his academic achievements, but for the determining role that his own life, and that of his working-class mother, played in those achievements (1998; 128, 135, 154–58). The finished novel would celebrate the dance of the English language through Sarah's extempore versifying, and also its beauty: as Eleanor hears Celia saying about the water,

> "Oh, but there's quite enough for everybody at present," . . . And for some reason she held the sentence suspended without a meaning in her mind's ear," . . . quite enough for everybody at present," she repeated. . . . What a lovely language, she thought, saying over to herself again the commonplace words, spoken by Celia quite simply but with some indescribable burr in

> the 'r's, for the Chinnerys had lived in Dorsetshire since the beginning of time. (1998, 151–52)[7]

Thus language and the family are linked through their common roots in the deep past.

Woolf's pleasure in language is that of "the most rich inheritor." For a moment, she allows herself to enjoy "the advantages of being Virginia Stephen," privileged daughter of Sir Leslie; for a moment, she is an insider revelling in traditions whose exclusions can be temporarily ignored; for a moment, and exceptionally, she catches up the modernist concern with a lost past, to be found in the work of T. S. Eliot, Ezra Pound, and W. B. Yeats.[8]

One seminal text for an understanding of Woolf's notion of Englishness is her 1919 essay, "Reading," set in a country house in a summer garden with views to the sea. Here she basks in the carved and paneled library, "lined with little burnished books, folios, and stout blocks of divinity" that house the long canon of English classics from Chaucer to Wordsworth and beyond. As she sits reading beside an open window, the book and the world beyond it become indistinguishable: "it seemed as if what I read was laid upon the landscape not printed, bound, or sewn up, but somehow the product of trees and fields and the hot summer sky, like the air which swam, on fine mornings, round the outlines of things. / These were circumstances, perhaps, to turn one's mind to the past" (1986–1994, *Essays* 3: 141–42).[9]

A sunlit avenue seems to stretch all the way back to Queen Elizabeth I, reminding her of an old favorite, Thomas Hakluyt's *Traffics and Discoveries*.[10] Its volumes were loved by the late Victorians for their foretaste of imperial trade and exploration, and by Woolf herself as a young girl for their outlandish adventures and general eccentricity. A more personal history is also written into this essay, for the garden described is that of Talland House, St. Ives, where the Stephens had spent their summer holidays. The escallonia hedges and the beds of fuschia and geranium, like the gardener mowing the lawn with his rubber-shoed pony, are remembered from Talland House, and so is the vivid account of a moth hunt by night in the second half of the essay (later to be reworked in *Jacob's Room*).[11]

"There is no difficulty in finding poetry in England," she announces. "Every English home is full of it." It is "sunk very deep," yet it is both as familiar and as "strangely persistent" as the climate, characterized by "the loveliness of the hurrying clouds, of the sun-stained green, of the rapid watery atmosphere, in which clouds have been crumbled with colour until the ocean of air is at once confused and profound" (1986–1994, *Essays* 3: 153).

Yet, as Woolf well knew, the country house, with its garden and well-stocked library belonged primarily to a world of masculine provision and privilege. "[I]n all the libraries of the world," she wrote in the following year, "the man is to be heard talking to himself and for the most part about himself" (1986–1994, *Essays* 3: 193).[12] Libraries were built by gentlemen for gentlemen, and the unidentified country house in "Reading," like Bourton or Pointz Hall, would have appeared very different to those "below stairs"—to Candish the butler, the gardener leading his pony, the scullery maid, or the cook. Servants only enter the library to dust the books, not to enjoy their contents. There is no danger here of finding "the kitchen maid curled up . . . reading Plato," or even of the cook coming in to borrow the *Daily Herald*.[13] Yet if it is class-blind, this essay is not entirely gender-blind, for the library bookshelves house, rather surprisingly, the writings of Lady Fanshawe, Lucy Hutchinson, and Margaret Cavendish. And the history of old houses and old families includes linguistic change, as local and particular manners gradually give place to the metropolitan, merging "the dialect of the district into the common speech of the land. . . . But what dignity, what beauty broods over it all!" (1986–94, *Essays* 3: 145).

"Reading" is a highly polished essay, substantially longer than her reviews, a piece on which she evidently lavished time and trouble. Which leaves the interesting question, why did she never publish it? It appeared for the first time in 1950 in *The Captain's Death Bed* as one of the few essays that had never been published before. Leonard apparently assumed that it was a draft chapter intended for the book that evolved into *The Common Reader*, perhaps as an introduction, though the first mention of this book occurs in May 1921, well over a year later.[14] His supposition was probably based on the fact that the essay and the book had identical titles at this stage, though the library contents outlined in her essay "Reading" actually anticipate the canon set out in *The Common Reader*. The essay underpins *The Common Reader*, rather as her essay "Professions for Women" would generate both *The Years* and *Three Guineas*.

The collocation of country house, landscape, and library reappears again in *Orlando* and finally in *Between the Acts*, where it is played out against a looming threat to that particular way of life. "Reading," by contrast, was written not in the expectation but in the wake of a major European war, some time during 1919, if internal evidence can be trusted, and probably after September, when her diary records her re-reading Sir

Thomas Browne, who figures largely in its final pages. It survives in a heavily corrected typescript among the Monk's House Papers.[15]

Was it abandoned unpublished because she was "almost ashamed" of creating a picture of an England that was "so English"? In another essay written in the same year, 1919, and published in Middleton Murray's *Athenaeum*, she caricatured the mood of national self-congratulation on display at the Royal Academy's Summer Exhibition. Here again, we encounter the English country house amidst its rural setting, but this time viewed from a dramatically different angle:

> The sun is exquisitely adapted to the needs of the sundials. The yew hedges are irreproachable; the manor house a miracle of timeworn dignity; and as for the old man with a scythe, the girl at the well, the village donkey . . . each is not only the saddest, sweetest, quaintest, most picturesque, tenderest, jolliest of its kind, but has a symbolical meaning much to the credit of England. . . . It is indeed a very powerful atmosphere; so charged with manliness and womanliness, pathos and purity, sunsets and Union Jacks, that the shabbiest and most suburban catch a reflection of the rosy glow. "This is England! these are the English!" one might explain if a foreigner were at hand. (1986–94, *Essays* 3: 92).[16]

Here England and Englishness have become an embarrassment, appealing to spurious emotions reflected in her choice of clichés. As a cultural critic, Woolf felt herself offended by the attitudes on display, the heroics, smugness and complacency of all kinds that seemed to pour down from the walls. As an aesthetic critic, she was offended by the provincialism of both the subject matter and the technique of the paintings. Art historians as well as close friends, Roger Fry and Clive Bell had sought to liberate painting from precisely this kind of extraneous sentiment, the narrative appeals made by the Academy's genre paintings. They had, instead, encouraged a focus upon form intended to lead provincial English painting toward postimpressionism and European modernism. In a final sentence, Woolf invoked Roger Fry's judgment on the 1,674 works of art exhibited, knowing perfectly well what he would have thought of them.[17]

The versions of Englishness on display at the Academy were factitious and politically conservative. Their aesthetic poverty endorsed widespread assumptions as to the relative strengths of literature and painting in England: whereas literature might be a legitimate source of national pride, it was usually conceded in Woolf's circle that Victorian painting had been a dead end, particularly in comparison with French painting of the same period. It was, in part, Fry's criticisms in his *Reflections on British Painting*

(1934) that prompted Pevsner, a European refugee, to defend the Englishness of English art by observing that "none of the other nations of Europe has so abject an inferiority complex about its own aesthetic capabilities as England" (1997, 25, 205). Mindful of Fry's strictures, Woolf briefly introduced a debate about the nature of English genius into *Between the Acts*. After lunch, Bartholomew Oliver challenges William Dodge, "Since you're interested in pictures, . . . why, tell me, are we as a race, so incurious, irresponsive and insensitive . . . to that noble art, whereas Mrs Manresa, if she'll allow me my old man's liberty, has her Shakespeare by heart?" (1992, 35).

By 1919, wider European ties had come to seem desirable, and not only in the field of aesthetics. The Great War had left England as a major voice at the Peace Conference Table, deciding national boundaries in Europe and war indemnities for Germany, as well as generally setting the agenda (one that would lead to another European war twenty years later). The Woolfs, like the rest of Bloomsbury, had been pacifist in their sympathies during the war, and were passionately committed to internationalism and the establishment of a League of Nations as the only way to build a better and safer Europe. Leonard had contributed substantially to the establishment and maintenance of the League through his book *International Government* (1916). In "Reading," then, it seems that Woolf had allowed her mind a private canter through her own particular English/Elysian fields, while recognizing that such pleasures must be indulged in private.

"In times of peace and tranquillity the vocabulary of patriotism is not much used. . . . Trouble changes this. . . . If England seems threatened you feel that in losing her you would lose yourself; she becomes plainly and decidedly 'this dear realm of England,'" wrote the poet Edward Thomas, with yet another allusion to John of Gaunt's speech, so often invoked in the context of a national threat.[18] Both before and during the Great War, Woolf felt repelled by displays of chauvinism. They induced in her a sense of alienation that was enhanced by (or perhaps contributed to) her breakdown during the early years of the war. Her disgust with these "most violent and filthy passions" seems to have distracted her from anxieties about England under threat that would later characterize *Between the Acts*.[19] One exception, however, is her use of Scarborough in *Jacob's Room*. In December 1914, German gunboats had shelled Scarborough from the sea, creating the first civilian casualties of the war on English soil. Hundreds of people were killed or injured. Woolf's earliest readers would have read her account of the town's sea front, bandstand, and aquarium, and the houses and streets beyond, with the added knowledge of their fate to come. Her use of Scarborough is one of the novel's several deliberate reminders of the devastation wrought by the war, like the fates of the young men in the submarine, of Jimmy and Peggy, or of Jacob himself.[20]

Woolf particularly disliked the kinds of sentiment about England and Englishness licensed by army recruitment campaigns, sentiment that appears at its most rhetorical in Rupert Brooke's sonnet, "The Soldier": "If I should die, think only this of me / That there's some corner of a foreign field / That is forever England . . . " Woolf had known and admired Brooke, but she disliked the cult of hero-worship that he attracted after his death.[21] Yet national pride in the institutions of democracy and empire had begun well before the Great War, and are already being satirized in her first novel, *The Voyage Out* (completed before the war, though not published until 1915). Here she explores the meanings of England and Englishness for a right-wing, conservative, imperialist politics. At Lisbon, the little party on board the *Euphrosyne* are joined by the Tory MP Richard Dalloway and his pretty, silly wife, Clarissa, who announces that her favorite play is Shakespeare's *Henry V* (another key source for patriotic sentiment).[22] With absurd inconsequence, she parrots her husband's views: "I can't help thinking of England. . . . Being on this ship seems to make it so much more vivid—what it really means to be English. One thinks of all we've done, and our navies, and the people in India and Africa, and of how we've gone on century after century sending out boys from little country villages—and of men like you, Dick, and it makes one feel as if one couldn't bear not to be English! Think of the light burning over the House, Dick!" (1992, *Voyage Out*, 46).

"Dick" himself is only a little more self-aware than she is, while being, if anything, more racist. In conversation with Rachel, he admits with apparent reluctance that "the English seem, on the whole, whiter than most men, their record cleaner" (identifying skin color with moral superiority, in a revealing linguistic strategy) (1992, *Voyage Out*, 56). The full significance of the Dalloways' politics emerges at the end of chapter 4, when "two sinister grey vessels [appear], low in the water, bald as bone . . . with the look of eyeless beasts seeking their prey." This is "the Mediterranean fleet," Dick announces, as the Euphrosyne dips its flag, and Clarissa squeezes Rachel's hand, exclaiming "Aren't you glad to be English!" (60).

The vessels are Dreadnoughts, the first built in 1905, and a significant step in the arms race against Germany. Virginia Stephen had examined one at close quarters in 1910, when she took part in "the Dreadnought hoax," in which she, her brother, Adrian, Horace Cole, and others dressed up and blacked up. Upon proclaiming themselves to be Abyssinian princes, they were taken on an inspection tour of the battleship, which the navy regularly showed off to foreign powers. "The hoax combined all possible forms of subversion," Hermione Lee observes: "ridicule of empire, infiltration of the nation's defences, mockery of bureaucratic procedures, cross-dressing and sexual ambiguity" (1996, 283). Back in *The Voyage Out*, at lunch that day, while Willoughby and the Dalloways are praising British admirals, Rachel's aunt Helen remarks that "it seemed to her as wrong to keep sailors as to keep a Zoo, and that as for dying on the battlefield, surely it was time we ceased to praise courage . . ." (1992, 60). Woolf recognized how ideas of Englishness might be exploited even before the war had produced its particular appeal to patriotism.

When Woolf dusted off the Dalloways and set them at the center of her fourth novel, *Mrs Dalloway* (1925), she made them substantially more sympathetic. Richard is nowhere referred to as Dick.[23] At once less arrogant and more likeable, he sits on committees investigating the plight of the downtrodden: at home, victims of the police; abroad, the Armenians (1992, *Mrs Dalloway*, 126–27, 131).[24] Clarissa becomes one of the novel's centers of consciousness and it is difficult for readers to judge just how far to identify with her. Meanwhile, several of the couple's former foibles are displaced onto other characters: Dalloway's uninvited kiss is here transferred to Hugh Whitbread (he had kissed the proto-feminist Sally Seton in the smoking room, or so she claims) (80). Clarissa's patriotism is transferred to Lady Bruton, whose love for "this isle of men, this dear, dear land, was in her blood (without reading Shakespeare)." The earlier Clarissa's sense that she couldn't bear not to be English becomes entangled with the sentiments of Rupert Brooke's "The Soldier": "one could not figure [Lady Bruton] even in death parted from the earth or roaming territories over which, in some spiritual shape, the Union Jack had ceased to fly. To be not English even among the dead—no, no! Impossible!" (198).[25]

Both *The Voyage Out* and *Mrs Dalloway* play out insular, Anglo-Saxon attitudes in contexts that expose their limitations. In the earlier novel, the Dalloways in their cabin on board the *Euphrosyne* pit themselves against the "set of cranks" (i.e., Ridley, Helen, and Mr. Pepper) (1992, *Voyage Out*, 42). The little community of the English in their hotel at Santa Marina also seem isolated, dwelling on the edge of the jungle into which they make occasional forays. In the end, the jungle appears to retaliate, seizing upon Rachel as upon its prey. And although *Mrs Dalloway* is set in London, at the center rather than on the periphery, it too can be read as a conflict between the insularity of Westminster and a wider, more threatening world beyond. Clarissa herself withdraws to her narrow bed in the attic, with the sheets turned down—a symbol of death (1992, *Mrs Dalloway*, 33–34). She deliberately refuses to think of the suffering Armenians, just as she does not want to invite poor, shabby Ellie Henderson to her party (129–32). Her reaction to Septimus Smith's suicide can be read either as a momentary reversal of this process, an impulse of sympathy for the outcast, or else as a confirmation of it, in which she accepts his death as enabling the party to go on, as if the millions of war deaths have served only to guarantee the continuance of her way of life: "she felt glad that he had done it; thrown it away while they went on living" (202–4).[26]

In *The Voyage Out*, Woolf had represented the Dalloways' chauvinism as politically provocative, the kind of attitude that had brought war closer, whereas in *Mrs Dalloway* her critique is directed against a society that has accepted the bloodshed without seeking further change or reform, a society that has picked up life where it left off before the war: Clarissa and her friends are absorbed in the London season with its sequence of "Lords, Ascot, Hurlingham," as if the war had never taken place (1992, *Mrs Dalloway*, 18).[27] What goes on elsewhere—whether in Albania or Armenia, or even in the parks and mean streets beyond the little enclave of Westminster—has a minimal impact upon her way of life. The politics of *Mrs Dalloway* reflect British policy between the wars, when the country looked toward the empire, rather than Europe, for alliance and trade. Woolf's distaste for imperialism is reflected in her essay on the great Empire Exhibition of 1924, entitled "Thunder at Wembley," which envisages a fantastic storm blowing away all the old machinery of colonialism and empire.[28] Her next novel, *To the Lighthouse* (1927), celebrated a lost English past with a nostalgia that risked becoming sentimental (as she herself acknowledged), although its central section, "Time Passes," explores the impact of the war and was written during the General Strike of May 1926.[29] *Orlando* (1928) reworks the nexus of ideas present in her 1919 essay, "Reading," but its narrative is so shot through with sexual and historical subversion that we are never in danger of taking it seriously. "Englishness," like several of the book's other risky topics, seems to slip through customs undeclared, as Woolf affectionately parodies Vita/Orlando's aristocratic love of "The Land."[30] In reality, British agriculture was as depressed as its industries, and the thirties were marked not only by a reluctance to be drawn into European conflict, but by massive unemployment, marches, and hunger strikes at home.

In 1938, the year that Chamberlain returned from Munich with Hitler's paper promises, thus staving off war for a further year, Woolf published her most explicit critique of patriotism, with its often militarist implications—*Three Guineas*. To define patriotism, she turned to the words of the Lord Chief Justice: "Englishmen are proud of England. . . . There are few loves stronger than the love we have for our country. . . . Liberty has made her abode in England. England is the home of democratic institutions. . . . Yes, we are greatly blessed, we Englishmen" (1993, *A Room of One's Own and Three Guineas,* 123). But then she goes on to ask whether such sentiments can ever mean the same to a woman: Do women have the same reasons for being proud of England, for loving England, for defending England and for feeling greatly blessed? Because of their different stakes in the community, they are made to feel like outsiders, and what can "our country" mean to an outsider? "[A]s a woman, I have no country. As a woman, I want no country. As a woman my country is the whole world." This much-quoted assertion is often read as implying that for women, as outsiders, "our country" has no meaning. Yet it is followed by a less familiar qualification: "some obstinate emotion remains" for Woolf, "some love of England dropped into a child's ears by the cawing of rooks in an elm tree, by the splash of waves on a beach, or by English voices murmuring nursery rhymes" (1993, *A Room*, 233–34).[31] Even while making her most unequivocal assertion about the irrelevance of patriotism, Woolf could not fully disengage from the deep pull of the English landscape, the English language of her childhood.

By 1938, as threats to England's island fastness were growing, ideas of England and Englishness were themselves undergoing further transformations. Though, in *Mrs Dalloway*, the world of upper-class privilege apparently continued much as it had done before, fundamental social and economic changes were taking place. The days of the country house, with its "upstairs, downstairs" split, were numbered, and "middle England" was beginning to find a voice for itself, its values often expressed by sensible, humorous, provincial or suburban ladies. The nation of explorers and conquerors had become a nation of gardeners, decent ordinary people who muddled through with a combination of cheerfulness and good sense, more appropriate to uncertain times.[32]

During the thirties, many small towns and villages acted out their own (imaginary) pasts in secular pageants, often performed on Empire Day (May 24th), though such entertainments could reflect a range of political attitudes. In London in 1936, for example, the Communist Party performed its own "March of History" pageants, evoking a past of radicalism and resistance (Samuel 1998, 207). Woolf's friend E. M. Forster wrote two pageants. The "Abinger Pageant" of July 1934, with music by Ralph Vaughan Williams in the form of folk song settings, is set in the garden of the old Rectory at Abinger and asks, in its epilogue, "Are [houses] man's final triumph? Or is there another England, green and eternal, which will outlast them?" His second pageant, "England's Pleasant Land," was performed at Milton Court, near Dorking in July 1938.[33] Its title refers to Blake's poem "Jerusalem," another key text for "Englishness." It had been broadcast by John Reith at the end of the General Strike of 1926 to signify that England had been saved; today it is always sung on the last night of the promenade concerts at the Royal Albert Hall, as well as by the Women's Institute, archetypal supporters of English country life.[34] By the spring of 1940, Woolf had herself become "an active member of the Women's Institute, "who've just asked me to write a play for the villagers to act. And to produce it myself. I should like to if I could" (1975–80, *Letters* 6: 391).[35] In the event, she didn't. It was an instance of life imitating art, for she had already written Miss La Trobe and her village pageant into her final novel.

Woolf began *Between the Acts* in the atmosphere of increasing international tension of 1938, reverting to the fantasy of her essay on "Reading," and of the country house and village fete sketched out in the 1911 section of *The Years*—yet developing these too. It was to be "composed of many different things," among them, "English country; & a scenic old house—& a terrace where nursemaids walk," as well as a library, for she planned to discuss "all lit.," as well as "all life, all art, all waifs & strays—a rambling capricious but somehow unified whole—the present state of my mind?" (1977–1984 *Diary* 5: 135).[36]

The sense of an imminent ending to a way of life that has gone on uninterrupted for centuries is very strong in the novel. While the present is enough for William Dodge, Isa and Giles look forward, though in different ways and for different reasons, to an uncertain future—and it is such anxieties that make *Between the Acts* Woolf's most English novel, the novel that records most fully her complex feelings about the English past, the English way of life, the nature of English genius and of English society, sharply ranked and distrustful of outsiders as it is. The first draft was particularly focused upon English literature, and opened with Isa and the gentleman farmer, Rupert Haynes, recognizing each other through a shared reference to the poet Edward Thomas, and his poem about memory and the past, "Old Man" (misremembered by Isa as "Old Man's Beard").[37] Thomas speaks to Isa's generation as Byron had spoken to that of her father-in-law (1992 *Acts*, 51). Woolf's initial choice of Edward Thomas to open, and perhaps preside over, the novel reflects the centrality of English landscape and literature to her initial conception of the book, for these had been the main subject matter of Thomas's prose and poetry (1983, 38–40).[38] In a second draft, she cut away most of this opening scene, and in the process entirely removed the discussion of Thomas, yet his poem "Old Man" left its shadow across the moment when Isa "stripped the bitter leaf that grew, as it happened, outside the nursery window. Old Man's Beard" (1992, *Acts*, 123).

Between the Acts catches up the theme of insularity, treating it socially, rather, than politically. "Our island history" unfolds within a smaller island, a microcosm of English society quietly absorbed in its activities, "as if warm days would never cease." At the same time, Giles (and thus the novel) cannot forget Europe, "bristling with guns, poised with planes," at once so far away yet so dangerously close, "just over there, across the gulf in the flat land which divided them from the continent" (1992, 34, 30), as Gillian Beer's essay "The Island and the Aeroplane" has brilliantly shown. Giles is a lone Cassandra in a society preoccupied with the advent of the cesspool or the building of new bungalows (5–6, 47), yet Woolf herself recognized during the crises of 1938 that the thought of war was so overwhelming, that one could only deal with it by averting one's eyes, by concentrating on the local and trivial: "One ceases to think about it—that's all. Goes on discussing the new room, new chair, new books. What else can a gnat on a blade of grass do?" (1977–1984, *Diary* 5: 162).

The village society of *Between the Acts* is rooted in the past. Many of the local families have lived there time out of mind, and they are well aware of who has insider or outsider status, gossiping and speculating about Mrs. Manresa's Tasmanian background, and about her Jewish husband, Ralph, and the money he has made, as well as about Miss La Trobe (1992, 47, 26, 37). Characteristically, it is the two outsiders who revitalize the flagging community. Between them, if in rather different senses, they are always "getting things up." Miss La Trobe's name reveals that she is "not pure English"; indeed, she is not pure anything, being both a sexual and a social outsider (37). In this role, she offers the insiders an image of themselves, an image of an England affectionately observed yet at the same time comically parodied, simultaneously mocking and reproducing England's favorite narratives of itself as a seafaring nation under Queen Elizabeth I, as a cheerful eighteenth-century squirearchy and as a harmonious Victorian family, with father at home, reading to the children by lamplight (a myth approached, yet finally avoided in *To the Lighthouse*). Once again Woolf turns Englishness into a joke, thus dispersing the embarrassment of sentiment in permissive laughter.

Ultimately, the novel reaches beyond its vision of England in 1939 to something altogether darker, older, and more enduring. Miss La Trobe turns, as Woolf herself used to, from the work she has just completed to envisaging her next project, to be enacted in a time and place before England: "It was land, merely, no land in particular," where a couple stand among rocks, though she does not yet know what they will say (1992, *Acts*, 124). Her vision reaches beyond the novel's preoccupation with the current condition of England to something timeless. The final paragraphs of *Between the Acts* reenact Miss La Trobe's vision, so that love and hate, which have engendered all the plots, are finally seen in their full nakedness, as the explanation of what we are and what we do—not just as the English, but as all people forever, reproducing and making war. The final words of the novel are couched in the theatrical terms that Miss La Trobe had used ("the curtain would rise"), and, as in her vision, English history is annihilated in a moment that simultaneously evokes an impossibly distant past and anticipates the anarchy of war to come: "Our English past" has been reduced to "one inch of light."[39]

It was difficult for Woolf to reconcile the countercurrents of her socialism, and even more, of feminism and modernism, with her love of that patriarchal myth, "England" itself, distinctive and elaborated, with its own recorded history.[40] As a sharp observer and analyst of prevailing ideologies, she recognized that ideals of Englishness were intended to arouse the envy of foreigners, the pride and protectiveness of natives, and to disguise the increasingly divided and disheartened nature of a nation slipping from world leadership into economic decline. Patriotism for Woolf was normally a matter for censure or satire, or at least ironic distance, yet she was also in love with the English language—poems and verses remembered from childhood, as well as downland walks and tumultuous clouds, and at moments her dream of a fair country merged with the reality around her—her England of the mind assumed a body.

Near the end of her life, when air raids had exiled her from it, she identified London as her only patriotism (excepting a vision of spring in Warwickshire),[41] but in the essay on "Reading" of twenty years earlier she had created her own private England, a vision that had gathered power from being suppressed. Its country house is re-created in *Between the Acts*, where the hills and woods of the parish epitomize England. Pointz Hall may owe its name to Shakespeare (Pointz is one of Hal's companions in Shakespeare's *Henry IV*), while the name of the village, Bolney Minster, combines Bolney, a South Downs village not too far from Rodmell, with the suffix "Minster," perhaps glancing backward to her visit to Iwerne Minster of 1926. Though *Between the Acts* is as humorously critical of English insularity as ever—of its snobbery, conservatism, xenophobia—it is also imbued with love for a country expecting a foreign invasion. Woolf could not resist the upsurge of patriotic feeling that the war brought, resulting in what Raphael Samuel has described as "a country in love with itself" (1998, 218). Even Churchill, a former bugbear of hers, was now redeemed. The sense of imminent danger around her—and perhaps also within her—restored the ideal vision. "The searchlights are very lovely over the marsh," she wrote to Ethel Smyth in the summer of 1940, "and the aeroplanes go over—one, a German, was shot over Caburn, and my windows rattled when they dropped bombs at Forest Row. But its [sic] like a Shakespeare song today—so merry, innocent, and very English" (1975–80, *Letters* 6: 402).[42]

Notes

The author would like to thank Alison Light and David Stocker for their contributions to this article.

1. See Brooker and Widdowson (1986, 119). Stefan Collini observes that "Britain's twentieth-century wars, large and small, have invariably been accompanied by renewed celebrations of the achievements of the Elizabethan period, without . . . exhibiting any very firm hold on the distinctions between William Shakespeare and Sir Francis Drake" (1999, 13).

2. Samuel, in *Island Stories* (1998, 4), and Philip Dodd, "Englishness and the National Culture" in Colls and Dodd (1986, 1) locate the origins of "Englishness" in the late nineteenth century.

3. See Howkins (1986, 62–84) and Brooker and Widdowson (1986, 141) for discussions of rural England as nostalgic landscape. Richard Jefferies himself wrote *Wild Life in a Southern County* in 1879 (London: Smith, Elder), a work often considered his best.

4. Dodd (1986, 16–19; see note 2), Samuel (1994, 218–19), and Howkins (1986, 79) describe these changes.

5. Brian Doyle outlines the history of English as a discipline (1989, 1–4).

6. "A Talk about Memoirs," first published in the *New Statesman* (March 6, 1920).

7. This section, 1911, is centrally concerned with ideas of "traditional country life," as well as with England in relation to the question of patriotism and experiences of empire or abroad, though the logic of its ideas is more obvious in the manuscript notebooks

for the novel: "The Pargeters," M42, the Henry W. and Albert. A. Berg Collection, New York Public Library—whereas patriotism is discussed extensively in the preceding section.

8. The reference to "the most rich inheritor" is from the third section of W. B. Yeats's "Meditations in Time of Civil War," published in *The Tower* (1928). Winifred Holtby entitled the first chapter of her memoir (1932) "The Advantages of Being Virginia Stephen." While T. S. Eliot's outlook ("royalist in politics, and anglo-catholic in religion") was very different from that of Woolf, at times the *Four Quartets* and *Between the Acts* seem to echo one another in their celebration of England, as Gillian Beer has pointed out in her introduction to the novel published by Oxford University Press (1992, xii, xxvii, 134, 142).

9. Sonya Rudikoff describes the "dark Jacobean paneling" of the moated Elizabethan manor house at Blo' Norton, where the young Stephens stayed in August 1906, though she does not specifically mention a library (2000, 83).

10. "It was the Elizabethan prose writers I loved first & most wildly, stirred by Hakluyt," Woolf wrote on December 8, 1929, in her diary (1977–84, 3: 271). Woolf first wrote on *Traffics and Discoveries* either just before or during her stay at Blo' Norton (1986–1994, *Essays* 1: 120–123); other mentions occur in 1917 and 1918 (1986–94, *Essays* 2: 91–93, 329–333); briefly in 1924 (1986–1994, *Essays* 3: 450); and in "The Elizabethan Lumber Room" in *The Common Reader* (1925). The influence of *Traffics and Discoveries* is apparent in *The Voyage Out* and *Orlando*, and is discussed by Alice Fox (1990, 20–50).

11. Woolf described the garden of Talland House in "A Sketch of the Past," published in *Moments of Being* (1985, 128–29) where she also records the moth hunts (104), and in *Jacob's Room* (1992, 25).

12. Libraries are seen as distinctly male-determined spaces in "A Society" (1985, *The Complete Shorter Fiction*), and in the scene in the British Museum Library in *Jacob's Room* (1992, 90–94).

13. Woolf avoided introducing servants by having "a sallow priest . . . dusting the books and the carved birds at the same time" (1986–1994, *Essays* 3: 141). The maid reading Plato occurs in the full text of "Professions for Women" and *The Pargeters* (xlii). The Georgian cook borrows the *Daily Herald* (from the drawing room, rather than the library) in "Character In Fiction" (1986–1994, *Essays* 3: 422).

14. "Reading" is MH/B11.d of the Monk's House Papers held by the University of Sussex Library, at B.11.d. A note by Leonard refers to it as "Typescript of Chapter for 'Reading' Unfinished book." The last two pages (numbered 33, 34) also survive in manuscript, M120, in the Berg Collection of the New York Public Library. Woolf wondered "how to shape my Reading book" on May 23, 1921 (1977–84, *Diary* 2: 120).

15. "[E]ven in the year nineteen hundred and nineteen a great number of minds are only partially lit up by the cold light of knowledge," she wrote in "Reading" (1986–1994, *Essays* 3: 154), *a propos* of Sir Thomas Browne's *Vulgar Errors*. Narrower dating is difficult, but the discussion of Browne suggests that it was written after a diary entry for September 12, 1919: "I was making way with my new experiment, when I came up against Sir Thomas Browne, & found I hadn't read him since I used to dip & duck . . . hundred of years ago." It's possible that the "new experiment" was "Reading" (unless it was one of her short stories), and it may be relevant that by September the Woolfs had surrendered the house at Asheham and just moved into Monk's House, which at first

she compared unfavorably with their old home—a fantasy of an ideal house could well have been the outcome of that moment of doubt (though by the end of the month she wrote, "Monk's House improves, after the fashion of a mongrel who wins your heart") (1977–1984, *Diary* 1: 297, 302). For details of the typescript, see note 14. Another possible context, of rather a different nature, was the railway strike that ran from September 27 to October 6, 1919, a spectacle of national division—see entries for the 28th and 30th of September and for the 1st and 7th of October (1977–84, *Diary* 1: 301–304).

16. Woolf must have written this in July and early August 1919, whereas "Reading" is unlikely to have been completed before September (see note 15). Chapter 19 of *Howard's End* begins similarly: "If one wanted to show a foreigner England . . ." (1941, 126). Woolf's brief notice of the Royal Academy's Summer Exhibition contributed to the *Nation* and *Athenaeum* in May 1924 made several of the same points as her 1919 review: "As a compliment to ourselves it is magnificent. As a contribution to art . . ." (1986–94, *Essays* 3: 406).

17. See, for examples: Clive Bell (1923, 28–30), Roger Fry (1928, 12, 15), and Woolf, "The Royal Academy" (1986–94, *Essays* 3: 93).

18. Quoted from page 91 of *The Last Sheaf* (London: Jonathan Cape, 1928) by Edna Longley (1981, 222). This point is frequently made; see, for example, C. F. G. Masterman in *The Condition of England* (1909): "Never . . . has the land beyond the city offered so fair an inheritance to the children of its people, as today, under the visible shadow of the end" (Brooker and Widdowson 1986, 136), and compare with Slavoj Žižek: "national identity constitutes itself through resistance to its oppression—the fight for national revival is therefore a defence of something which comes to be only through being experienced as lost or endangered" (1991, 802).

19. The phrase is from a letter to Duncan Grant, November 15, 1915 (1975–80, *Letters* 2: 71); see also an earlier letter to Grant, January 3, 1915 (2: 57), and a diary entry for the same date: "I think patriotism is a base emotion" (1977–84, *Diary* 1: 5).

20. The raid was witnessed by the sixteen-year-old Winifred Holtby (Gilbert 1995, 110).

21. "I never think his poetry good enough for him, but I did admire him very much indeed," Woolf told Ka Cox on January 12, 1916 (1975–80, *Letters* 2: 75). Woolf was particularly critical of Edward Marsh's hagiographic account of Brooke's life—see letter to Ka Cox of August 13, 1918 (1975–80, *Letters* 2: 267–268), and diary entries for July 23 and 27, 1918 (1977–84, *Diary* 1: 171–72).

22. On patriotic readings of *Henry V*, see Howkins (1986, 119). (The first dissenting voice was that of Gerald Gould, significantly in 1919.)

23. Woolf may have been familiar with the slang sense of "Dick" as the penis, in military use from circa 1860 according to Eric Partridge (*The Penguin Dictionary of Historical Slang*, 1972).

24. Lyndon Peach suggests that Dalloway wŽas involved in negotiations for the Lausanne Treaty, "the final act of betrayal of the Armenians" (Mrs Dalloway, 1992, 104–5) (as was Harold Nicolson, who described the conference in *Some People* in 1928).

25. The allusion is, once again, to John of Gaunt's speech, although we have been told that Lady Bruton "never read a word of poetry herself" (Mrs Dalloway, 1992, 115). A very different juxtaposition of John of Gaunt's speech and Rupert Brooke's "The Soldier" occurs in A. S. M. Hutchinson's best-selling novel, *If Winter Comes* (1921), as John Lucas discusses (1997, 58).

26. "Mrs Dalloway in Bond Street," the short story that provided the starting point for the novel, was even more explicit: "Thousands of young men had died that things might go on . . ." (Woolf 1985, *Complete Shorter Fiction*, 158–59).

27. Gertrude Bell, writing at the time of the General Strike, 1926, made the same point: "It is so amazing that the world seems to go on just the same—Ascot and parties are what I read of in *The Times*" (quoted in Gilbert 1995, 708).

28. "Thunder at Wembley" is reprinted in *Essays 3*: 410–13; see also Samuel (1988, *Island Stories* (88–90).

29. Woolf acknowledged her own sentimental nostalgia on September 5, 1926 (1977–84, *Diary 3*: 107). Kate Flint discusses "Virginia Woolf and the General Strike" (1986). For an account of the General Strike as "a battle for England," culminating in the broadcasting of "Jerusalem," see John Lucas (1997, 217–221). Lyndon Peach notices that Lily Briscoe first appears in the manuscript as an "English" painter of thatched cottages and hedgerows (2000, 116).

30. For Orlando's love of the land see Woolf 1993, *Orlando*, pages 183, 54, 192, and 215.

31. Woolf's "As a woman, I have no country" deliberately echoes the Communist Manifesto: "The working people have no country" (Marx and Engels 1950, 44). On Woolf's further qualification see Erin Carlston (1998, 157).

32. For a discussion of these changes in British class structure see Samuel (1994, 218–19; 1998, 68, 82–83). Lucas cites Orwell on the "cult of cheeriness and manliness, beer and cricket, briar pipes and monogamy" (1997, 35). Alison Light explores "Femininity, literature and conservatism between the wars" as well as self-division in Woolf in *Forever England* (1991), especially on pages 2–19.

33. "The Abinger Pageant" is reprinted in Forster's *Abinger Harvest* (1967, 369–84). Woolf refers to "England's Pleasant Land" in a diary entry for July 17, 1938 (1977–84, *Diary* 5: 156), and in letters to Ethel Smyth (July 15, 1938) and R. C. Trevelyan (July 5, 1938) (1975–80, *Letters* 6: 255, 258).

34. For Reith broadcasting "Jerusalem," see Lucas, who comments "the absurdity . . . is matched by its nastiness" (1997, 220).

35. Letter to Margaret Llewelyn Davies, April 6, 1940.

36. Probably "capricious" should read "capacious."

37. Although she misnames it "Old Man's Beard," it is quite clear that Isa is thinking of the poem "Old Man," in which the speaker shreds and sniffs a handful of southernwood (also known as "Old Man" or "Lad's Love"), and meditates upon childhood, love, and loss. It is not known when Woolf first read the poem, and a reference to the crushed leaves of verbena and southernwood in her 1919 essay "Reading" may also include an allusion to Thomas's poem: "If we could see also what we can smell—if, at this moment crushing the southernwood, I could go back" (1986–1994 *Essays* 3: 145).

38. Reviewing Thomas's *A Literary Pilgrim in England* for the *Times Literary Supplement* many years earlier, in October 1917 (and six months after his death in France), Woolf found "He had a passion for English country and a passion for English literature"; she had seldom read a book "which gives a better feeling of England than this one"—"Flumina Amem Silvasque" (1986–94 *Essays* 2: 161, 163).

39. From *The Waves* (1992, 74).

40. Brooker and Widdowson note that these countercurrents failed to produce a literature of "socialist-feminist modernism" before 1920 (1986, 158).

41. In a letter to Ethel Smyth, January 12, 1941 (1975–80, *Letters* 6: 460).

42. Churchill had been a notoriously right-wing Home Secretary in November 1910, at the time of "Black Friday" and the Tonypandy strike, and had later been militantly opposed to the General Strike, which the Woolfs had supported. See Woolf's diary for May 6, 1926 (1977–84 *Diary* 3: 78), and in a letter to Vanessa Bell, May 12, 1926 (1975–80, *Letters* 3: 261). Woolf had made fun of his style in the first draft of *A Room of One's Own*: "huge leather arm chairs & vast mahogany tables & turkey carpets so thick that the foot sinks in them somehow write like this when they are alone after dark in an office" (1992, *Women and Fiction* 156). Yet by April 13, 1940, he has become "Winston" (1977–84 *Diary* 5: 279), and a letter to Ethel Smyth records "the admiration this war creates—for every sort of person: chars, shopkeepers, even much more remarkably, for politicians—Winston, at least," September 25, 1940 (1975–80, *Letters* 6:434).

Works Cited

Beer, Gillian. 1990. "The Island and the Aeroplane: The Case of Virginia Woolf." In *Nation and Narration*. Edited by Homi K. Bhabha. London: Routledge.

———. 1992. "Introduction." In Virginia Woolf, *Between the Acts*. Edited by Stella McNichol. London: Penguin.

Bell, Clive. 1923. *Art*. 1914. London: Chatto and Windus.

Brooker, Peter, and Peter Widdowson. 1986. "A Literature for England." In *Englishness: Politics and Culture, 1880–1920*. Edited by Robert Colls and Philip Dodd. London: Croom Helm.

Carlston, Erin. 1998. *Thinking Fascism: Sapphic Modernism and Fascist Modernity*. Stanford, CA: Stanford University Press.

Collini, Stefan. 1999. *English Pasts: Essays in History and Culture*. Oxford: Oxford University Press.

Colls, Robert, and Philip Dodd, eds. 1986. *Englishness: Politics and Culture, 1880–1920*. London: Croom Helm.

Doyle, Brian. 1989. *English and Englishness*. London: Routledge.

Flint, Kate. 1986. "Virginia Woolf and the General Strike." *Essays in Criticism* 36: 319–334.

Forster, E. M. 1941. *Howard's End*. 1910. Harmondsworth, UK: Penguin.

———. 1967. *Abinger Harvest*. 1936. Harmondsworth: Penguin.

Fox, Alice. 1990. *Virginia Woolf and the Literature of the English Renaissance*. Oxford: Clarendon Press.

Fry, Roger. 1928. *Vision and Design*. 1920. London: Chatto and Windus.

Gilbert, Martin. 1995. *First World War*. London: HarperCollins.

Holtby, Winifred. 1932. *Virginia Woolf: A Critical Memoir*. London: Wishart.

Howkins, Alun. 1986. "The Discovery of Rural England." In *Englishness: Politics and Culture, 1880–1920*. Eds. Robert Colls and Philip Dodd. London: Croom Helm.

Lee, Hermione. 1996. *Virginia Woolf*. London: Chatto and Windus.

Light, Alison. 1991. *Forever England: Femininity, Literature, and Conservatism between the Wars*. London: Routledge.

Longley, Edna. 1981. *A Language Not to be Betrayed: Selected Prose of L. Edward Thomas*. Manchester, UK: Carcanet.

Looker, S. J., ed. 1937. *Jeffries' England*. London: Constable.

Lucas, John. 1997. *The Radical Twenties*. Nottingham, UK: Five Leaves Publications.

Marx, Karl, and Frederick Engels. 1950. *Selected Works*, vol. 1. London: Lawrence and Wishart.

Partridge, Eric. 1972. *The Penguin Dictionary of Historical Slang*. Harmondsworth, UK: Penguin.

Peach, Lyndon. 2000. *Virginia Woolf*. Basingstoke, UK: Macmillan.

Pevsner, Nikolaus. 1997. *The Englishness of English Art*. 1956. Harmondsworth, UK: Penguin.

Rudikoff, Sonya. 2000. *Ancestral Houses: Virginia Woolf and the Aristocracy*. Palo Alto, CA: Society for the Promotion of Science and Scholarship.

Samuel, Raphael. 1994. *Theatres of Memory*, vol. 1. London: Verso.

———. 1998. *Island Stories: Unravelling Britain. Vol. II.: Theatres of Memory*. London: Verso.

Woolf, Virginia. 1975–1980. *The Letters of Virginia Woolf*, vols. 1–6. Edited by Nigel Nicolson with Joanne Trautmann. London: Hogarth Press.

———. 1977–84. *The Diary of Virginia Woolf*, vols. 1–5. Edited by A. Olivier Bell with Andrew McNeillie. London: Hogarth Press.

———. 1978. *The Pargeters: The Novel-Essay Portion of "The Years."* Edited by Mitchell A. Leaska. London: Hogarth Press.

———. 1983. *Pointz Hall: The Earlier and Later Typescripts of Between the Acts*. Edited by Mitchell A. Leaska. New York: University Publications.

———. 1985. *Moments of Being*, 2nd ed. Edited by Jeanne Schulkind. London: Hogarth Press.

———. 1985. *The Complete Shorter Fiction*. Edited by Susan Dick. London: Hogarth Press.

———. 1986–1994. *The Essays of Virginia Woolf*, vols. 1–4. Edited by Andrew McNeillie. London: Hogarth Press.

———. 1989. *Congenial Spirits: The Selected Letters of Virginia Woolf*. Edited by Joanne Trautmann Banks. London: Hogarth Press.

———. 1992. *Jacob's Room*. Edited by Sue Roe. 1922. Harmondsworth, UK: Penguin.

———. 1992. *Between the Acts*. Edited by Stella McNichol. Introduction by Gillian Beer. Harmondsworth, UK: Penguin. 1941.

———. 1992. *Mrs. Dalloway*. Edited by Stella McNichol. Introduction by Elaine Showalter. 1925. Harmondsworth: Penguin.

———. 1992. *Night and Day*. Edited by Julia Briggs. 1919. Harmondsworth, UK: Penguin.

———. 1992. *The Voyage Out*. Edited by Jane Wheare. Harmondsworth, UK: 1915. Penguin.

———. 1992. *The Waves*. Edited by Kate Flint. 1931. Harmondsworth, UK: Penguin.

———. 1992. *Women and Fiction: The Manuscript Versions of A Room of One's Own*. Edited by S. P. Rosenbaum. Oxford: Blackwell.

———. 1993. *Orlando*. Edited by Brenda Lyons. Introduction by Sandra Gilbert. 1928. Harmondsworth, UK: Penguin.

———. 1993. *A Room of One's Own and Three Guineas*. Edited by Michele Barrett. 1929, 1938. Harmondsworth, UK: Penguin.

———. 1995. *Roger Fry*. Edited by Diane F. Gillespie. 1940. Oxford: Blackwell for Shakespeare Head Press.

———. 1998. *The Years*. Edited by Jeri Johnson. 1937. Harmondsworth, UK: Penguin.

Žižek, Slavoj. 1991. *For They Know Not What They Do*. London: Verso.

Hyphenated Identity in the "Woman's Novel": Racisms and Betty Miller's *Farewell Leicester Square*

CLAIRE M. TYLEE

ALTHOUGH BETTY MILLER'S *FAREWELL LEICESTER SQUARE* WAS NOT published until 1941, it is essentially a novel of the 1930s. In fact it was finished in 1935 and offered to Gollancz, who had published her last three novels, but rejected this (Jane Miller 2000, x; Beauman 1998, 3).[1] Betty Miller had announced to Victor Gollancz that her novel concerned "the social and psychological conflicts of a Jew in the modern world" (Jane Miller 2000, ix); that "modern world" is England of the 1930s. Although dates are not specified in the novel, allusions suggest that its climactic events have implicitly to be understood as taking place between January 1933, when Hitler became Chancellor of Germany, and *kristallnacht*, November 10, 1938, when his intentions toward those whom nazism classified as "Jews" became unmistakable. How much that would make Miller's book a hostage to fortune she could not have foreseen in 1935, but it determined that there would be an ironic distance between the novel and its readership. This could only grow more pointed after its public appearance during World War II, by which time the British were fighting for their lives against nazism.[2]

Not that the grounds for the irony are immediately apparent from the opening chapters. The reader is skillfully seduced by a novel that is by turns lyrically responsive, visually impressionistic, and gently comic. This is a novel that disguises its political designs within the apparent format of familiar generic conventions, conventions it artfully subverts. While paying homage to the formal elegance and subtlety of English culture, particularly the "woman's novel" of the interwar period, Miller savagely exposes the ugliness behind the screen of middle-class decorum. A brilliantly original chapter at the center of her novel rends that screen with a sequence of frank revelations and caustic jokes. Comparing the anti-Semitic demonstrations of the East End with the orderly crowds on the pavements in the West End, one of her characters remarks on the "potentialities of evil and violence that lay beneath that surface of good humour and good manners" (1941, 181–82). The resentment and hostility so sharply revealed make plain the conflicted identity of being both Jewish and English: "There are moments when it's *intolerable* being a Jew" (180). They also make plain the problems involved in writing a Jewish-English novel—and in getting it published.

Set in middle-class family life in southeast England during the period when it was being written, between the wars, *Farewell Leicester Square* might seem at first to fit neatly into the genre of the woman's novel. This is a twentieth-century tradition of British women's writing which feminist critics have carefully traced since the publication of Nicola Beauman's *A Very Great Profession: The woman's novel, 1914–1939* in 1983. It consists of novels that, as Beauman defined them, are not concerned with adventure or dramatic action but with the "steadfast dailiness" of (domestic) life where what is important is intensity of emotion and, above all, human relationships. Such novels are said to be marked by an unmistakably "middle-class/female tone of voice" and, as Clare Hanson points out, they construct their reader as feminine, interpellating women to recognize their shared (contradictory) identity and knowledge in the text (2000, 1–2). Among the novelists who contributed to the tradition, influenced by Virginia Woolf, are Rosamund Lehmann, Rose Macaulay, Jean Rhys, Elizabeth Taylor, and, above all, Elizabeth Bowen.

Alison Light also includes E. H. Young, E. M. Delafield, and Jan Struther among the writers of what she terms "the middle-brow novel" that brought "the culture of domesticity to public awareness" (1991, 139). Olga Kenyon has extended our understanding of the tradition beyond the Second World War. The later generation of authors such as Anita Brookner continue to display "a 'feminine' sensibility in the subtle descriptions of appearances, textures, social nuances" and to represent the "social frustrations and intimate thought processes of gifted, undervalued women" (1988, 149). The daily life with which these writers were concerned was the mundane life of contemporary, comfortable middle-England. This places them as heirs to Jane Austen, and distinguishes their work from other traditions of British women's writing.[3] For instance, Betty Miller had the choice of following the extremely popular G. B. Stern if she wanted to write about a Jew in modern Britain. The first three novels in

Stern's baroque saga about the Rakonitz family had been republished as *Rakonitz Chronicles* in 1932 and had resulted in a successful West End play, *The Matriarch*, starring Mrs. Patrick Campbell, in 1929. Stern's was a fresh voice in English literature, her rich, everflowing style of story-telling mirroring the exuberant, abundant lives she described. Such loud tones and unstoppable generosity were quite alien to the cool restraint of the woman's novel. However, unlike Stern, Miller had not the confidence of a wealthy cosmopolitan background to draw on when confronting the conservative English tradition. Rather than divert sedate sensibilities with an exotic entertainment, her novel masqueraded as home-grown. It convincingly mimicked the woman's novel in style and tone until, as if pushed beyond endurance, it suddenly affronted English notions of good taste by openly speaking its mind.

The woman's novel was a product of certain social changes for women brought about by three major factors: the entry of women into secondary and higher education, the availability of birth control,[4] and (thus) more leisure for married women, and the development of mass publishing and lending/circulating libraries—Mudie's had given way to Boots, which made 25 to 35 million book loans annually from 1928 to 1939. It is the first of these factors that directly affected the content of the new genre. Kenyon identifies the woman's novel which first emerged as a significant form in the 1920s and 1930s as "the novel written by and for educated middle-class women" (quoted in Hanson 2000, 7). This category of "middle-class" was problematized by Alison Light in *Forever England*. There she suggests that the complex nature of class references was undergoing radical revision in the interwar period: "being middle-class, in fact, depends [*sic*] on an extremely anxious production of endless discriminations between people who are constantly assessing each other's standing" (1991, 13). These novels might themselves be seen as part of that anxious process of assessment and discrimination amongst educated women as they jockeyed for intellectual status while critiquing middle-class women's social power. "Discrimination" is, of course, a double-edged word when used in connection with the work of a Jewish-British novelist. It indicates the knife-edge Miller's writing had to negotiate.

According to Hilary Radner (1989), the women's novel bridges the gap between the public, dominant discourse of intellectual mastery, and the private, occluded discourse of domesticity and (female) embodiment. The public discourse tends to be gendered as masculine, and is esteemed by patriarchal culture, which, by contrast, derogates the private discourse of emotion and the responsive body as feminine, thereby setting up a binary opposition of value and exclusivity. Despite this constructed opposition, educated women laid claim to both discourses and to both the domains they denoted; the fictions of the woman's novel have been discussed by Clare Hanson as attempts to deal with the contradictory position their authors thus found themselves in. The novels claim a right to interrogate the transcendent life of the intellect and spirit but they also defend and explore the material life events of the viscous lived body made taboo by patriarchy: menstruation, pregnancy, birth, lactation, and dying. As a result the novels may present themselves as generically part of the popular form of romantic fiction which has essentially to do with women's feelings; but the novels also belong to the higher generic form of the literary novel; they are novels of ideas. As Hanson argues (following Radner 1995), they therefore offer both the (feminine/hysterical) pleasures of an emotional wallow in the imaginative reading process and in the imaginary events conveyed, and also the (masculine/obsessive) pleasures of being intellectually stimulated to reflect on the text itself and its arguments and enigmas. However, polarities between public and private, masculine and feminine, intellectual and emotional, become far less clear-cut when patriarchal society is seen to be constructed on a complex hierarchy of race and class as well as gender.

Farewell Leicester Square certainly straddles the two areas of discourse identified by Radner: on the one hand it explores the personal problems of a mixed marriage within the nexus of uninvolved sexual encounters, friends' perceptions, and family relations; on the other hand it interrogates the public world of the film industry and the culture it (re)produces. Miller achieves this by marrying the popular world of romantic fiction to the traditional high-art form of the European *bildungsroman*, and more specifically to its subgenre of the *kunstlerroman*—the novel about the growth and development of the artist. Novels such as Stendhal's *The Red and the Black*, Dickens's *Great Expectations*, and Joyce's *A Portrait of the Artist as a Young Man* portrayed the development of a young man as a conflict between individual and society as he progresses from his parental home to the choice of a life and career of his own. Novelists have used the genre as an opportunity to display the corrupt social values of the wider society, particularly with regard to religion and class. The young man's coming of age as a mature adult is marked by his recognition of those corrupting forces and his ability to resist them. Despite the limitations on women's achieving a career, there have been attempts at female *bildungsromans*, for instance, *Jane Eyre*, *The Mill on the Floss*, and *The Voyage Out*. Yet, since the expected career for a woman has been marriage, both the heroines and the plots of such novels, however much they press to escape, tend to be hemmed in by the domestic world of emotion which pertains to the domain of popular romantic fiction.

What primarily makes Miller's novel unlike other woman's novels of the 1920s to 1930s is her choice of a male protagonist. The reader is called in, interpellated, to identify not with a female heroine like Olivia in Rosamund Lehmann's *Invitation to the Waltz* (1932) and *The Weather in the Streets* (1936) or Portia in Elizabeth Bowen's *The Death of the Heart* (1938). The reader is called upon to share his/her feminine sensibility with a man, the film director, Alec Berman. This is less odd than it sounds since Berman, as a Jew, is feminized by British culture. He lacks the power of English patriarchal networks that would construct him as masculine and his vulnerability to negative evaluations of his physical appearance mark him as feminine. In fact, the narrative focalizing of Miller's novel is quite complex—more akin to Jean Rhys's *Wide Sargasso Sea* (1966) than to *Invitation to the Waltz*. The novel opens with a chapter centered on a spectacular event rather than on any named character, the premiere of Alec Berman's successful film *Farewell Leicester Square*. It then moves in flashback to Alec's adolescence as perceived by himself. He remains the central focus, like Antoinette/Bertha in *Wide Sargasso Sea*, but part 2 of the novel ends with two chapters narrated from the point of view of his new (gentile) wife, Catherine: chapters 9, "Gynaecological," and 10, "Dinner for Four." Part 3 includes another, chapter 12, "The Agent," which centers again on Catherine's experience in the absence of Alec. Just as Rhys interposes a sequence from the perspective of Rochester, Antoinette's spouse, so Miller interleaves Catherine's viewpoint with Berman's. Such a shift of focalizer is even more pronounced in Bowen's *The House in Paris* (1935)—a novel exactly contemporaneous with Miller's. However, Bowen presents the gender shift across generations, between mother and son, rather than between sexual partners.

This narrative technique of shifting focalizer is particularly appropriate to these three novels since they all deal with figures construed as racially Other. The changing perspective is a novelistic device that encourages the reader to shift identification and to imagine alien viewpoints. The reader must cross not only a gender divide, but also a racial one. However, whereas Rhys's novel was written in awareness of postimperial anti-Caribbean racism, Bowen and Miller are both dealing with the complexities of anti-Semitism at the time of the European-wide political crises between the world wars. It is hardly coincidental that Gollancz published Bowen's novel in the same year he refused Miller's.[5] Setting

Farewell Leicester Square against *The House in Paris* highlights not only their similarities but also their differences, enabling us to perceive what is special about Miller's attempts to politicize the woman's novel. This may help us to "read slant" and fill in the silences of Bowen's more circumspect novel; more importantly it may help us to understand why Miller's openness was censored by Gollancz. The evasiveness of Bowen's approach, which may have suited Gollancz's assimilationist policy, may also then be seen to maintain a tacit political position—exemplifying precisely the unspoken politics that Miller was critiquing: British liberalism.

The second aspect of *Farewell Leicester Square* that makes it unlike many other 1930s novels, beyond its focus on a male protagonist, Alec Berman, is its critical positioning of the female characters, especially the novel's English, middle-class "heroine," Catherine Nicolls. She becomes Alec's wife and the mother of his son, David. (It is David who—at the age of six—precipitates the novel's crisis and Alec's mature disengagement from illusion.) The novel places Catherine against two other representative types of womanhood: on the one hand, Hetty Follet, the glamorous parvenue star of Alec's films who had been his mistress, and on the other, his careworn mother, Mrs. Berman. Although, unlike Catherine, these two other women in Alec's life are not agents of any action that propels the plot, they do signify not only contrasting forms of emotional attachment but also two poles of value. With regard to the intellectual reading of the novel they establish the criteria by which Alec's films and English culture are to be judged. The novel traces Alec's spiritual journey away from spell-binding, sterile spectacle (represented by Hetty) and the cool, gracious, regulated emptiness of English bourgeois culture (represented by Catherine); both are only superficially attractive. Alec finally returns to the nourishing warmth of his "common" shop-keeping family, fashioned into enduring value by the artistry of his mother's house-work-roughened hands (1941, 13).

Such a journey may sound clichéd, too obviously in the mold of *Great Expectations* to impress the reader greatly at its ending. The emphatic contrast between surface appearance and underlying reality, between beauty and character, snobbery and sincerity, aesthetic values and moral ones, is hardly new to European culture. The strength and originality of *Farewell Leicester Square* lie in the third aspect I want to stress: its depiction and interrogation of racisms in British society. Alec Berman comes from a Jewish family and the novel traces the growth of his awareness of what this means for his sense of his own identity. This is the political design that links the two domains of the novel, the personal, domestic life (of marital breakup) with the world of public culture. I say "racisms" because alongside the anti-Semitism which Alec fights and which eventually destroys his marriage, is the anglophilia that drives his ambition, and which Miller depicts as the mirror image of the "judaeophobia" (the anxiety about and aversion to Jewishness) from which he also suffers. That is, his desire for what he perceives as English, which includes Catherine, is not merely a class snobbery against the vulgarity of his petit-bourgeois family; Miller displays it as fueled by self-denigration, and both are continually expressed in terms of race.[6] Discourses of race, which are essentially evaluative, infect both the private and the public domains, structuring bodily feeling as well as intellectual perception.

This is the strength of Betty Miller's sensitivity to the "subtle nuancing" which for Kenyon typifies the woman's novel. Miller does not revel in social nuance for its own sake. Nor is she merely creating a comedy of manners—although there is plenty of humor to enjoy. She shows, to quote the *Guardian*, "the discreet discrimination of the bourgeoisie . . . in shaping the intellectual heritage of the United Kingdom" (Anon. 2000, 11). Her novel makes a trenchant challenge to the cosy nationalism of the early British film industry constructed by such Jewish filmmakers as Michael Balcon (Kardish 1984, 43–44).[7] It also voices criticism of British liberalism in the face of dictatorship abroad. British social discrimination, which may strike us as comic with regard to class, is anything but comic when it comes to race, and Miller's brilliance lies in her depiction of the intimate interrelationship between snobbery and racism.[8] Miller does not rest on the polite social surface. Taking advantage of the woman's novel's exploration of the material, bodily life, she shows how Catherine's physical and undoubtedly sexual attraction for Alec is based on racial values: her non-Jewish, madonna-like beauty is seen in terms of paintings of Christian martyred saints and, perhaps ominously, as Pre-Raphaelite: "a martyr in an old painting" (33), "a Rosetti" (120), a "painting of a martyr-saint" (135).

What is finally original in *Farewell Leicester Square* is Miller's demonstration of the power and importance of the ethnic-minority community, and particularly the role of the family, in supporting individuals to resist racism. Counterbalancing Alec's insecurity and his anglophilia, is his nostalgia for being "one in a community," a longing for protection, solidarity, and oneness (132). Miller offers a peculiarly Jewish-feminist analysis.[9] This prefigures the theories of third-wave feminism exemplified in the writing of Nira Yuval-Davis and others, and implicitly offers a reply to Ros Coward's rhetorical question, "Are Women's Novels Feminist Novels?" (1980). Catherine is a principled if unimaginative mother, a mother who breast-feeds her baby (in a comic section in chapter 10) and who eventually leaves her husband in order to raise her son to be different from his father, free from the insecurities and "stigma" of being identified as Jewish. Although, in accordance with the conventions of the woman's novel, the (female) reader may seem to be interpellated to identify with Catherine, it is actually another woman who haunts the novel: Alec's mother. Unnamed and practically invisible, she is the epitome of the self-denying Jewish mother—a figure who is so much the butt of jokes that even Miller's lips twitch.[10] Such women, along with Alec's vulgar sister and sister-in-law, maintain the enduring Jewish culture in which "decent, average human-beings" can survive the charges that a Jew is "degenerate, parasite, effluvium from the ferment of rottenness" (181). It may have been that, in England in the 1930s "The concentration camp [wa]s only spiritual" (144), but (as we know only too well) Miller was not naive in her reminder that "potentialities of evil and violence lay beneath that surface of good humour and good manners" (181). This sense of a threatened community in which "a state of intent communicativeness" (175) provides underground support, provides the reader, too, with a powerful alternative to dominant "English" culture. It interpellates the Jewish woman reader and any other reader threatened by the rallying cry: "England for the English!" (175) in a way that such novels as Elizabeth Bowen's *The House in Paris* fail to do. Thus, *Farewell Leicester Square* offers subversive pleasures to which the woman's novel is usually insensible.

It also offers discomforts unknown to the run-of-the-mill woman's novel. I suggest that Miller's *Farewell Leicester Square* takes advantage of the generic conventions established by the woman's novel in order to shake the ordinary educated woman reader of such novels out of her liberal English bourgeois complacency, so that she may recognize Catherine's blindness to racism in herself. Criticizing what she called the "nice novel" written for "ladies," Elizabeth Bowen commented that pre-assumptions are bad: "they limit the novel to a given circle of readers. They cause the novel to act immorally *on* that given circle. . . . outside the given circle a novel's pre-assumptions must invalidate it for all other readers" (1950, 258). However, I believe that Bowen's own novel on the Jewish issue in 1930s Europe, *The House in Paris,* suffers precisely from (liberal, middle-class) racial pre-assumptions which it implicitly (if unintentionally) confirms. Miller, by contrast, has tried to *use* racial pre-assumptions. It is this that makes her novel such an interesting and affirming read for people outside that circle of ladies to whom the woman's novel was typically directed. Comparing the two novelists and their novels may help to identify the exclusivity by which the British bourgeoisie maintained its own (racial and class) status.

Bowen and Miller shared a background, but were also divided by it in ways that are illuminating for a reading of their novels. They were both born in Ireland in the years before World War I (Bowen in 1899, Miller in 1910); County Cork was common home to their childhoods. But for Bowen that meant Bowen's Court, an Anglo-Irish Great House in its own rural estate, of the kind that figures in Bowen's *The Last September*;[11] for Miller it meant a cigar and jewelry shop in the city streets of Cork, of the kind that figures in *Farewell Leicester Square*. Whereas Bowen came from the landed gentry, with roots in both Ireland and England, Miller was the daughter of Jewish immigrants from Eastern Europe, who were "in trade." (Her father became a JP and secretary of the local synagogue.) Both Miller and Bowen were exiled to England, where they took university courses in journalism. After their respective marriages, in the 1930s they each set up home in the select Regent's Park area of Central London: Miller in a flat above her husband's consulting-rooms at 23 Park Crescent, Bowen a stone's throw away in the house she and her husband bought at 2 Clarence Terrace. Both authors moved in London literary circles, but these seem to have been distinct. In spite of their ten-year age gap, they shared some mutual friends, such as Isaiah Berlin and Rosamund Lehmann, but that does not seem to have led to any friendship (or even meeting?) between the two women. Despite all they had in common, is it only that Miller had three children while Bowen remained childless that accounts for their separateness?

The critic Heather Bryant Jordan has identified what she called Bowen's "hyphenated identity" as important to her writing: "From her childhood experiences, the writer discerned the significance of the hyphen in Anglo-Irish, and her pervasive sense of being an outsider, both personally and nationally, originated in the disruption of those early years [when she lived alternately in England and Ireland]" (1989, 82, 70–71). We may hypothesize that Miller's sense of herself as British-Jewish gave her, too, a sensitivity to "hyphenated identity." These hyphenated terms point to family backgrounds by which Bowen and Miller inherited critical areas of European history, areas that helped create what it was to be British or English in the twentieth century. However, through their families they stood in different relations to that history. Whereas Bowen's family benefited from the exploitation of the dispossessed native Irish, Miller's family itself belonged to another such dispossessed people, European Jewry.[12]

Bowen's alignment is made clear in her 1942 remark: "We have everything to dread from the dispossessed" (1942, 338). She may have been emotionally insecure because of her parents' personalities, but cultural dominance was Bowen's birthright, a right she could take for granted in London. The centuries-old threats to the very survival of Miller's minority culture give the commemoration of Passover in *Farewell Leicester Square* special poignancy. Their experiences and ideas about being an outsider or an insider are manifested very differently in the two novels that Miller and Bowen wrote about European-Jewish identity in the 1930s.

Written at the beginning of one of the greatest dispossessions in European history, *The House in Paris* and *Farewell Leicester Square* depict states of unbelonging. The structural similarities of their central situations are striking: both plots revolve around a sexual liaison between a young, privileged middle-class Englishwoman and an older Jewish man, which results in the birth of a son. According to strict Jewish orthodoxy the child inherits its ethnic Jewishness through the mother and so these boys would not necessarily be recognized as Jewish. Nevertheless, they were growing up in the 1930s, when according to Nazi racial ideology—regardless of whether they were claimed, recognized, or educated to be Jewish—these boys would be racially Jewish (through having at least one Jewish grandparent). They were highly vulnerable at a dangerous time.[13] The novels by Miller and Bowen were published before the worst Nazi atrocities commenced, but the anxious emigration of impoverished European Jewish refugees was already being thwarted by the quota systems of foreign governments.[14] Like the literature about apartheid in South Africa and segregation in the United States, the plight of mixed-race children brings into focus the pain, injustice, and irrationality of racist politics, and interpellates the reader to bear responsibility for the fate of the innocent.

However, Bowen and Miller flesh out their structural skeleton from diametrically different standpoints. Whereas Miller's novel foregrounds the developing perceptions of the Jewish man from late adolescence, before switching to the Englishwoman's consciousness, Bowen offers a point of view barely alluded to by Miller: the uncomprehending feelings of the mixed-race child of their union. Bowen then switches to the Englishwoman's consciousness, but the experiences, beliefs, and values of the adult Jewish male are never directly revealed to the reader of *The House in Paris*. In fact, although he is variously recognized as an English-French Jew (the son of a French mother married to an English-Jewish father), he apparently has no immediate family and no sense of a Jewish cultural heritage. Nor does the sense of being Jewish form any part whatever of his son's consciousness and so it is not presented to Bowen's reader. By contrast, in Miller's novel it is precisely that Alec's six-year-old son has been fighting in the playground over taunts that he is a Jew that leads to the breakup of Alec's marriage. That explicitness, that sense of the power of the word-out-loud, is symptomatic of the whole difference between the novels.

Bowen's novel commences when the English-(French-)Jewish child, Leopold, is about nine. He is introduced to the reader through the bewildered eyes of an eleven year-old girl, Henrietta. She sees "a dark-eyed, very slight little boy who looked either French or Jewish" (17). (What it is to "look Jewish" or how Henrietta could already recognize it are not elucidated, although this is the usual basis for prejudiced, discriminatory treatment and is directly confronted in Miller's novel.) Bowen's ironic method of narrating through the sexually innocent yet intelligent perceptions of a young girl in the charge of an incompetent, middle-aged spinster obviously owes much to Henry James's *What Maisie Knew*. Bowen's overriding purpose is much the same as his: to display the sexual hypocrisy of the English middle classes. However, for James the sophisticated moral joke he shares with the reader at the expense of Maisie's naivete is sufficient, his novel is mainly comic. The irony in Bowen's novel leads up to tragedy. Henrietta is incidental to the plot but her blinkered helplessness prepares us for that of Leopold's mother, Karen. The novel flashes back ten years and tells what happened to place Leopold in his present predicament: having traveled from Italy he is expecting to meet his birth-mother for the first time in Paris.

The main bulk of *The House in Paris* concerns Karen, who, while engaged to be married, had a brief, secret affair with Max, the Jewish fiancé of her closest friend, Naomi. Apprehending not only that Karen will not marry him but that the affair has destroyed his precarious position in Paris, Max commits suicide before Karen discovers that she is pregnant. Naomi arranges for the baby to be adopted, and Karen goes ahead and marries Ray. The narrative is a psychological study of the fatalistic way in which Karen behaves. She simply allows things to happen as if she had no power over them, rather like Lois Farquar in *The Last September*. Karen succumbs to sexual desire but is incapable of openly confronting her mother's values. The book is largely a study of her bad faith as she submits to the aims of others and evades any self-analysis or responsibility for the effects of her actions. But it is not merely a psychological study, any more than *The Last September* is simply a study of Lois, whose moral limitedness also leads to tragedy. Just as Lois's behavior is displayed as woven into the ultimately myopic and selfish fabric of upper middle-class Anglo-Ireland, so Karen's limitations are gradually revealed to be typical of the emotionally restrictive nature of her people. The decorum of middle-England is shown to be kept in place by silence, secrets, deceit, and hypocrisy, a veneer of respectability maintained by women like Karen's mother. This results in a stultifying failure of emotional imagination. It comes almost as a relief when the moral inertia of the women's world is suddenly cut through by the masculine decisiveness of Ray, by this time Karen's husband, who comes to claim Leopold.

Bowen has satirically displayed the cowardice, selfishness, and coldness of English middle-class culture—but the novel can suggest no alternative because it itself is symptomatic of that very culture. It is a liberal novel. Her aesthetic position belongs to what Hanif Kureishi has identified as the "tolerant, reasonable, civilised" English way of life, the world of the British tradition of "understatement, civilised discourse and respect for reason" that gives no sense of the racism faced by racial minorities in Britain: "violence, abuse and discrimination in jobs, housing, policing and political life."[15] Miller gives one restrained example of the verbal abuse that Catherine unthinkingly inflicts on Alec by her casual use of the term "Dago" (170). It acts like a silent whiplash on Alec's consciousness as he recognizes the racist contempt. In his mind he follows the remark with typical excuses such as "some of my best friends . . ." and then curses such "tolerance": "their damned shallow self-satisfied *tolerance*" (108). Bowen gives no example of such overt abuse, only what Jean Radford calls the "genteel anti-Semitism" of Karen's mother in alluding to Max's Jewish "astuteness" over money (1999, 42). As Tony Kushner demonstrates, the much-lauded English liberalism exalts the value of toleration, but toleration is only a conditional acceptance: the outsider must conform to the values and manners of bourgeois English society. This conditional acceptance is actually the "central driving force of British racism" (Kushner 1989, 18) for all difference must be ironed out. There is no active welcoming of diversity, no sense that the outsider might bring new cultural riches—a fierce sense of humor would not be the least of these, to judge by what Beauman has rightly called "the great central scene" of Miller's novel (Beauman 1998, 2–3).

For Bowen, Max is simply a token, a cipher of the outsider, an indication of the fate of unbelonging that Leopold is saved from by Ray. For Bowen, to be a Jew is simply not to belong to the dominant culture. This evinces a very tenuous tolerance at best. More important, Max is a "cad" (Lassner 1996, 204). This is a mild term for a man who, following a long-term liaison with a woman older than himself, forms a loveless engagement to her daughter in the prospect of money, then betrays her for unprotected sex with yet another woman, a wealthy virgin whom he leaves pregnant. He is not only a "cad" but a coward who commits suicide to evade the mess he has created. This is the token Jew Bowen has created. If Karen's mother can be accused of genteel anti-Semitism for suggesting that Max conforms to the Jewish stereotype of financial astuteness, what should we say of the author who created Max and his selfish, mercenary behavior? The contrast with Ray, the English public-school product who shoulders Max's responsibilities, could hardly be more marked. In fact, if Ray is the impossibly heroic figure from adolescence romances like *Tom Brown's Schooldays* and *Tell England*, then Mme Fisher and Max Ebhart are the villains of gothic melodramas such as *Great Expectations* and *Oliver Twist*.

By contrast, Miller deconstructs stereotypical ideas of both English (wo)men and Jews by including a range of characters from both sides of the divide, with varying strengths and failings. Bowen's canvas is more intensely focused on fewer people and a tighter time period; Miller depicts a wider range of society over a lengthier time span. Not only does this enable her to produce a looser, larger picture, but it demonstrates more fully the interrelation between public and private which is one of the strengths of the interwar woman's novel. However, in both novels there is a narrative progression to the assimilation of the part-Jewish boy. In neither novel is the prospect for this "hidden child" very promising: Bowen and Miller at least shared distaste for the bourgeois English family, distrust of the English public-school education that awaited these boys, and pessimism about race relations, particularly about mixed marriage. However, there is some hope for the future presented by Miller.

The final words of *Farewell Leicester Square* chime with the song from which the title is taken: It's a long, long way back for Alec to find where his heart is, back from a bondage to false values and home to the welcome of his Jewish family and the ceremonial Friday evening meal. Alec had jokingly predicted to Catherine that if he should lose his claim on England, unlike his Jewish ancestors he would sit on the banks of a river in Zion weeping when he remembered Babylon (142). In losing Catherine he does lose his stake in bourgeois England. Yet he returns to his family strong in the recognition that although he and Catherine had tried and failed, the mixed marriage had been an attempt worth making. We might say that he returns to Zion *in* Babylon. To end her Jewish-English woman's novel, Miller leaves the atheist Alec amongst his family singing the blessing from the Book of Psalms. She concludes her text with the words that celebrate the return from exile. They are being sung with the door open so that Alec's mother, ill in bed, can hear them in unison. The blessing is presented to the reader not in the original Hebrew that they sing but in the familiar words of the Authorized Version: "Then was our mouth filled with laughter, and our tongue with exaltation. . . . They that sow in tears shall reap in joy." This tactful, emotional, ironic reminder of a shared culture, one that has endured and sustained both Christians and Jews for centuries, forms a graceful ending. It demonstrates with what artistry Miller had adapted the conventions of the woman's novel to her own purposes.

Notes

1. Victor Gollancz published books by such best-selling authors as Vera Brittain, Katherine Burdekin, Elizabeth Bowen, Ivy Compton-Burnett, and Dorothy L. Sayers, so his rejection of Betty Miller was highly significant for her career. Beauman identifies the reasons for his rejection of Miller's novel as "twofold," in that it was both "embarrassingly angry" and, "given that its author was only 24, it was overall too controversial, too uppity" (1998, 3). Gollancz's "ambivalence toward his [own] Jewish roots" is discussed by Tony Kushner in chapter 6 of his *The Holocaust and the Liberal Imagination* (1994). Although Gollancz "veered away from Jewish particularity" between the wars, in 1942 he produced what Kushner calls "one of the most astonishing pieces of polemical literature published in war-time Britain": *Let My People Go* (1994, 176). This was followed by three more pamphlets in 1945 and 1946, including *What Buchenwald* Really *Means*.

2. Miller's epigraph to her novel, from the Book of Jeremiah, is taken from a prophecy by Jeremiah that predicts the fate soon to be suffered by the ancient nations surrounding Israel. It would be interesting to know whether it was attached to her original manuscript or added to the 1941 version of *Farewell Leicester Square.*

3. They were not "social explorers" like Elizabeth Gaskell or Margaret Oliphant: they did not seek to write novels of historical reconstruction like George Eliot or Naomi Mitchison; nor did they produce fantasies such as Virginia Woolf's *Orlando* or Angela Carter's *Nights at the Circus*, or works of the gothic imagination, such as the Brontës or Emma Tennant.

4. And disposable sanitary napkins, according to Alison Light (1991, 101).

5. These were not the only writings by British women that engaged with anti-Semitism in the 1930s. See Phyllis Lassner, 1992 and 1996, for a discussion (with bibliographies) of fiction by Virginia Woolf and Stevie Smith between 1936 and 1938, and Lassner, 1998, for a development of her earlier discussion.

6. Readers of American literature may have become familiar with this perception about racial discourse fueling self-denigration. It is the theme of such works as Toni Morrison's *The Bluest Eye* and Arthur Miller's *Broken Glass.* However, I have not found this insight presented in British literature before Miller's novel. The issue with regard to

German-Jewish American identity is discussed by Sander L. Gilman in *Jewish Self-Hatred* (1986).

7. Nicola Beauman remarks on "the many similarities between his [Alec's] career and that of the real-life Alexander Korda" (1998, 2). Balcon seems to me a more appropriate comparison—especially since Miller's brother was apprenticed to him, and she went to visit Balcon's studios for background for the novel (see Jane Miller's introduction to the 2000 edition). Michael Balcon (1896–1977), a central figure in the creation of a British film industry between the wars, was, like Alec, a first-generation Englishman born into a Jewish family in the English provinces. Adrienne Mancia's comments about Balcon's films give us an insight into what Miller implies about Alec's films and his self-delusion: "Balcon's celluloid England was as he believed it to be, or wanted it to be, and how he wanted the audience to believe it. It was liberal, traditional, comfy, and parochial" (Fluegel 1984 14–15).

8. Miller is not ignorant of working-class anti-Semitism. The novel alludes to the overt violence in London's East End, later to be depicted in Arnold Wesker's trilogy *Chicken Soup with Barley*. But her main purpose was to detect the more covert racism in which fascism takes root.

9. So-called "third-wave feminism" revised what it saw as second-wave feminists' tendency to essentialize women. In particular, it distinguished the differences among women due to their varying ethnicities, economic situations, and historical backgrounds (as well as their sexualities). Nira Yuval-Davis, while problematizing the nature of Jewishness and the heterogeneity of Jewish experience, movements, and ideologies in different countries, nevertheless stresses the importance of the mother in Jewish life. She outlines women's specific Mitzvot, their duties as wife, housewife, and mother, to emphasize how "women are constructed as the guardians of the Jewish home, which is the foundation of the Jewish people" (1992, 214). She presents this imposition as actually empowering women, and her analysis is corroborated by other Jewish feminists such as Adrienne Baker and Rabbi Julia Neuberger. Miller certainly presents some of the differences between Alec's wife and his mother in terms of his mother's preservation of religious culture in the home, specifically through mealtime ceremonial. Incidentally, Julia Neuberger's account of feeling "German-Jewish" is particularly relevant to the present paper about hyphenated identity (1979, 29–59).

10. The question, "The Jewish Mother—Myth or Reality?" was addressed in the session, "Meet My Jewish Mother" at the annual Jewish Culture Day on the South Bank, in London, November 28, 1999, by a range of Jewish writers including Bernice Rubens and Michelene Wandor. Jokes abounded.

11. There is a photograph of this property in Patricia Craig's *Elizabeth Bowen* (1986). Other, fuller biographies of Bowen include Victoria Glendenning's *Elizabeth Bowen: Portrait of a Writer* (1977) and Hermione Lee's *Elizabeth Bowen: An Estimation* (1981). There is a photograph of Betty Miller on the front cover of the *Persephone Quarterly* 5 (March 2000). A brief account of Miller's literary circle is given in Frances Spalding's *Stevie Smith: A Critical Biography* (186–188). This also details Smith's extraordinary tactlessness with regard to the "feeling of profound uncertainty" Miller experienced as a Jew, her anxieties about what she perceived as the "strong growing anti-Jewish feeling" in England in the late 1940s, and the fears she had for her children as a result. Miller did not forgive Smith for making this intimate knowledge public in her short story "Beside the Sea: A Holiday with Children" (1949).

12. Theoretical discussions of Irish history raise issues that parallel those raised about recent Jewish history. For a discussion of the apocalyptic nature of the Great Famine and the inadequacy of language to express the "unspeakable memory" of such a historic trauma see Brewster and Crossman (1999). Of course, the very term 'Anglo-Irish' indicates that Bowen belonged to the Protestant Ascendancy, Irish landowners of English origins.

13. Restrictive Jewish policies had gradually been enacted in Germany since March 1933, after Hitler's accession: anti-Semitism was formalized by the Nuremberg Laws in autumn of 1935, which stripped Jews of all rights to citizenship, confiscated their property, and forbade intermarriage or miscegenation between "Jews" and "Aryans."

14. Britain's 1919 Alien's Act had "stopped almost all immigrants" even before the Nazi rise to power (Kushner 1994, 32).

15. In "Bradford" Hanif Kureishi was discussing racism in 1980s Britain, but I see no difference between it and the English liberalism of the 1930s as delineated by Miller.

Works Cited

Anon. 2000. "Review of Persephone edition of *Farewell Leicester Square*." *The Guardian*, London (April 15): 11.

Baker, Adrienne. 1993. *The Jewish Woman in Contemporary Society: Transitions and Traditions*. London: Macmillan.

Beauman, Nicola. 1998. *A Very Great Profession: The woman's novel, 1914–39*, 2nd ed. 1983. London: Virago.

———. 2000. *Persephone Quarterly* (March): 5.

Boruma, Ian. 1999. "Churchill's Cigar." *Granta* 65 (Spring): 327–343.

Bowen, Elizabeth. 1935. *The House in Paris*. London: Gollantz.

———. 1942. *Bowen's Court*. London: Longman Green.

———. 1950. "Notes on Writing a Novel." *Collected Impressions,* 258. 1945. Longmans.

Brewster, Scott, and Veronica Crossman. 1999. "Re-writing the Famine: Witnessing the Crisis." In Brewster et al., 42–58.

Brewster, Scott, Veronica Crossman, Fiona Becket, and David Alderson, eds. 1999. *Ireland in Proximity: History, Gender, Space*. London: Routledge.

Byatt, A. S. 1976. Introduction to *The House in Paris* by Elizabeth Bowen, 7–16. Harmondsworth, UK: Penguin.

Coward, Rosalind. 1980. "'This novel changes lives': Are Women's Novels Feminist Novels? A Response to Rebecca O'Rourke's Article 'Summer Reading.'" *Feminist Review* 5.

Fluegel, Jane, ed. 1984. *Michael Balcon: The Pursuit of British Cinema*. New York: Museum of Modern Art.

Gilman, Sander L. 1986. *Jewish Self-Hatred: Anti-Semitism and the Hidden Language of the Jews*. Baltimore: Johns Hopkins University Press.

Gollancz, Victor. 1942. *Let My People Go*. London: Gollancz.

Hanson, Clare. 2000. *Hysterical Fictions: The "woman's novel" in the Twentieth Century.* Harlow, UK: Macmillan.

Jordan, Heather Bryant. 1989. "The Territory of Elizabeth Bowen's Wartime Short Stories." *Library Chronicle of University of Texas at Austin* 48. 69–85.

Kardish, Lawrence. 1984. "Michael Balcon and the Idea of a National Cinema." In *Michael Balcon: The Pursuit of British Cinema.* Edited by Jane Fluegel. 43–73. New York: Museum of Modern Art.

Kenyon, Olga. 1988. *Women Novelists Today: A Survey of English Writing in the Seventies and Eighties.* Brighton, UK: Harvester.

Kiberd, Declan. 1995. *Inventing Ireland.* London: Cape.

Kureishi, Hanif. 1986. "Bradford." *Granta* 20 (Winter): 149–70.

Kushner, Tony. 1989. *The Persistence of Prejudice: Anti-Semitism in British Society During the Second World War.* Manchester, UK: Manchester University Press.

———. 1994. *The Holocaust and the Liberal Imagination: A Social and Cultural History.* Oxford: Blackwell.

Lassner, Phyllis. 1992. "A Cry for Life: Storm Jameson, Stevie Smith, and the Fate of Europe's Jews." In *Visions of War: World War II in Popular Literature and Culture.* Edited by M. P. Holsinger and M. A. Schofield, 181–90. Ohio: Popular Press.

———. 1996. "'The Milk of our Mothers' Kindness has Ceased to Flow': Virginia Woolf, Stevie Smith and the Representation of the Jew." In *Between "Race" and "Culture": Representations of "the Jew" in English and American Literature.* Edited by Bryan Cheyette, 129–209. Stanford, CA: Stanford University Press.

———. 1998. *British Women Writers of the Second World War: Battlegrounds of Their Own*, Basingstoke, UK: Macmillan.

Layton, Geoff. 1992. *Germany: The Third Reich, 1933–45.* London: Hodder and Stoughton.

Light, Alison. 1991. *Forever England: Femininity, Literature and Conservatism Between the Wars.* London: Routledge.

Miller, Betty. 1942. *Farewell Leicester Square.* London: Robert Hale.

———. 1945. *On the Side of the Angels.* London: R. Hale.

Miller, Jane. 1985. Introduction to *On the Side of the Angels*, by Betty Miller. London: Virago.

———. 2000. Introduction to *Farewell Leicester Square.* London: Persephone Books.

Neuberger, Julia. 1979. Introduction to *The Matriarch*, [*The Tents of Israel*, 1924] by G. B. Stern. London: Virago.

———. 1995. *On Being Jewish*, London: Heinemann.

———. 1995. "A True Survivor." In *Mothers by Daughters.* Edited by Joanna Goldsworthy, 149–158. London: Virago.

Radford, Jean. 1999. "Late Modernism and the Politics of History." In *Woman Writers of the 1930's: Gender, Politics and History.* Edited by Maroula Joannou, 33–45. Edinburgh: Edinburgh University Press.

Radner, Hilary. 1989. "Extra-curricular Activities: Women Writers and the Readerly Text." In *Women's Writing in Exile.* Edited by M. L. Broe and A. Ingram, 251–67. Chapel Hill: University of North Carolina Press.

———. 1995. "'Out of Category': The Middlebrow Novel." In *Shopping Around: Feminine Culture and the Pursuit of Pleasure*, 105–15. London: Routledge.

Rhys, Jean. 1966. *Wide Sargasso Sea*. London: Deutsch.

Smith, Stevie. 1981. "Beside the Seaside: A Holiday with Children." *Holidays and Happy Days*. Edited by Oswell Blakeston. 1949–London: Phoenix House; reprinted in *Me Again*, edited by Jack Barnera and William McBrien, 13–25. London: Virago.

Spalding, Frances. 1989. *Stevie Smith: A Biography*. New York: W. W. Norton.

Stern, G[ladys] B[ronwen]. 1924. *The Tents of Israel*. London: Chapman Hall.

Yuval-Davis, Nira. 1992. "Jewish Fundamentalism and Women's Empowerment." *Refusing Holy Orders: Women and Fundamentalism in Britain*. Edited by Gita Sahgal and Nira Yuval-Davis, 198–226. London: Virago.

Colonizing an Anti-Imperialist Text: Marguerite Yourcenar's Rendering of *The Waves* into French

GENEVIÈVE BRASSARD AND
MARIANNE GUÉNOT-HOVNANIAN

IS LITERARY TRANSLATION A FORM OF CULTURAL COLONIALISM? WHAT happens when a well-meaning but forceful entity appropriates original material for its own purposes, in the process transforming the source into a hybrid product, no longer pure yet somewhat reminiscent of its native origins? In actual colonization, the native country inevitably begins to look and sound like its conquering metropole, while retaining unassimilable elements. Similarly, when "annexing" or "conquering" a foreign text, the translator, especially one who writes novels herself, will to a greater or lesser extent alter the original to the point that it betrays the author's implicit intentions. Analyzing a translation foregrounds the translator's critical lenses, that is, her relationship to literature, language, and those internalized social rules that tell how much of the Other national culture and language can take in. We propose to examine the intersection of poetics and politics in two translations of Virginia Woolf's *The Waves* into French; the original text and its translations are particularly fruitful cases to uncover aesthetics and political slippages in the process of literary transmission. We argue that French translators Marguerite Yourcenar and Cecile Wajsbrot transform Woolf's novel to the extent that they diffuse and even erase its underlying critique of imperialism. Ironically, then, well-meaning linguistic "conquerors" literally impose a form of cultural domination on a text filled with subtle jabs at imperialism in all its ramifications.

While recent scholarship on the reception of Woolf abroad has looked closely at French translations of her major works, these critics attend more to matters of style than content.[1] It is worth noting that translation itself, let alone the rendering of a celebrated author's major novels into foreign languages, is a process fraught at best, and perilous at worst, as Yourcenar herself would admit if she were around today to read critical assessments of her work. As Pierre-Eric Villeneuve puts it, "Translation imposes its range of limitations, contradictions and often after publication of a text, it creates polemics" (2002, 24). In the case of Yourcenar's *Les vagues*, this polemic continues: Mary Ann Caws and Sarah Bird Wright lament the way Yourcenar "makes things unnecessary explicit" in a language "heavy [and] unsuited to Woolf's subtlety" (2000, 355–56). If, as Francoise Pellan suggests, "All translations are damaging, but they are nonetheless a necessary evil" (2002, 55), what rules govern its practices and what happens when transmission goes awry?

Translation theorist Jean-Louis Cordonnier argues that translating practices reveal the way a society understands its relationship to the Other. Looking at the history of translation, Cordonnier draws a link between poetics and the political history of western Europe, between the Conquest of the New World ("expulsion de l'Autre extérieur") and the Reconquest of Granada ("expulsion de l'autre intérieur") (1995). He pictures a tradition of translation as appropriation that answers the necessity of establishing a national culture through the expulsion of the Other. More recently, French linguist, translator, and poet Henri Meschonnic has designed a methodology useful to our purposes in this essay. He identifies four kinds of teratology in translation that are committed for the sake of preserving the so-called natural [fluency] of the target language. The first is suppressions and omissions: words or group of words are omitted, generally under the pretext of eliminating redundancy or nationalizing the syntax. The second consists of additions, most often because the translator feels the need to explain, to say more than the original. Third, Meschonnic brings attention to displacements of words or group of words committed to respecting the practices of the target language. Lastly comes what he identifies as nonconcordance or anticoncordance: A single unit of meaning is rendered by several or several by one.

The practice of translation bears on notions of alterity and identity, while its politics shows that conflicts between identity and alterity matter greatly to the linguistic and poetic act of translation. It is worth noting that Malherbe coined the term *belle infidèle* to describe translation at the height of French Absolutism. The codification of national languages required French, for instance, to be seen as superior and as so refined that it could not bear repetitions; this nationalistic imperative demanded proper reordering and sequencing of the discourse. For Cordonnier, those practices of *annexion* or *décentrement* in translation mirror our relation to the Other.[2]

These considerations of Otherness and national character, of *annexion* and *décentrement* in translation are particularly relevant for the study of *The Waves*'s translation into French. The French were the first to translate and publish Woolf's works, and Laura Marcus suggests, "Translations into French have been of particular interest not only because of these early beginnings, but because of the literary status of the translators, who included Charles Mauron and Marguerite Yourcenar" (2002, 330). Woolf's friend Roger Fry "spoke of 'the dangerous ease of French,' arguing that it could eclipse a person's original ideas because of the 'many attractive and ready-made moulds into which one's thoughts can flow" (Caws and Wright 2000, 351). Our work is grounded in recent critical analyses that foreground culture making, national character, and critique of empire in the text. Marguerite Yourcenar published the first translation of *The Waves* in 1937.[3] A second translation was published in 1993 by Cécile Wajsbrot, an accomplished novelist and translator.[4] Wajsbrot's first novel features a young journalist who sets out to write a book on madness that Woolf never wrote. It tells of the young writer's discovery of Woolf and her obsession with Woolf's sentences.[5]

As a rising young novelist whose family inheritance had run out, Yourcenar needed translation to make a living: "On the advice of the influential Edmond Jaloux, an early admirer of Woof's and Yourcenar's works, she accepted the translation of *The Waves*" (Jacobs 1988, 2). A conscientious translator and self-conscious admirer, Yourcenar was thrilled to spend two hours with Mme Woolf in Bloomsbury on February 22, 1937. She wished to know how Woolf wanted her novel to be translated. However, her idol viewed translation itself darkly, and dismissed Yourcenar's eager questions.[6] Woolf expressed skepticism about translation and any actual access to foreign literature. In "The Russian Point of View," she wonders how we are to judge a literature we read in translation, without having "even *heard* the language *spoken* by natives." Readers of translations may share Woolf's annoyance at having to judge a "whole literature stripped of its style. When you have changed every word in a sentence from Russian to English, have thereby altered the sense a little, the *sound*, *weight*, and *accents of the words in relation to each other completely*, nothing remains except a crude version of the sense" (Woolf 1984, 174). Woolf's words recall Meschonnic's insistence on rhythm, and his defiance of semiotic approaches to translation. Woolf's annoyance with the French translator's visit most likely came from Yourcenar's questions, which bore on interpretation and meaning rather than poetics: "What does 'See, here he comes' mean?" Woolf may not have wanted to know which of her "clothes" were to be "stripped" by this Melle Youniac . . . as she tried to recall Yourcenar's name after her visit. Woolf describes translation as an "earthquake," a "terrible catastrophe," a "mutilation." Who would care to meet someone about to inflict such a treatment on her play-poem? (Woolf 1980, *Diary* 5:61, n. 18).

Inevitably, comparisons between Yourcenar's work and Wasjbrot's have been detrimental to the former; to be fair, Wajsbrot's task has benefited from greater biographical knowledge of Woolf, the development of feminist studies, and even postcolonial theory as a useful lens to read *The Waves* and other novels. Wajsbrot's work also benefits from positioning itself as a critical response to Yourcenar's text. Wajsbrot writes in her preface to *Les vagues*, "la conception de la traduction a évolué, aujourd'hui, par exemple, personne ne songerait à convertir les livres sterling d'un texte anglais en francs français" (1993, 29).[7] She adds that identified quotations will be respected and not replaced under the pretext that those works may not be known to the French reader. She does not go on to explain how her own treatment of quotations inscribes itself in the system of the translated text;[8] however, Wajsbrot's familiarity with Woolf scholarship as well as changes in translating practices since Yourcenar's time inflect her text with a greater awareness of the Other.

Our purpose here is not to denounce either Yourcenar's or Wajsbrot's work, but rather to explore the inner workings of translation, with two versions of *The Waves* as examples. Using Meschonnic's methodology, we focus on Yourcenar's extreme semiotism, which opens the way for the creation of a *belle infidèle*. It is worth noting that Yourcenar's language in *Les vagues* is often more elevated than in her own works. Caws and Bird Wright note how her version "gives a classisizing view" of Woolf's novel, and they deplore Yourcenar's heavy-handedness: "Yourcenar's surprisingly literal rendering veers toward the novelistic and the narrative as opposed to the poetic and deliberately 'subjectless' and rhythmical text that Woolf wanted for her poem-novel. Yourcenar's language is heavy, unsuited to Woolf's subtlety. She delights in the pointing word and the situating adverb, elements that can impede the lyric flow" (2000, 355). Yourcenar's reimposition of narrative order and re-inscription of the text into the visual can also be seen as *annexion* and *décentrement* of the original, *le corps sain.*

Wajsbrot rightly suggests that Yourcenar's translation is Yourcenar's text rather than Woolf's. Yet she fails to show how Yourcenar's translation appears to be an exercise in contrapuntal *dissonance*, as suggested by Beatriz Vegh (1997). Drawing from Yourcenar's reference to Bach's *The Art of the Fugue*, Vegh sees the compositional form of the fugue as an embodiment of Yourcenar's translating processes in *Les vagues*. Yourcenar, while respecting the narrative elements set out in the original, inscribes onto it a counterdiscourse: the "lisible" (readerly) text becomes "scriptible" (writerly). Yourcenar's pace follows Bach, whereas Woolf, when struggling with the form of *The Waves*, listened to Beethoven's late quartets and sonatas. Yourcenar's reference to *The Art of the Fugue*, Bach's major work of codification, may indicate that although she is sensitive to Woolf's play on music, she anchors herself onto something more structured than Beethoven's late works. A fugue obeys fixed compositional rules quite remote from the formal innovation that characterizes Beethoven's quartets. On December 22, 1930, Woolf records in her diary that she was listening to Beethoven's quartets when "it occurred to [her] . . . that [she] would merge all the interjected passages in Bernard's final speech," (1980, *Diary* 3:339).

Translators, Yourcenar in this case, may be tempted to give precedence to the habits and manners of the target language, and their renderings become a practice of *annexion*. Those practices of additions, omissions, and nonconcordance, when at work in a translation, will inevitably owe a great part to the passive ideology of the translator and produce a cultural translation oblivious of itself. Instead of holding closely onto the signifier and the system of the text as she has identified it, the translator renders a "probable and plausible" core of "reality," losing sight of the processes of *signifiance*. So could Yourcenar's semiotic approach be summarily described. In Yourcenar's *Les vagues,* French sounds beautifully classical; the diction is well paced. Yourcenar does not question order, rather she finds comfort in it. It is not *The Waves* as many of us read it now, rather an astonishing counterpoint to it.

Reacting to Yourcenar's *re*construction, Wajsbrot stays much closer to the original, and this often works quite beautifully. Her translation improves Yourcenar's and is much more accurate in terms of references and syntax. Wajsbrot's translation was very well received and praised notably by Mona Ozouf in *Le Nouvel Observateur* February 25, 1993. Yet, in a polemical notice published in *Le Monde* on April 23, 1993, Viviane Forrester, novelist and author of the preface to the translation into French of *Moments of Being*, condemns Wajsbrot's prose as *dialecte*, *charabia*, *galimatias*. Although Forrester denounces a *manque de rigueur* and *volonté de séduire* in Marguerite Yourcenar's prose, she calls against Wajsbrot's suppression of repetitions. One could argue that Wajsbrot translates against

Yourcenar and accentuates traits Yourcenar's text obscures or elides. She also reacts against Yourcenar's tendency to impose order and erase abstraction by *re*constructing a visual world. Wajsbrot demonstrates in her introduction how Yourcenar privileges her own vision of the order of things. Yet one could also see a link between the technique of juxtaposition Wajsbrot uses in *Les vagues* and the syntax of *Atlantique*, her second novel, also published in 1993. One can hear Wajsbrot's own voice in her translation—but how could it be otherwise?[9]

Because of the novel's phonic play on language, the process of translating *The Waves* blurs the line between translating poetry and prose; it is therefore imperative that the translator listen to the text and grapple with its shape and form. In her introduction, Wajsbrot grounds her reading of *The Waves* in Woolf's reflections on the novel in, for example, "Women and Fiction," as well as in Woolf's biography. She indicates the poetical references and provides helpful notes at the end of the text, but regrettably leaves out examples of her approach to close reading. Through references to Woolf's essays and diaries, Wajsbrot explains how Woolf reacted to the Victorian novel, yet she does not show how the text exemplifies such reaction nor does she explain how to render it in translation. Preparing a third translation into French, Michel Cusin writes that when translating *The Waves*, "one should give priority to translating the signifier, and yet not lose signification." He identifies as a "crucial obstacle . . . the near impossibility to sustain leitmotifs throughout the novel," which "both Yourcenar and Wajsbrot ignore" (1999, 4).

In 1984, French critic Jany Berretti provided a remarkable study of Yourcenar's rendering of the play of repetitions in the interludes, revealing that although Yourcenar is aware of lexical repetitions, she fails to see how Woolf's technique destabilizes the apparent harmony of the text. The play of repetitions and the phonic play of language in the interludes create a musical effect in which language closes in on itself, introducing a rupture in the function of language as communication. Yourcenar, in turn, gives a rhetorical response to the text. She imposes her own vision of the world on *The Waves*, mainly through syntax (nonconcordances, additions, and omissions), thus reversing its politics. In other words, Yourcenar's lexicon participates in the logic of imperialism. Her explanatory additions to the original not only bring back the "order of things"; they erase abstraction and re-inscribe visually what was aural in the original.

Moreover, at the syntax and meter levels, the sequencing of Yourcenar's sentences reintroduces linearity. As Beatriz Vegh suggests, Yourcenar's processes explain what Woolf's omit and impose a certain course to the reading: one thing leads logically to another, as we can see from the following example taken from the first interlude:

> Gradually the fibres of the burning bonfire were fused into one haze, one incandescence which lifted the weight of the woollen grey sky. . . . [A]ll around it the sea blazed gold. (*The Waves*, 1978, 7–8)
>
> [Peu à peu les fibres se fondirent en une seule masse incandescente; la lourde couverture grise du ciel se souleva, se transmua. . . . Et la mer tout autour ne fut plus qu'une seule coulée d'or. (MY 1982, 17–18)]
>
> [Peu à peu les fibres du feu se fondirent en une brume, incandescence qui souleva le poids de la laine grise, transformant le ciel. . . . Tout autour la mer s'embrasait d'or. (CW 1993, 35–36)]

Here Yourcenar omits "haze," which, juxtaposed to "incandescence," had an oxymoronic effect. Instead of "haze," she brings in "masse." The "burning bonfire" is also dealt away with and, in the second part of the sentence, she changes the subject, that is, the operating agent. Although Wajsbrot is much more accurate, both translators add a verb recording the occurrence of the transformation, which in the French text becomes *told* as much as it is *shown* by the text processes. Yourcenar uses "transmuer," a verb recalling alchemy, by which she also introduces her ending on "coulee d'or," being precisely what alchemy is about. Yourcenar doubly re-inscribes the text into a plausible and linear reality, while Woolf forcefully resisted such narrative order visual re-inscription: one could argue that her politics found expression in this resistance.

Wajsbrot rightly points out that in this "text by" Yourcenar, the latter feels the necessity of personifying what Bernard, after the death of Percival, simply addresses as "what is abstract," and which becomes "L'Etre invisible," with a capital E, in *Les Vagues* (MY 1982, 152; *The Waves*, 1978, 154).[10] Wajsbrot shows how Yourcenar's meter imposes her vision of the world and how she works against the polyphony that characterizes the modern novel. For instance, in *Le denier du rêve* Yourcenar still resorts to free indirect discourse to supplement her characters' narrative commentary. Yourcenarian discourse articulates itself as a correction of surrounding discourses. In Yourcenar's novels, only Hadrian has a voice, yet it is the voice of authority and the voice of Yourcenar. Dissenting voices are silenced or dismissed by correction.[11]

Wajsbrot, respectful of a tradition that tends to erase the translator as producer of discourse, explains the purpose of a new translation in a self-effacing voice:

> L'objet d'une nouvelle traduction, c'est tenter de restituer le rythme . . . de redonner à chaque voix son écho intérieur et sa solitude . . . de rester dans les limites du possible, au plus près d'un texte dont la question centrale est celles des limites (le dedans et le dehors de l'être, l'un et l'autre, le moi et le monde), y compris celles de l'écriture. (CW 1993, 32)
>
> [The purpose of a new translation is to attempt to restore the rhythm . . . give back to each voice its interior echo, its solitude . . . to stay within the limits of the possible, as close as possible to a text, of which the central question is the one of limits (the inside and the outside of being, one and the other, the self and the world), including the limits of writing.]

According to a poetics of translation, such a paragraph could be the opening of an introduction explaining the translator's project as a critical act. It should situate the text in its context, but also identify its processes of *signifiance* by providing examples of close reading. Wajsbrot explains that she will attempt to correct a translation that betrays her own reading of the original. Yet she does not take into consideration her own reading perspective and gives no examples of poetic choices she has made.

Both translators are oblivious to the sustained interweaving of politics with poetics in *The Waves* and miss the critique of empire, patriarchy, and male bonding frequently highlighted by recent scholarship.[12] Whether one completely accepts "Woolf's irony about an author figure like herself in the portrait of Bernard" (Jane Marcus 1992, 1380), or whether one has reservations about the transparency of Woolf's critique of the ideology of white British imperialism (McGee 1992, 3), Woolf's relationship to *Britannia* needs to be taken into consideration here. Both translators also fail to make sense of the silence, absence, and death of Percival, the Saxon hero, who grounds the Eurocentric subject and yet figures as a void at the center of the text. As Laura Doyle has shown, "Percival serves as organizing principle for the English community figured in the three male and three female" personae of the "play-poem" (1996, 338). Doyle suggests that "as woman writer, Woolf lets us know she speaks a double voice, at once inside and outside the circle of an imperialist sublimity" (344). The positioning of Percival brings to mind Kristeva's argument in *Revolution in Poetic Language*: the bourgeois republic is a society with no hero in which power, both called for and rejected, has become the problem around which everything revolves and is measured against.[13]

Yourcenar sees *The Waves* as "a meditation on life" that reads as an "essay on human isolation." Talking about composition, she refers to "l'Art de la Fugue," in which "*les pensées*" (thoughts) of childhood, and "*réflex-*

ions" of youth give way to long soliloquies about experience, solitude, and mature age. She sees Woolf's work as opposed to Proust's and defines *The Waves* as a "biographie de l'Etre." Woolf's references to Proust in her diary would rather indicate that she felt a kinship with him in their shared attempt in modern fiction to work against egotism and grapple with the plurality of the self: "The six characters were supposed to be one . . . I come to feel more and more how difficult it is to collect oneself into one Virginia" (Lee 1997, 612). In 1925, while she is "embedded in" Proust, she sees how he will "both influence me and make me out of temper with every sentence of my own" (Woolf 1980, *Diary* 3: 7).

The mere fact that Yourcenar sees the soliloquies as "thoughts" or worse, "reflections," hints at the coherence she will impose on the text. For instance, when Bernard, recalling school years in his final summary, says "we are not always aware by any means; we breathe, eat, sleep automatically," Yourcenar translates "nous ne faisons pas que penser; nous respirons, nous mangeons, nous dormons avec l'exactitude d'une machine" (*The Waves*, 1978, 246; MY 1982, 239). Here Yourcenar omits both "always" and "by any means." Between "penser" (to think) and "être conscient" (to be aware of), one may see the distance that separates those two minds. "Penser" brings in Déscartes, sitting by his fire, and beginning his *Méditations*. "Penser" brings back order, organized thoughts. Here Wajsbrot writes "la conscience n'existe pas toujours; nous respirons, mangeons, dormons machinalement" (CW 1993, 2). Wajsbrot is more abstract than Woolf was. Yet she also changes the subject, thus the statement seems less about the speaker. It is no longer a discovery about oneself but a piece of knowledge that is put forward. Such a shift changes the reading perspective and the reader is not invited to the same level of participation with the text.

Yourcenar does not seem concerned with revealing, as Woolf claims in "Modern Fiction," "the flickerings of that innermost flame which flashes its messages through the brain," but rather with presenting the "thoughts" of a mind disciplined by Cartesian logic and coherent/normative language. She is far from ready to disregard "probability" or "coherence" in order to record "the atoms as they fall upon the mind in the order in which they fall" (1984, 155). Yourcenar presents herself as a full subject of discourse in her introduction and gives her reading grid. Reading Yourcenar's *Les vagues* informs us less about Woolf's poetic incarnation of "atoms" than it does about Yourcenar's vision and processes of creation.

Most crucially for our purpose here, Yourcenar's text displaces and even suppresses Woolf's critique of imperial dominance. For instance,

Yourcenar refuses to let the sun sink on the Empire. This can be seen in the penultimate paragraph of the text when, just before seeing death approaching, Bernard says: "The canopy of civilisation is burnt out" (*The Waves*, 1978, 296). Yourcenar returns safely to the vision of a city at night: "les lumières chatoyantes de la grande ville n'éclairent plus le firmament" (MY 1982, 285). Wajsbrot proposes here "le dais de la civilisation a été consumé," which is much closer to the original. Paying absolutely no attention to the signifier, Yourcenar invents a text that fits the immediate narrative context, and disregards the indeterminacy of the original without endangering her own sense of narrative order. The preceding sentence shows Bernard seeing before him "the usual street," therefore in the city, and the next begins with "the sky is dark." Thus, Yourcenar pictures things for herself, and *re*constructs a text. She cannot picture the abstract "canopy of civilization," so she tries her mind at it. Civilization must mean city—so says the mid-1930s ethnocentric discourse. So there she has it : "les lumières chatoyantes de la grande ville n'éclairent plus le firmament." It is not what Woolf wrote, yet it is true to the immediate narrative element, thus producing a *belle infidèle*.

Not only does Yourcenar elide Woolf's critique of imperialism, she goes so far as "colonizing" the original text with her problematic diction. Three lines above the final "O Death," Yourcenar sees Percival galloping "aux Indes" (although she uses the singular in most of the text). In French, using India in the plural form (aux Indes) refers strictly to colonial India. When, early in his summary, Bernard recalls how Percival would have "done justice" to the "people dying of famine" and the "many obscure Indians" bubbling up the tube, Yourcenar translates "Indians" as "Hindus." She thus assimilates religion and nationality (*The Waves*, 1978, 243; MY 1982, 237): besides ignoring the reality of India, by using "Hindus" for "Indians" Yourcenar *orientalizes* the text. Furthermore, when Bernard retells the death of Percival in India a little later, the exoticized Other is also eroticized. Yourcenar adds that the "men in loin-cloths" are otherwise "naked/nus." Yourcenar leaves out the metaphor and speaks of "turbaned waves" instead of "turbaned warriors": she holds captive the imagination of the reader who is no longer free to envision "turbaned warriors" endangering "the white sheep." Wajsbrot accurately translates "des hommes en pagne," without adding that they are naked or that the "pagne" is "worn around their loins" (CW 224; MY 256). In the fifth interlude, the one introducing the episode about the death of Percival in India, the "southern village" and "southern hills" become the "villages d'Orient" and "collines d'Orient" in Yourcenar's Orientalist translation.

Yourcenar extends this "Othering" of Woolf's text when she obscures Woolf's indictment of empire's patriarchal underpinning. When in Bernard's summary and just after he understands being "the inheritor," "the continuer," "the person miraculously appointed to carry on," and the question "what is to be done about India, Ireland, or Morocco" is asked, Yourcenar elides the fact that it is "the old gentlemen standing decorated under chandeliers" who answer the question (*The Waves*, 1978, 255; MY 1982, 247). She misses Woolf's attack on such a society of "decorated old men" sitting in English clubs, oblivious to the forces that "roar" outside. She does not see how the syntax implies a critique of male bonding and its effects on government. Thus, in Yourcenar's text, Bernard is "remarkably" supplied with information instead of "surprisingly." Wajsbrot also misses the weight on "what is to be done" and translates "Que faut-il faire" instead of "Que faire," which has a broader meaning, and was also the title of Lenin's work in French translation (CW 1993, 150). In the following paragraph, when Bernard feels that "this extreme precision, this military and orderly progress" is a mistake, a convenience, a lie, Yourcenar adds that it is "a convention that seems useful." One may be tempted to ask: to whom is the convention useful and what purpose does it serve?

In "The Politics of Modernist Form," Patrick McGee shows how Woolf's style challenges the "view that reality can be captured or adequately mapped by a traditional narrative which privileges coherence and continuity between the representation and the represented" (1992, 640). Yourcenar, in her translation, applies herself to reestablishing coherence. Short, abstract sentences become well-sequenced French ones, following classical diction. For instance, when confronted with a sentence like "Faces loom," Yourcenar uses well-structured language and renders a poetic image instead of the abstract proposition of the original: "le *mirage* des figures *humaines* s'élèvent *à l'horizon*" (*The Waves*, 1978, 240; MY 1982, 234; emphasis added). This fourteen-syllable sentence is closer to classical French diction than to Woolf's rhapsodies. We now know that the faces are *human*, that it is a *mirage*, and that they loom on the *horizon*. Yourcenar makes us see what Woolf makes us hear, she narrates rather than attempting to record the atoms as they fall upon the mind.

Yourcenar's choice cannot be explained by some constraints of French since Cécile Wajsbrot manages to say, accurately at all levels, whether syntactic, semiotic, or poetic: "Des visages surgissent" (CW 1993, 206). This is a good example of the differences between these two approaches to translation. Wajsbrot stays as close to the text as she can. Sometimes it works beautifully, as it does here, but in some instances she stretches the language beyond its possibilities. According to Michel Cusin, "in reaction to Yourcenar's expanding tactic, [Wajsbrot] deliberately accentuates Woolf's thrifty use of English, thus constraining French syntax beyond the range of its flexibility." He adds that Wajsbrot's translation "though much improved" is "still unsatisfactory because it suppresses repetitions which are part and parcel of Woolf's poetic prose" (Cusin 1999, 3).

Another example of Yourcenar's tendency to re-create a visual world can be found at the beginning of the fourth episode (the dinner in honor of Percival's departure for India). Woolf begins with: "How fair, how strange, said Bernard, glittering, many-pointed and many-domed, London lies before me . . ." (1978, 111). Yourcenar introduces first "Londres," thus erasing any possible doubt as to what is described here; the magic does not appear before the reader is well grounded. She then adds, "Londres aux mille tours, aux mille dômes *sommeille* devant moi" (MY 1982, 144; emphasis added). She must have felt it was reassuring to say that the city was sleeping, since Bernard rides the early morning train. Wajsbrot is again thriftier than Woolf here, and omits the repetition of "many," which Yourcenar had tried to keep with "mille."

Whenever she feels the narrative context receding, Yourcenar brings it back. For example, further down "we draw a curtain as we pass" becomes "nous tirons le rideau de la portière." By simply adding *portière* (the door of a car or a railway carriage), Yourcenar reminds her reader that Bernard is in a train, watching outside, and that it's early morning—time to draw curtains. She erases the indeterminacy of the original. The "portière" added by Yourcenar does modify the text and closes the range of possibilities. She authoritatively situates the action in the train. Again Wajsbrot stays closer to the original and writes "nous tirons le rideau au passage." When looking for a second breath, early in his final summary and after the memory of Percival as imperial hero overtakes him, Bernard asks his listener to "let me dip again and bring up in my spoon another of these minute objects . . . characters of our friends" (1978, 243). Yourcenar almost surreptitiously adds "a potage" into which Bernard dips his spoon. So we are back in context, sitting at a table, having dinner, talking to someone, and at least Bernard is dipping his spoon into something. Here, by adding *potage*, Yourcenar anchors the reader into the immediate narrative context, while Wajsbrot takes the reader away from it. She transforms the spoon into an "apostate," a term she will use again later, thus establishing a leitmotif. The *apostate*/shrimp net belongs to the register of childhood and sea. Wajsbrot re-inscribes the sentence in the larger context of the fin passing in the waste of waters, a recurring image in the novel.

At the beginning of his final summary, when Bernard explains that he is tired of phrases and "long[s] for some little language such as lovers use," Yourcenar calls such a language "naïf" instead of "little," and "broken words" become "des mots sans suite" (*The Wave*, 1978, 238; MY 1982, 233). She reintroduces here the notion of continuity, or *suite* between words, thus implying that the words themselves become broken, when the chain of language as communication is broken. For instance, when Bernard, about to explain how he felt before Susan's tears, recalls the time when he "first became aware of those enemies . . . who are always there" and understands that "to let oneself be carried on passively is unthinkable" 'That's your course, world,' one says, 'mine is this,'" one may see how Yourcenar gives away her own mental processes. Thus, "unthinkable" becomes "contraire à la nature même de notre pensée," and the "course" of the wold becomes a "law," a more normative term (MY 1982, 234). Here again, Yourcenar favors traditional narration over a language freed from its shackles.

Moreover, when Bernard recognizes that the mind, even in the midst of anguish, goes on registering "myriad of impressions," and says "that little piece of dramatisation shows how incompletely we are merged in our own experience," Yourcenar is unable to mock her own powers of dramatization, or to accept a mind's loss of control. Thus, she writes "ce coin pittoresque prouve qu'une part de notre âme échappe à nos émotions." Her proposition reverses the original: "dramatisation" becomes a "picturesque corner," belonging to the visual, to description. She introduces "âme," which belongs to Christian vocabulary and "émotions" instead of experience. The *décentrement* at work here is quite impressive. This "little piece of dramatisation" brings Bernard to recognize the presence in himself of some "observant fellow" who "directed [him] . . . to that which is symbolic, and thus perhaps permanent," which he challenges right away. Yourcenar safely evacuates the abstract notion of the symbolic, which becomes "symboles," something more tangible. Furthermore "the chaos of life" becomes "un monde surpeuplé et chaotique (The Waves, 1978, 249; MY 242)."

Yourcenar's resistance to questioning traditional narration is further shown as we move toward the moment when Bernard will give up narrative language and call for silence. Yourcenar cannot say "but there are no stories," which becomes "si toutes les histoires sont fausses [if all stories are false]." Refusing also to recognize that "life is not susceptible perhaps to the treatment we give it when we try to tell it," she proposes "paint" instead of "tell," which confirms her constant re-inscription of the text into the visual, and allows her to continue dealing with linear narration and making stories (*The Waves,* 1978, 267; MY 1982, 259).

Yourcenar seems quite comfortable with the "man's sentence" and with the narrative "shape that has been made by men out of their own needs for their own uses" of which Woolf complains in *A Room of One's Own* (1957, 76–77). She does not understand Woolf's work on the sentence and its sequencing, and thus she erases Woolf's refusal of plot and narrativity by operating lexical displacements, by avoiding any "unsafe, unstable" indeterminacy, and by privileging narrative structure over verbal texture at the sentence level. Yourcenar produces a text that keeps the narrative elements of the original but transforms its *signifiance,* or meaning. She elides Woolf's search for what is untouched in the fragments of phrases.

As Wajsbrot notes, Yourcenar needs "phrases [to be] laid like Roman roads across the tumult of our lives, since they compel us to walk in step like civilized people with the slow and measured tread of policemen" (VW 1978, 259; CW 1993, 221). Instead of letting the disorder of life enter the text, she finds comfort in that kind of semantic order. Those two translations show that when the translator remains unaware of her reading and translating processes, her politics will potentially inform and even transform the translated text. Forgetting she is reading a "modern novel," Yourcenar uses *The Waves* as a point of departure to write a story of her own; as such she practices what Meschonnic qualifies as "annexion." More crucially, by annexing a novel "so rich in its dialogue with the Greeks" through her "classical" rendering (Villeneuve 2002, 35), Yourcenar obscures the political preoccupations of Woolf as public intellectual present throughout the text. Yourcenar not only annexes Woolf's novel, as thirties dictators were soon to annex conquered territories, she inflicts upon Woolf's work the same pernicious process Woolf herself deplores in *The Waves* and other texts from that decade: ideological coercion through linguistic, social, and cultural means.

Notes

1. See Laura Marcus, Françoise Pellan, Carole Rodier, and Pierre-Eric Villeneuve, among others, in Mary Ann Caws and Nicola Lockhurst, eds. (2002), *The Reception of Virginia Woolf's Reception in Europe.*

2. According to Henri Meschonnic, "Le décentrement est un rapport textuel entre deux texts dans deux langues-cultures jusque dans la structure linguistique de la langue . . . L'annexion est un effacement de ce rapport, l'illusion du naturel" (1973, 380).

3. Marguerite Yourcenar, *Les vagues*, (1982). All subsequent references to Yourcenar's translation will be cited as MY in the text. In the 1920s, Yourcenar had already published several poems, two novels, various essays, and three tales. A first version of some pages of Yourcenar's translation appeared in *Revue Hebdomadaire* (August 8, 1936): 133–53.

4. Cécile Wajsbrot, *Les vagues (1993)*. All subsequent references to Wajsbrot's translation will be cited as CW in the text.

5. A third translation, by Michel Cusin, is also in the works. Cusin argues that "novelist translators" are a drawback, rather than an advantage, especially when translating a novel as "poetic" as Woolf's *The Waves*: "it is genuine bilingualism, i.e. two maternal languages, which is here a prerequisite" (Cusin 1999, 4).

6. As Françoise Pellan tells the story, Yourcenar "was to be disappointed, since after a few brief, non-committal replies, Virginia Woolf quickly turned the conversation to the current political situation in Europe . . . since she was working on *Three Guineas* at the time, and nervously awaiting the publication of *The Years*, she would have been particularly reluctant to cast her mind back to such a different type of book as *The Waves*" (Pellan 2002, 54).

7. "The notion of translation has changed; today, for example, no one would think of converting the sterlings in an English text into French francs." Wajsbrot, Introduction to *Les vagues* (1993).

8. Wajsbrot identifies quotations in notes and uses their translations into French as "authorized versions."

9. Cusin similarly criticizes Wajsbrot's version (as well as Yourcenar's): "Her translation, though much improved, is still unsatisfactory because it suppresses repetitions which are part and parcel of Woolf's poetic prose and because Wajsbrot's French sounds stilted whereas Woolf's English sounds naturally fluent" (1999, 3). Such pronouncements set up very high expectations for Cusin's own version, still forthcoming at press time.

10. Wajsbrot's translation reads as follows: "M'addressant à l'abstraction sans regard, là haut, qui me fait face au bout de l'avenue" (1993, 143).

11. In many interviews, Yourcenar also corrected what she believed was her readers' misreading of her work. She would say, "My culture is built on a foundation of religion, something of which my readers are completely unaware—they don't see it" (1984). For a study of Yourcenar's dismissive discourse, see Brian Gill, "Technique de l'argumentation" (1997).

12. See especially Kathy Phillips, *Virginia Woolf against Empire* (1994), 153–83.

13. Julia Kristeva 1974, 480: in *La révolution du langage poétique*: "Dans une république bourgeoise, le pouvoir se donne comme nécessaire, mais pluralisable, défaillant et éphémère, ce qui veut dire qu'il est devenu un problème, voire même le problème majeur; tout tourne autour de lui, s'y mesure, le convoque et le rejette."

Works Cited

Berretti, Jany. 1984. "Lectures et traductions de Virginia Woolf: Les interludes de son roman *The Waves*." *Lectures et systèmes de lecture*. Edited by Jean Bessière, 91–102. Paris: Presses Universitaires de France.

Caws, Mary Ann, and Nicola Lockhurst, eds. 2002. *The Reception of Virginia Woolf in Europe*. London: Continuum.

Caws, Mary Ann, and Sarah Bird Wright. 2000. *Bloomsbury in France: Art and Friends*. Oxford: Oxford University Press.

Cordonnier, Jean Louis. 1995. *Traduction et culture*. Paris: Hatier, Didier.

Cusin, Michel. 1999. "On Translating *The Waves* into French." *Virginia Woolf Miscellany* (Fall): 3–4.

Doyle, Laura. 1996. "Sublime Barbarians in the Narrative of Empire; or Longinus at Sea in *The Waves*." *Modern Fiction Studies* 42.2: 323–347.

Gill, Brian. 1997. "Technique de l'argumentation: La topique de Marguerite Yourcenar." *Lectures transversales de Marguerite Yourcenar*, 17–26. Tours, France: Société Internationale d'Etudes Yourcenariennes.

Jacobs, Peter. 1988. "Mlle Youniac (?) et Mme Woolf, or the French Translator's Visit." *Virginia Woolf Miscellany* 31 (Fall): 2.

Kristeva, Julia. 1974. *La révolution du langage poétique*. Paris: Le Seuil, Tel quel. Translated by Margaret Walker as *Revolution in Poetic Language*, New York: Columbia University Press, 1984).

Lee, Hermione. 1997. *Virginia Woolf*. New York: Alfred Knopf.

Marcus, Jane. 1992. "Britannia Rules *The Waves*." In *Decolonizing Tradition*. Edited by Karen Lawrence 136–162.Chicago: University of Illinois Press.

Marcus, Laura. 2002. "The European Dimensions of the Hogarth Press." In Caws and Lockhurst, 328–356.

McGee, Patrick. 1992. "The Politics of Modernist Form." *Modern Fiction Studies* 38.3 (Fall): 631–650.

Meschonnic, Henri. 1973. *Pour la poétique II: Epistémologie de l'écriture, Poétique de la traduction*. Paris: Gallimard.

Pellan, Françoise. 2002. "Translating Virginia Woolf into French." In Caws and Lockhurst, 55–59.

Phillips, Kathy. 1994. *Virginia Woolf against Empire*. Knoxville: University of Tennessee Press.

Rodier, Carole. 2002. "The French Reception of Woolf: An *Etat Présent* of *Etudes Woolfiennes*." In Caws and Lockhurst, 39–53.

Vegh, Beatriz. 1997. "The Waves/Les vagues: Traduction, écriture, contrepoint." *Lectures transversales de Marguerite Yourcenar*, 67–74. Tours, France: Société Internationale d'Études Yourcenariennes.

Villeneuve, Pierre-Eric. 2002. "Virginia Woolf among Writers and Critics: The French Intellectual Scene." In Caws and Lockhurst, 19–38.

Wajsbrot, Cécile. 1993. *Les vagues*. Paris: Calman Levy.

Woolf, Virginia. 1957. *A Room of One's Own*. 1929. New York: Harcourt.

———. 1978. *The Waves*. 1931. New York: Harcourt Brace Jovanovich.

———. 1980, 1984. *The Diary of Virginia Woolf*, vols. 3 and 5. edited by Anne Oliver Bell. London: Hogarth Press.

———. 1984. "Modern Fiction." *The Common Reader*, 150–158. 1925. New York: Harcourt Brace Jovanovich, Harvest edition.

———. 1984. "The Russian Point of View." *The Common Reader,* 173–82. 1925. New York: Harcourt Brace Jovanovich.

Yourcenar, Marguerite. 1982. *Les vagues*. 1937. Paris, France: Stock. Le Livre de poche Biblio.

———. 1984. *With Open Eyes: Conversations with Mathieu Galey*. Trans. Arthur Goldhammer. Boston: Beacon Press.

Nancy Cunard's *Black Man and White Ladyship* as Surrealist Tract

TORY YOUNG

NANCY CUNARD (1896–1965) WAS A POET, A PUBLISHER, AN EDITOR, A translator, a journalist and an activist. She was born in rural England to Sir Bache Cunard, English heir to the shipping line, and Lady Maud, American hostess and patron of the arts. When Maud left her husband for the conductor Sir Thomas Beecham in 1911, she changed her name to Emerald and took her daughter to London with her. Cunard's teenage years were spent in the company of renowned artists, writers, and musicians. But although this metropolitan upbringing introduced her to the buzz of the literary salon, when she began to write, her most powerful verse was a rejection of the values of her mother's society. The concluding plea of "Prayer" in *Outlaws* (1921), her first volume of poetry, may be read as her creed: "Make me symbolic'ly iconoclast, / The ideal Antichrist, the Paradox" (8–9). When contemporaries dismissed her poetry, she responded in "Answer to a Reproof" with the assertion that they had failed to recognize its radical political purpose.

Cunard moved to France in the 1920s where she continued to inhabit fashionable and artistic circles. She established her own press, *The Hours Press*, publishing work by Samuel Beckett, Ezra Pound, and Laura Riding, amongst others. She had a turbulent relationship with the Surrealist writer Louis Aragon and through the Surrealists became interested in issues of race, ethnography, and empire. These interests were to take a personal dimension when in 1928 she began a relationship with Henry Crowder, an African-American pianist; the racism she experienced as a result sparked her lifelong commitment to racial equality. But as with her verse, Cunard's politics were not always taken seriously and her commitment was—and continues to be—doubted. Although she and Crowder devoted three years to the collection of material for *Negro*, the massive anthology of black culture that she published in 1934, her interest in African and African-American art and society has been dismissed as an example of her negrophilia—a purely sexual interest in black men. Petrine Archer-Straw's *Negrophilia* is a striking example of this. Similarly, the polemical tract that Cunard wrote in 1931, the subject of this essay, *Black Man and White Ladyship*, which boldly denounced her mother's racism alongside slavery and imperial oppression, has been disregarded as impassioned and unscholarly, a petulant outburst at her mother. Cunard's political activism has been derided because of her name, her gender, her wealth, her upbringing, her race, and her sexuality.

But recently scholars have followed the lead of Jane Marcus in questioning this account of Nancy Cunard; they have investigated the reasons for the damning focus upon the woman and have begun to reignite an interest in her words. Maureen Moynagh has edited and republished her essays on race and empire (including *Black Man and White Ladyship*); Lawrence Rainey includes her verse and essays in his anthology of Modernism; and John Lucas has edited and republished her poems.[1] As Harlem *flâneur* and publisher in Paris, Cunard is beginning to be recognized as a key figure in the transatlantic circulation of ideas, and recent work by British critics has called for a renewed focus on Cunard's significance in Britain. Mary Joannou has chronicled her work with black communities in Liverpool and London and her specific contribution to the archive of black British history; Lola Young and Sheila Gopaulen have argued that attention to *Negro* has led to the neglect of such British campaigns for racial equality.[2] It is true that *Negro* has dominated serious discussion of Cunard's work; where she is known by academics it is generally for this tome. Furthermore, the anthology is often perceived as being a discrete component of her life, unrelated to the rest of her political activism. Her affiliation with the International Brigades during Spain's Civil War, subsequent poetry, and prolific political journalism tend to be compartmentalized, although in fact her concern for racial equality united many aspects of her work and life.

I suggest that there are two significant reasons for this reading of Cunard's output. The implication of Anne Chisholm's biography (for a long time the main source of information on Cunard), which represents Cunard's life in chapters, is that *Negro* was compiled because of her affair with Henry Crowder and that her interest in race ended when the relationship did. Secondly, much of the research, until recently, into Cunard's political and race campaigns has been undertaken by U.S. scholars who have focused on *Negro* for its obvious American import. British scholars have tended to write about her poetry, particularly of the 1920s. Whilst her archives, stored in the Harry Ransom Center for Research in the Humanities (HRC), reveal that her output was enormous and that most of her life was devoted to writing about racial and political concerns throughout Europe, North and South America, North Africa, and the Caribbean, a lack of awareness about this real body of her work leads to misrepresentation of the texts that are more widely available.

Cunard once said that the thirties were "her years" (Wineapple 1989, 79). Cultural and political events at the beginning of the decade were to transform her life. In January 1931 she arranged the first British screening of *L'Âge d'Or*, Buñuel's sexually provocative and consciously blasphemous film, which had been banned following right-wing protests in Paris. In Scottsboro, Alabama, in April 1931, nine impoverished young black men, the youngest only thirteen, were sentenced to death for the alleged rape of two white women on a train. The case of the Scottsboro boys became the focus of worldwide attention. Cunard began to campaign for their release through a series of fundraising events in London (notoriously including mixed-race bathing parties) and many letters and articles which were published in periodicals as diverse as *The Daily Worker* and Bryher's film journal *Close Up*. Despite the insubstantial evidence against those charged, and the international campaigns, the case was dragged through the courts for over six years and the last of the nine remained incarcerated until 1950. Cunard's outrage at the injustice strengthened her intent to publish a "new book on COLOR" with "outspoken criticism, comment and comparison from the Negro on the present day civilizations of Europe, America, South America, the West Indies, African Colonies, etc." (Chisolm 1979, 191–92). Between 1931 and 1934 she researched and compiled material for this monumental volume whilst continuing her ardent campaigning for the release of the Scottsboro boys. In 1934 the collection was published as *Negro* by Lawrence and Wishart. The anthology of over 800 pages chronicled transatlantic black history, culture, and society through the contributions of black and white authors, artists, and political leaders.

Although the 1920s saw the publication of poems by Cunard, now more widely reinterpreted by critics such as John Lucas as expressive of a political desire to change society, she tends to be remembered not for her writing but through her image commemorated in the 1920s by the pen, lens, and brush of male artists. Even a sympathetic new biography is titled *Nancy Cunard: Heiress, Muse, Political Idealist* with a hierarchy of attributes in which only the third and final denotes the subject's agency. Fictionalized accounts of her conduct by Michael Arlen and Aldous Huxley have contributed to the substance of retrospective and contemporary 1920s' mythology. Cunard has been "textually consumed" (Clements 1986, 191). As Iris March, the déclassé heroine of *The Green Hat*, Arlen's best-selling novel (1924), she appears as a fashionable dilettante: he depicts her as gallantly defending Imagist poems, "but it turned out she hadn't read any, and wasn't at all sure what they were" (24). She is presented as a restless traveler whose not staying in London "let England down" (51). Her "nymphomania" is portrayed as a threat to English values: "We are of this soil, Iris, of this air, of this England which is still our England," and her promiscuity "stabs at the roots of our life, Iris" (306–7). Arlen's sketch of Cunard as a woman who blindly championed fashionable movements, empowered by a sexuality so aggressive as to drive men to suicide, has dominated her reception. She was publicly configured as unpatriotic; her promiscuity and lack of patriotism are symbiotic.

Whilst *The Green Hat* is no longer a bestseller, the photographs by Man Ray and Cecil Beaton which appeared in *Vogue* throughout the 1920s are still widely circulated. By the mid 1920s Cunard was known for her trademark armfuls of ivory bracelets. And although his photographs celebrate this stylish primitivism, Cecil Beaton also caricatured Cunard in his series "Portraits in Passing—that little group of the celebrated and the chic in whom all the world is interested" (Beaton 1929, 52). The caption accompanying Beaton's 1929 sketch reads "Miss Nancy Cunard, the daughter of Lady Cunard, whom we all know, spends most of her time in Paris, but lately came to London to buy more barbaric bracelets—a selection of which is shown here in a silk handkerchief and on her arm." Just as Arlen's heroine was dangerously iconoclastic, Beaton's jibe about the "barbaric" bracelets indicates his underlying sense that Cunard's bangles signified something far more disconcerting and threatening than mere fashion. But in the 1920s British print portrayals of Cunard attempted to subsume all that was genuinely radical in her behavior and to position her instead as voguishly nonconformist. She was publicly denied the outlaw status so defiantly sought and stated in her 1921 volume of poetry of that name. The publication and circulation of *Black Man and White Ladyship* in 1931, however, was an act of iconoclasm by Cunard and surely a bid to gain agency. It is my intention in this essay to further current critical enquiry into Cunard's significance as a political agitator in Britain; to consider *Black Man and White Ladyship* as a moment of contiguity between anticolonialism and modernism in London, reading the 1931 pamphlet in the context of Surrealism, especially *L'Âge d'Or*. I also hope to initiate a reevaluation of Cunard's preoccupations in 1931, which will indicate *Black Man*'s proximity to Surrealist tracts, thus confirming Cunard's agency within that movement.

The Polemics of *Black Man and White Ladyship*

> An anniversary is coming and that is why this is printed now, and the reason for its having been written will, I imagine, be clear to those who read it.
>
> By anniversary I am not, indeed, referring to Christmas, but to the calendric moment of last year when the Colour Question first presented me personally with its CLASH or SHOCK aspect. (Cunard 1931, 1)

Black Man was privately printed and circulated in December 1931 like a Christmas card *manqué* to associates and family friends. The text is breathtakingly bold; with utter disregard for the niceties of social convention, Cunard capitalizes on a personal incident to illustrate her polemic. The pamphlet, with a somewhat heavy-handed irony, "celebrates" the first anniversary of the occasion when her mother discovered that she had a black lover, Henry Crowder. One year earlier, in December 1930, Emerald was hosting a party when one of her guests, the notoriously brazen Margot Asquith—wife of the former prime minister of Britain, Herbert Asquith—confronted her with a question about Nancy: "Hello Maud, what is it now—drink, drugs or niggers?" (1). In *Black Man* Emerald's reaction to the slur and details of her own private life are surprisingly juxtaposed with a short history of slavery and an account of contemporary American lynchings. Cunard presents Emerald's anxiety about decorum and ease about profound injustices as in metonymical relationship with the behavior of Britain's ruling and imperial authorities. This juxtaposition of shocking intimate revelation with global affairs, and the use of a religious festival to denounce the sacred dyad of mother and country, is suggestive of Surrealism. It is plausible to read the pamphlet as perhaps a petulant attack upon the mother, simply a stage in Cunard's psychic development, but focusing upon the mother/daughter relationship can blind readers to its real polemic.

The pamphlet is composed of two sections: "Her Ladyship" and "Black Man." The first refers to her mother and the second to her lover. But whilst these figures are more significantly employed as metonyms for colonial white Britain and enslaved black Africa, respectively, Emerald, as signifier of oppression and the dominant discourse is more of a presence than Crowder who signifies the silenced and abused. In the second printing of the pamphlet the heading "Black Man" is omitted altogether—presumably an accident of the printer—creating an even sharper juxtaposition of the two sections than Cunard hoped for. As in the title, Cunard's polemic gains its power through the structured contrasts of black and white, private and public, power and oppression. Those who criticize it as an impassioned outburst, an unthinking attack, fail to see this considered form. The shifts in register and variations in presentational style are not the failings of a careless writer but quite the reverse, a calculated and effective methodology. Cunard's sensitivity to language has perhaps been underestimated. Her experience as a translator and poet informs the arrangement and thus the rhetoric of *Black Man*.

The rhetorical power of Cunard's argument is in part derived from close attention to lexis. She records her mother's response to Margot Asquith's question ("what is it now—drink, drugs or niggers?"): Emerald immediately telephoned "half of London society asking 'Is it true my daughter knows a Negro?'" (1). To "know" or associate with a black man was in itself unspeakable for Emerald but the outrage implied by Asquith's slur was in its euphemism, that her daughter "knew" one sexually. Cunard's polemic is centered around an exploitation of this duality of meaning; it explores the gap between what is "known" and what is spoken of in the aristocratic social world that her mother inhabited and embodies in *Black Man*. Emerald's question was clearly resonant for Cunard. Her first article for *The Crisis*, the journal of the National Association for the Advancement of Colored People (NAACP), in September 1931,was titled "Does anyone *know* any Negroes?" and concerned the public attitudes and reception of mixed-race couples in Europe and America.

In *Black Man* Cunard proceeds to name all the tabooed subjects that her mother liked to gossip about but could not explicitly name (including homosexuality, adultery, and personal wealth). She accuses Emerald of hypocrisy when she says, "Her ladyship has a definite fear of certain words. Some days she will even shy at the word 'lover'" (5). For Emerald was enjoying "an imperturbable life of licensed indecency" with Beecham whilst still married to Sir Bache (Douglas 1996, 275). This hypocrisy is emphasized in Cunard's explication of Emerald's delight in being scandalized by gossip: "as for the tabooed subject of pederasty it is frequently introduced and worried like a fox in death-throes by a whole pack of . . . allusions. An unsafe enough topic in this milieu but made positively, imminently hot by the hostess' concern" (5). Whilst Emerald cannot say the word "pederast" or "homosexual" (for the two seem to be employed synonymously), she delights in gossip about "those dreadful people who . . . well, you know those horrid . . ." (5). Cunard portrays her as equally repelled by the word as by the deed. She cannot name her own adultery, or homosexuality, or, we are to infer, her daughter's relationship with a black man.

When *Black Man* was first reprinted in edited form in Hugh Ford's collection of her writings and then in the same form in Bonnie Kime Scott's influential modernist anthology, *The Gender of Modernism*, Cunard's critique of her mother's attitude toward homosexuality was omitted. Perhaps Ford cut the passage referring to homosexuality because he felt it irrelevant, or somehow damaging, to Cunard's main argument about racism. Conversely, however, Cunard's polemic is, in fact, composed through the cataloguing of all that was known and yet could not be openly discussed by those in Emerald's social class; mixed-race relationships, adultery, homosexuality, left-wing politics, personal finances. Cunard writes explicitly about taboos to remove the frisson of pleasure from speaking the unspeakable. In daring to print the spoken prejudices of the aristocracy as used by her mother, Cunard aimed to expose the relationship of discourse to the maintenance of class, sexual, and racial hegemonies. Cunard ridicules her mother's self-depiction as being too aristocratic to discuss money by quoting a recent interview given to the *Sunday Express* in which Emerald flaunts her wealth. She then creates a striking contrast to this refusal to discuss figures by following the quotation with a list of statistics of the slave trade.

Thus, in the first section of the pamphlet, Cunard portrays Emerald as leading a fashionable and essentially frivolous life in order to emblematize the hypocrisies and petty concerns of white aristocratic Britain. The textual presentation of this section clearly indicates her outrage. Points of particular indignation are italicized or capitalized and Emerald's racist and homophobic utterances are isolated on the page for maximum effect. This style creates the sense of a verbatim recording. The reader feels faintly embarrassed about witnessing a private argument until Emerald's words are sharply juxtaposed with the gruesome brutalities of the slave trade (under the heading "Black Man") and suddenly the reader's discomfort at reading one side of this personal exchange is exposed as insignificant. Cunard's text provokes the reader to consider that eavesdropping upon a mother and daughter is a different shade of immorality to the passive sanctioning of slavery, lynching, and racism. "Her Ladyship" closes with a reported telephone conversation between Emerald and an unnamed acquaintance: "You mean to say my daughter does know a Negro and that you know him too? Well, don't speak of it to anyone—nobody knows anything about it. *Good Bye*" (1). This is immediately followed with an invitation to:

> Consider the following extract of what happened. From 1619 to after the middle of the 19th century hundreds of thousands of Negroes, men, women and children, were sold, stolen and torn out of Africa. They were herded into boats at one time specially built for their transport. The trade prospered; more profits were made at it, and more quickly, than at any other trade in history. Its apex, in number of slaves shipped from Africa to the New World, was the last two decades of the 18th and the first two of the 19th centuries—about the time there was most agitation for its abolition. An estimate puts the figure at over 100,000 slaves a year. On special boats the slaves were manacled to each other two by two and to the ship itself; a space of 6ft. by 1ft.4 was allotted each on deck for the many weeks of the voyage. At night they were stuffed into the hold. Many would be found dead in the morning. Those that looked for death from starvation were forcibly fed—many hanged themselves, leapt overboard, died of the flux and of despair. They were made to jump up and down in their irons after eating; this was called 'dancing,' to obtain exercise. They were flogged, tortured and maimed. After three or four such passages the slave ships had to be abandoned—having become unusable from filth. The stench of them spread some four miles out at sea. Once landed the slaves were sold by auction. Everyone knows how things went for them till 1863. 244 years of slavery in America, and Charles Lynch existed—a Virginian *Quaker*. From the World Almanac figures—*admitted official* figures,—3,226 Negroes have been lynched in U.S.A. between 1885 and 1927, an average of over 6 a month. (7)

Cunard's synopsis is relatively sober and factual. In appearance, whilst some italicized emphasis is retained, the denser text, longer paragraphs, and more conventional structure clearly signify a change in tone. The language and content still shock—lynching is undertaken in the "name of white american womanhood" and yet their ancestors "were in a very great number of cases suckled at the black breast" (8)—but the desire seems to be to shock the reader out of ignorant complacency. Cunard aimed to unsettle the reader's passive sympathies; of a daughter's obeyance of her mother and a national's obedience to his country.

In citing Emerald's attempt to hush up her daughter's relationship with Crowder next to an account of the barbarous atrocities of slavery and lynching, Cunard invites consideration of the relationship between the two. The jarring clash of white aristocratic society and the historical abuses it was built on enacts the shock of the meeting between Emerald and Crowder that Cunard yearned for but that never happened. Instead both figures are employed as metonyms and their two worlds collide only on paper. The reference to the wealthy white woman's attempt to silence something socially unpalatable next to the survey of racial abuses and inequity thus points to the refusal of white society to engage with its own brutal practices. For Cunard the figure of her mother, American by birth but imperiously resident in Britain, formed a fertile matrix from which to explore transatlantic stories of racism.

The content of *Black Man* was thus inspired by a collocation of political concerns and personal experience; the manner in which they are represented is characteristic of Surrealism. Cunard's relationship to the movement, as opposed to relationships with individual Surrealists such as Louis Aragon, has only begun to be explored, for example, by Laura Winkiel in her consideration of *Negro*'s format as borrowing "from surrealist ethnography" (Winkiel 2006, 521). Anne Chisholm records the geographical proximity of *The Hours Press* to the Galerie Surréaliste, notes her love affair with Aragon, and her sustained friendships with Tristran Tzara, Georges Sadoul, and René Crevel, but does not examine the intellectual exchange between Cunard and the Surrealist group beyond suggesting the appeal of their desire to shock. This is not only a reductive reading of Surrealism but also an emphasis that contributes to the continued reading of Cunard's actions, including *Black Man,* as temperamental outbursts designed simply to scandalize rather than politically agitate. In her memoir of this period, *These Were The Hours*, Cunard argues the reciprocity of the Surrealist movement's revolutionary "social-political" aims and "aesthetic-iconoclastic" effects (1969, 41). She emphasizes its political dimension: "All jingo values of *La Patrie* and *La Gloire*, the militarism so real to official France, were anathemized, and colonialism was consistently denounced" (41). Until the famously schismatic decision to formally politicize the group, the Surrealists, like Cunard, reviled the institutions of the state through acts of collective and individual iconoclasm.

Surrealism evolved out of Dada, the nihilistic movement that expressed the anger of the postwar world through violence and destruction. Whilst the Surrealists continued to abhor traditional values, their fight against all forms of oppression became more positive aiming not just to destroy but to radically transform society. However, as Helena Lewis argues in *Dada Turns Red,* in the mid-1920s the Surrealist "concept of revolution had a purely metaphysical value" (1990, 32). "Revolution" indicated not political revolt but the overturning of Western belief systems. In the third edition of *La Révolution Surréaliste*—the journal the group published irregularly between 1924 and 1929—the "spirit of the East" is employed as a shorthand signifier of spiritual freedom. As individuals the group rebelled against marriage, the Church and State, endorsing ideals of free love which were inspired by socialist traditions and the Russian Revolution. Indeed, it is widely perceived, for instance in the recent Tate/MOMA exhibition, *Surrealism: Desire Unbound,* that this eclectic group were only united in their sexual freedom and exploration of unconscious desires. This reading neglects not only the origins of this sexual liberation, but the political commitment that differentiated Surrealism from Dada. Furthermore, a focus on their art with an ahistorical emphasis on Freud's writings as its inspiration fails to recognize that psychoanalysis was appealing to the Surrealists precisely because of its rejection of Church and State sanctioned relationships, in other words its rejection of society as it stood. The recent exhibition's emphasis on the Surrealists as captivated by dreams is misleading: the Surrealist approach to psychoanalysis is directed toward a critique of social norms and is not distinct from political life.

The Surrealists had always been activists, agitators, demonstrators, writers of manifestos. A more explicit engagement with Marxism and left-wing politics began when André Breton took over the editorship of *La Révolution Surréaliste.* Breton's developing political consciousness and the war in Morocco initiated the group's movement toward the Communist Party. By 1930 *La Révolution Surréaliste* had been superseded by *La Surréalisme au service de la révolution* with its clearly significant shift in the title. Whilst the themes of anticlericalism and antimilitarism remained in the new journal, it was more overtly political and less literary in content. Aragon, Buñuel, Crevel, Dalí, Eluard, Ernst, Thirion, and Tzara were amongst those who signed the opening declaration in support of Breton and their intention to "prepare for the turning of current intellectual forces toward aiding the inevitable Revolution" (Alexandre et al. 1930, 41). Inevitably for a group developed out of an anarchist collective, support for the party was not unilateral. One "pivot of dissidence" (in Michel Leiris's phrase) to Breton's authoritarian conception of Surrealism was centered around *Documents*, the journal edited by Bataille. The journal published ethnographic photos next to bourgeois family portraits; like the seemingly haphazard juxtapositions of *Black Man*, the contrasts were a deliberate assault on conventional ways of seeing and ordering the world.

L'Âge d'Or (1930), produced by Luis Buñuel (in collaboration with Salvador Dalí) also bears witness to preoccupation with ethnography, drawing upon its discourse of detached, comparative and scientific study of myths, ceremonies, and social organization. The "one uncontested masterpiece of Surrealist film" became something of a cause célèbre in its attack on bourgeois society through Surrealist aesthetics (Williams 1981, 106). In France, *L'Âge d'Or* was banned by the Prefecture of the police less than a fortnight after its public opening in November 1930, following violent protests by the League of Patriots and the Anti-Semitic League in which ink was thrown at the screen and an exhibition of Surrealist paintings in the cinema foyer was destroyed. The press was outraged by the film: *Le Figaro* saw it as a threat to "the grandeur that is France" containing "the most obscene, disgusting and tasteless episodes. Country, family and religion are dragged through the mud" (Edwards 1997, 63). In an act of characteristic single-mindedness Cunard obtained a print and invited an eclectic racially mixed audience of acquaintances—whom she recognized as opposed to censorship—to a private screening in London in January 1931. (It was not to be released to the wider British public until 1980). Indeed, this was the London visit that Beecham "strongly advise[d]" against, and which is commemorated in *Black Man* (1). Cunard records in the pamphlet that due to investigations made after Margot Asquith's jibe, Beecham discovered that Cunard was coming to England with a "gentleman of American-African extraction" and had sent a letter, then a telegram, "strongly advising" against this visit. He was alarmed, not by the screening of the controversial film, but by the race of her companion, and added that "while friendships between races were viewed with tolerance on the continent," the situation in England was different "especially as viewed by the Popular Press" (1). According to Cunard in her article for *The Crisis*, the press were scandalized by the film but "unmoved" by her companion.

Cunard's screening can be deemed as much a political act as a cultural event. Retrospectively recognized as "the most scandalous film of its generation," *L'Âge d'Or* was summarized by the Surrealists, and most subsequent critics, as following a couple's pursuit of the erotic ideal in a debased and amoral "civilization" (Edwards 1997, 63). In the program notes Dalí wrote that his aim in writing the scenario with Buñuel "was to present the straight and pure line of 'conduct' of a person who pursues love, meeting and cutting across vile humanitarian and patriotic ideals and other shabby mechanisms of reality" (Mundy 2001, 43). However, as Linda Williams has more recently suggested, "rather than using the lovers to exalt any impossible amour fou, Buñuel shows that sexual desire . . . is a product of the interdependence of law and transgression" (Williams 1981, 137).

Cunard's pamphlet, written one year after *L'Âge d'Or*, bears structural and thematic comparison with the film. Like *Black Man*, the film is composed of discrete segments, each one a complete diegesis apparently unrelated to the next. The viewer of *L'Âge d'Or*, like the reader of Cunard's pamphlet and of Bataille's journal, *Document*, is invited to make the links between the disparate subjects and thus to understand the world anew. Buñuel's film is composed of five sections that are prefigured in the introductory section: a documentary on the scorpion. The five segments of its tail are distinctly observed by the camera. The film's exposition of civilization and empire building makes reference to the colonial enterprise of and reliance upon anthropology in this opening documentary. The detached "scientific" style invites a distancing from the communities and events under scrutiny in the subsequent scenarios. In the third section, "The Founding of Imperial Rome," a crowd of Majorcans gathers on a rocky shoreline to witness the ceremonial laying of a foundation stone. The ceremony is interrupted by the passionate writhings of a couple embracing in the mud. Here, sex disrupts the founding of social law, as Linda Williams has argued, but the later couplings of the pair are conversely prevented by social law (as represented by a ceremonious party and concert in the fourth section). Frantic sexual desire is thus seen to threaten establishment values of patriarchy, family, and religion, but simultaneously only exists because of this forbidden status. And as with Emerald's "hot" topics, the more society forbids something the more desirable it becomes.

The fourth section of the film, "Scenes from Roman Life," is a luminously proleptic evocation of the disrupted gathering commemorated in *Black Man*. A marquis and marchioness hold a smart concert party in their country house. Their guests are the Majorcans, earlier the colonists in the film; as in *Black Man*, the aristocratic party-goers represent imperial powers. In the film the guests continue to socialize despite surprising intrusions. A farm cart carrying drunken laborers is pulled by mules through the gathering; smoke and flames follow a terrified servant as she runs from a fire in the kitchen before collapsing at the feet of the guests; distant gunshot is heard as the gamekeeper shoots his small son whose play irritated him. The party-goers' disregard for all this is clearly a comment upon the aristocracy ignoring the plight of the working classes (or even the true nature of the society around them). On a more superficial level it is also a salutary account of how social codes constrain the behavior and insight of individuals. It comes as a shock to the spectator, then, that the only event that disrupts the social oblivion of the party is relatively inoffensive; and not related to human suffering or violent death, but to desire. The lovers, played by Gaston Modot and Lya Lys, gaze enraptured at one another, until the girl's mother, the marchioness, sits beside Modot and tries to engage him in small talk. He becomes so enraged by her interference, her attempts at polite social intercourse, that when she spills a little from a proffered glass of wine, he slaps her in the face. Those present are appalled and he is forcibly ejected from the party. Meanwhile Lya Lys laughs with pleasure at her mother's mortification. Modot sneaks back into the party and the two lovers arrange to meet in the garden, scene of the concert. In an uncanny visual representation of Beecham's telegram to Cunard, advising her not to travel to London with Crowder, the two lovers are physically separated by the intervention of the orchestral conductor. Throughout the film, social ceremonies interrupt the lovers.

The relationship between mother and daughter is not the focus of *L'Âge d'Or*—in the scene described the marchioness represents conventional morality that steadfastly blocks the course of love. Cunard's reading of the film is in line with that of Dalí and Buñuel. Her synopsis proposes that the family, like the church, and the state must be destroyed to prevent all humanity being laid to waste. Reading *Black Man* in the light of *L'Âge d'Or,* then, suggests a revolutionary interpretation of Cunard's symbolic matricide. This becomes not a closed act of personal resolution but the first step toward the destruction of existing society.

But *Black Man* has been received as a personal attack alone. Despite its powerful political argument, it seems that contemporaries either could not see beyond the personal attack upon mother by daughter or chose not to. Circulation of the pamphlet understandably resulted in a permanent severance of the already desiccated ties between mother and daughter, as Cunard intended. Disinherited as a result of her relationship with Crowder, it seems that her bold words within the pamphlet, "I trust we shall never meet again" (2), were realized: "Nancy was never again received in Lady Cunard's world, the world in which she had been raised" (Douglas 1996, 276). Crowder himself thought that the text lacked judgment. In his account of their relationship he describes "Blackman and Her Ladyship" [*sic*] as an "atrocious piece" and "thought it a most idiotic thing to do" (Crowder 1987, 118–19). Cunard's friends also balked at her public break with her mother, perceiving as foolhardy what critics now regard as courageous. Edgell Rickword, the communist critic who assisted Cunard in the making of *Negro*, "thought it both scurrilous and hysterical" but conceded "that it had opened his eyes to the injustices of which previously he had only been partly conscious" (Hobday 1989, 145). In spite of this grudging admission, Rickword was typical in reacting only to the outrage of the confrontation with the mother and not the outrages of empire outlined within it.

The explosive public rupture of the mother/daughter relationship still continues to transfix interpreters of Cunard's life and works, even those undertaken as part of a revisionary feminism. Lois Gordon's recent synopsis of *Black Man and White Ladyship* concludes: "Although her essay has been praised subsequently for its vicious wit and brutal honesty regarding racism, for raising the same challenge as Lillian Smith in *Strange Fruit* a decade later, Nancy had been remarkably harsh" (Gordon 2007, 160). Susan Stanford Friedman has stated that what is striking about the piece is its "conflation of matrophobia and political radicalism" (1990, 65). Even a favorable reading sees Cunard's attempt to uncover the societal attitudes that create and legitimize appalling acts of racism as an act of matrophobia: are all critiques of mothers matrophobia? Again, such an account of the tract reads only the personal relationship with the mother and neglects even the symbolism of the break with her as a break with an older generation's views. In her recent analysis of white patrons and the Harlem Renaissance, Ann Douglas convincingly explicates Cunard's political and sexual drives, alcoholism, and anorexia as "in part an inevitable backlash against a willful, matricidal determination on a course of extreme oral deprivation on every level" (1996, 273). Cunard's drives can be neatly interpreted through feminist psychoanalytical theories of mother/daughter relationships. We can find abundant biographical evidence to understand her "desire to become purged once and for all of [her] mother's bondage, to become individuated and free" (Rich 1976, 236). Looking at contemporary newspapers, commentaries, and magazines we can see that Cunard is always referred to as her mother's daughter, and even now detractors use Lady Cunard's wealth and reputation in society to dismiss the authenticity of Cunard's own political acts. Despite the furore of *Black Man*, this pairing of Cunard with her mother and an assumed inheritance from the Cunard family was to continue throughout her life. In the Harry Ransom Center for Research in the Humanities there are many letters to the press in which Cunard is at pains to point out that she is not an heiress of fortune or title, in order to dissociate herself from the shipping line and her mother.

Emerald's facile preoccupation with the *beau monde* has continued to haunt Cunard's own reputation. In *Black Man*, Emerald is heard to complain "*that*—she would not feel *chic* in Paris any longer as she had heard that all the chic Parisians nowadays consorted with Negroes" (3). Cunard's campaigns for racial equality are often dismissed as stemming from negrophilia or a modish fetishization of the New Negro. If we turn to the pages of *Vogue* we may understand that maybe even her contemporaries interpreted Cunard's relationship with Henry Crowder as merely a chic way of upsetting her mother. One of many caricatures by the popular New York-based cartoonist, Miguel Covarrubias, from a series "The Negro de Nos Jours," and printed in British *Vogue* in 1925, reads: "In the 18th century we made money out of negroes. In the 20th they make money out of us. We used to send them missionaries; we now send them telegrams. Our mothers, when young, were taken to the Christie minstrels. Mothers are not taken now; the wise child would not think it suitable" (53).

It is easy to see, then, how the radical politics of *Black Man* have been ignored or only tacitly acknowledged only as part of a petulant rebellion against polite society. We can also see perhaps that in thinking about the mother, Cunard's critics, if not Cunard herself, have found "negative ways of clinging to her still" (Friday 1977, 61). And while I find this interpretation of the pamphlet and the events it describes entirely credible, I feel that concentration upon it turns *Black Man* into just an account, albeit a fascinating one, of personal psychic development—the story of a woman's attempt to overcome an absence of maternal love in adolescence. In her analysis of feminism and psychoanalytic theory Nancy Chodorow observes that "separation from the mother, the breaking of dependence, and the establishment and maintenance of a consistently individuated sense of self" are particularly difficult psychological issues for Western middle-class women (1989, 58). In focusing on *Black Man* as an account of a dysfunctional relationship between privileged Western women are we perpetuating the racial and class hierarchies Cunard sought to undermine?

L'Âge d'Or threw down the gauntlet to establishment France and Cunard did the same for Britain, not when she screened the film but when she rewrote it as *Black Man and White Ladyship*. This tract ends, after all, with the words "How come white man, is the rest of the world to be reformed in your dreary and decadent image?" (11). As Buñuel challenged the belief systems of contemporary Western society in France, Cunard wanted to disturb the complacency of the British establishment. Her pamphlet should be described as an act not of matricide but of parricide—an act of treason against her country. She broke with her mother to break with empire.

Notes

1. See Nancy Cunard, *Essays on Race and Empire*, ed. Maureen Moynagh (Peterborough, Ont: Broadview Press, 2002); Lawrence Rainey, ed., *Modernism: An Anthology* (Oxford: Blackwell, 2005); John Lucas, ed., *Poems of Nancy Cunard* (Nottingham, UK: Trent Editions, 2005).

2. See Maroula Joannou, "Nancy Cunard's English Journey," *Feminist Review* 78 (2004): 141–63); and Lola Young and Sheila Gopaulen's keynote address at the Nancy Cunard Conference, APU, Cambridge, UK, November 10, 2001.

Works Cited

Alexandre, Maxime, et al. 1930. "Declaration." *La Surréalisme au Service de la Révolution* (July).

Archer-Straw, Petrine. 2000. *Negrophilia: Avant-garde Paris and Black Culture in the 1920s*. New York: Thames and Hudson.

Arlen, Michael. 1924. *The Green Hat*. London: Collins.

Beaton, Cecil. 1929. "Portraits in Passing." *Vogue* (Autumn): 52.

Buñuel, Luis, director. 1930. *L'Âge d'Or*. France.

Chisholm, Anne. 1979. *Nancy Cunard*. London: Sidgwick and Jackson.

Chodorow, Nancy. 1989. *Feminism and Psychoanalytical Theory*. Cambridge: Polity Press.

Clements, Patricia. 1986. "Transmuting Nancy Cunard." *Dalhousie Review*. 60: 1–2.

Crowder, Henry, and Hugo Speck. 1987. *As Wonderful As All That?* Navarro, California: Wild Trees Press.

Cunard, Nancy. 1921. *Outlaws*. London: Elkin Matthews.

———. 1931. *Black Man and White Ladyship: An Anniversary*. Toulon: Privately printed.

———. 1934. *Negro: An Anthology*. London: Wishart.

———. 1969. *These Were The Hours*. Carbondale: Southern Illinois University Press.

Douglas, Ann. 1996. *Terrible Honesty: Mongrel Manhattan in the 1920s*. London: Picador.

Edwards, Gwynne. 1997. *The Discrete Art of Luis Buñuel*, 2nd ed. London: Marion Boyars.

Friday, Nancy. 1977. *My Mother/My Self: A Daughter's Search for Identity*. New York: Delacorte Press.

Friedman, Susan Stanford. 1990. "Nancy Cunard (1896–1965)." In *The Gender of Modernism*.

Gordon, Lois. 2007. *Nancy Cunard: Heiress, Muse, Political Idealist*. New York: Columbia University Press.

Hobday, Charles. 1989. *Edgell Rickword: A Poet at War*. Manchester, UK: Carcanet.

Huxley, Aldous. 2004. *Antic Hay*. London: Vintage. 1923.

———. 2004. *Crome Yellow*. London: Vintage. 1921.

Lewis, Helena. 1990. *Dada Turns Red: The Politics of Surrealism*. Edinburgh: Edinburgh University Press.

Lucas, John. 1997. *Radical Twenties: Aspects of Writing, Politics, and Culture*. Nottingham, UK: Five Leaves Publications.

Mundy, Jennifer, ed. 2001. *Surrealism Unbound*. London: Tate.

Rich, Adrienne. 1976. *Of Woman Born: Motherhood as Experience and Institution*. New York: W. W. Norton.

Scott, Bonnie Kime, ed. 1990. *The Gender of Modernism*. Bloomington: Indiana University Press. *Vogue*. (February) 1925.

Williams, Linda. 1981. *Figures of Desire: A Theory and Analysis of Surrealist Film*. Berkeley and Los Angeles: University of California Press.

Wineapple, Brenda. 1989. *Genet: A Biography of Janet Flanner*. London: Pandora.

Winkiel, Laura. 2006. "Nancy Cunard's *Negro* and the Transnational Politics of Race." *Modernism/Modernity* 13. 3 (September): 507–30.

The First White Rastafarian: Sylvia Pankhurst, Haile Selassie, and Ethiopia

BARBARA WINSLOW

WHEN SYLVIA PANKHURST DIED ON SEPTEMBER 27, 1960, IN ADDIS Ababa, the capital city of Ethiopia, some of the greatest tributes came from African and Pan-African leaders, such as Jomo Kenyatta, Kwame Nkrumeh, Amy Jacques Garvey (widow of Marcus Garvey), and members of the South African National Congress. W. E. B. DuBois, the African-American intellectual and activist, wrote, "the great work of Sylvia Pankhurst was to introduce black Ethiopia to white England" (1960, 52). Pankhurst was buried as an honored patriot in a state funeral in Addis Abba. For most suffrage, feminist, and communist historians in the West, Sylvia Pankhurst is best known as the socialist-feminist member of the Pankhurst family. Many who have written about Pankhurst find it puzzling (or opportunistic or pathological) that she traveled from Independent Labour Party socialist-feminism to Bolshevism to (at least according to Lenin) "ultraleftism" to motherhood and then to antifascism. Many are surprised that, as an avowed socialist and republican, Pankhurst's final political activities included embracing the reactionary emperor Haile Selassie.[1]

Pankhurst's involvement in anticolonial, antiracist, and Pan-Africanist politics began with her commitment to and involvement in women's suffrage, working-class feminism, and socialist-feminist politics. Always a gadfly, a rebel, a loner, and an outsider, Pankhurst was somewhat of a unique figure in English suffrage, socialist, and working-class history. Her challenge to long-standing English women's suffrage and social democratic traditions made her one of the few white English people to embrace antiracist, anticolonial, and Pan-Africanist political activity. In the context of her politicized understanding of the dynamics of gender, race, and ethnic and national oppression, her political trajectory makes sense. Sylvia Pankhurst was the middle daughter of Emmeline Goulden and Richard Pankhurst, Manchester political radicals. In 1903 Emmeline and her eldest daughter, Christabel, founded the Women's Social and Political Union (WSPU), a woman's suffrage organization known for its innovative tactics and daring use of militancy. Sylvia broke, both personally and politically, with her mother and sister, believing they had abandoned the socialist and labor ideals of her father. She disagreed with the WSPU's increasing use of individual militancy and arson, as well as with their developing political rapprochement with the Tories. In 1913 Sylvia went into the East End of London to organize working-class women into a local branch of the WSPU. By 1914 her differences with her mother and sister were so pronounced that she was expelled from the WSPU, ostensibly for participating in a rally supporting the Dublin General Strike. She then devoted all her energies to building the East London Federation of the Suffragettes (ELFS), which played an important role not just in the woman's suffrage movement but also in the struggle to overcome the dichotomies of class and gender, socialism and feminism, and grass roots political activism and representative democracy.

Pankhurst took an independent path in the women's suffrage movement. She joined her mother and sister, who broke with the constitutional suffragists, by embracing militancy—civil disobedience and deliberate property destruction. However, Pankhurst differed from both wings of the woman's suffrage movement in that she called for universal suffrage, including suffrage for the colonies of Ireland, Africa, and India. She disagreed with the class-based demands of both wings of the woman's suffrage movement, which called for enfranchising women on the same basis as men. Given that the majority of working-class men were denied the vote, suffrage legislation as supported by the woman's suffrage movement would equally deny the franchise to the majority of working-class women. In addition, Pankhurst disagreed with the radical wing within the British Liberal Party and the emerging Labour Party, which had historically argued for full adult suffrage—that is, adult male suffrage—and by implication full adult women's suffrage. In reality, labor and social-democratic organizations did little to support women's suffrage. The leadership of the Independent Labour Party (ILP), for example, opposed the women's suffrage movement, even though much of its rank and file membership was supportive. Pankhurst agonized over these early political conflicts. When the WSPU called for Votes for Women, in reality it meant votes for privileged women; on the other hand, when liberal, labour and social-democratic organizations spoke of adult suffrage, they meant asking women not to agitate for the vote until men were fully enfranchised. As far as the Pankhursts were concerned, and for good reason, the words "adult suffrage" were code words for adult manhood suffrage.

Pankhurst's appreciation for and understanding of forms of domination and oppression began with class and gender, as she supported the self-activity and organization of workers and women in their struggle for rights. Yet she experienced first-hand the contradictions of such work: labor and socialist movements, in the name of working-class solidarity, opposed women's demands for equal rights, while middle-class women, in the name of feminism, ignored or opposed the rights of working-class women (and men). Her organization, the ELFS, attempted to find ways, both in theory and in practice, to interconnect class and gender. The struggle to resolve this conflict heightened her awareness and strengthened her determination to support other struggles against oppression and domination. Both supporters and detractors have often characterized Pankhurst's understanding of and opposition to oppression as a generalized and unswerving support for the so-called underdog.[2] However, her anticolonialism and antiracism was political rather than emotional. Her support of the Irish, Irish nationalism, and Irish independence challenged the labor, socialist, and suffrage movements, who were complacent at best and complicit at worst with regard to British imperialism. Her early support of Irish independence opened doors to her later embrace of African and Pan-African politics. Historically, the English labor and socialist movement had supported Irish Home Rule, especially if resolved constitutionally. However, by the twentieth century and with the development of the Irish struggle for independence into an anti-imperialist and anti-British struggle, support from the radical movements was tepid at best, and some sections of the labor and radical movements joined the English ruling class in viewing the Irish in racialized terms, as undeserving, sometimes inhuman, and always less than English.[3] Pankhurst broke with that English tradition. For example, during the great Dublin General Strike in 1913, Pankhurst, along with Dora Montefiore (another antiracist socialist-feminist), stood out among both suffrage and socialist organizations by organizing the evacuation of Irish children from strike-torn Dublin to the homes of sympathetic trade unionists in England. The vital necessity of supporting the Dublin strikers was underscored by the social democratic newspaper, the *Daily Herald*, which organized a support rally in London. Pankhurst joined Delia Larkin, organizer of the women's section of the Irish Transport and General Workers' Union (ITGWU) and sister of the imprisoned socialist and labor leader, Jim Larkin; James Connolly, Irish socialist and another leader of the ITGWU; as well as other socialists and suffragettes in defending and supporting the Dublin labor movement. Pankhurst defied her mother and sister by speaking out at a rally to support the strikers, "I was glad to . . . 'show solidarity with the Dublin workers and keep the women's side of the struggle to the front'" (Winslow 1996, 62). That speech precipitated her mother and sister expelling her from the WSPU, for they did not wish anyone in the WSPU to connect women's suffrage with Irish nationalism or labor militancy.

Very few English socialists or women's suffrage activists sided with the Irish against the English. At the outbreak of World War I, Pankhurst was in Dublin compiling a firsthand report for her newspaper, the *Woman's Dreadnought*. British troops had fired on a crowd of unarmed civilians in the incident that became known as the Bachelor's Walk Massacre. This would not be the first time that Pankhurst stood alone in defending the Irish. On Easter Monday, 1916, Irish nationalists and socialists led by Padraic Pearse and James Connolly staged an abortive rising against the British government. Pankhurst and the *Dreadnought* defended the rising and argued against British rule, while other socialist groups either denounced the rebels or were silent. Pankhurst was devastated over England's brutal suppression of the rising and the subsequent execution of its leaders, including Connolly. Writing in *The Home Front*, Pankhurst explained her support for Irish nationalism and demonstrated her understanding of the links between nationalism, anti-imperialism, and socialism:

> To me the death of James Connolly was more grievous than any, because the rebellion struck deeper than mere nationalism. It is a truism that countries held under an alien dominance remain politically stagnant, and to a large extent are culturally repressed. Recognition of this made me a supporter of Irish nationalism. Yet after national self-government had been attained, the social problems with which we in England were wrestling would still be present in Ireland. I knew the Easter Monday rebellion was the first blow in an intensified struggle, which would end up in Irish self-government, a necessary step in Irish evolution. (1932, 322)

Pankhurst's support of and contribution to the struggle for Irish freedom was not forgotten. Fifteen years after the rising, Hannah Sheehy Skeffington, an Irish pacifist and feminist whose husband, Francis, was shot in the back by English soldiers after the rising had been suppressed, expressed her feelings about Pankhurst's contribution: "I know no English rebel who understands the Irish situation and the international so well. The comments and sympathy of some English on Ireland just drive me mad at times as they show such a blind spot where we are concerned, in fact, friends are the worst! Your paper *Dreadnought* was always fine on this and other war matters."[4] Such events in Ireland contributed to Pankhurst's developing antiracist and anti-imperialist ideas. Pankhurst also broke with traditional English feminism and social democracy around issues of race and nationalism. Much has been written about the ideology of the woman's suffrage movement in relation to race, nation building, and imperialism in the United States and Europe.[5] Individually and organizationally, the women's suffrage movement used the campaign for suffrage in part to enhance middle-class women's status, often at the expense of women of color, working-class women, and colonized women. Few supported women's suffrage in the colonies. Fewer had relationships or associations with people of color. In the same vein, the overwhelming majority of English socialists were not sympathetic or sensitive to issues of race and racism. Some social democrats, such as H. L. Hyndman of the Social Democratic Federation, were out-and-out racists; others, such as Kier Hardie, ILP member and Labour Party MP, believed that race relations would automatically be solved under socialism. James P. Cannon, founding member of both the U.S. Communist Party and the Trotskyist Socialist Workers' Party, describes the methodology of social democracy as depending upon theorizing the oppression of racial minorities as "an economic problem, part of the struggle between the workers and capitalists; nothing could be done about the special problems of discrimination and inequality this side of socialism." What this meant in practice, Cannon concludes, was "a formula for inaction on the Negro front, and—incidentally—a convenient shield for the dormant racial prejudices of the white radicals themselves" (1962, 230–32)

In regard to race, Pankhurst was one of the exceptions to Cannon's analysis. When she toured the United States in 1912, Pankhurst was horrified at racial injustice. She made attempts to speak with African-Americans. She opposed racism publicly and spoke to black audiences. Against the expressed wishes of U.S. suffragists and even though she was attacked by the press, she spoke at an African-American college in Tennessee, publicly argued against the poll tax, and visited prisoners so that she could comment on prison conditions in the States. She also insisted upon visiting an Indian reservation and critically commented on the "sweated" labor of Indian women who sold their woven rugs for a pittance.

Her commitment to antiracist politics was tested during World War I. An antiwar activist, she used her newspaper, the *Workers' Dreadnought*, to agitate against the war and expose horrendous wartime conditions. Reuben Samuels, an Afro-Caribbean sailor, was a frequent correspondent. Claude McKay, the Jamaican revolutionary writer, became acquainted with Pankhurst after trying to get a number of his articles published in socialist journals such as the *Daily Herald*. McKay was horrified by the racism in the *Herald*. "The headlines were harrowing," he later wrote of those referring to the presence of African troops stationed in Europe: "'Black Scourge in Europe,' 'Black Peril on the Rhine,' 'Brutes in French Uniform,' 'Black Menace of 40,000 Troops,' 'Appeal to the Women of Europe.'" He continued:

> I wrote a letter to George Lansbury, the editor of the *Daily Herald*, and pointed out that his "black scourge" articles would be effective in stirring up more prejudices against Negroes. I thought it was the duty of his paper as a radical organ to enlighten its readers about the real reasons why the English considered coloured troops undesirable in Europe instead of appealing indirectly to illogical emotional prejudices. Lansbury did not print my letter, but sent me a private note saying that he was not personally prejudiced against Negroes. (1970, 74)

McKay was then introduced to Pankhurst, who hired him to write articles about life on the London docks from an antiracist perspective. He was also assigned to read articles in the American, Australian, and Indian presses and comment on them for the *Dreadnought*. He eventually wrote on a wide range of issues, including the Garvey movement and Black Nationalism in the United States.

In early 1920, McKay met a young English sailor named Springhall, who gave him information about revolutionary activity among sailors in the royal navy. McKay and Pankhurst edited the letter and published it as "Discontent on the Lower Deck," under the pseudonym "S.000 (Gunner)." A few days after the article was published, the police raided the *Dreadnought* offices. Pankhurst was arrested for publishing seditious articles. She refused to implicate McKay as the author of the article, and was tried, convicted, and sentenced to five months hard labor. At her trial, Pankhurst defended the sailor's article, as well as another antiracist article called "The Yellow Peril":

> This article is a plea that the workers should not turn around and assail their coloured brethren. . . . I was returning home one evening down the

> West India Dock Road and I found the place thronged. "What is the matter?" And I was told, "They are stabbing coloured men." Some were killed that night and for three nights that went on in Poplar [a working-class neighborhood in the East End of London]. Out of work soldiers and other unemployed were stabbing the coloured men. This is some time now since the war; we have had it in other towns and docks as well as East London. The fact is that the trade union was objecting to the employment of these coloured men. They were left here in this country, and the men out of work, seeing them, thought they were going to get their jobs, took to stabbing them. . . . Leon Lopez, being a coloured man—who is not a British subject perhaps—felt this keenly, and he put his letter in this paper; and I, as editor, felt he had a right to put it there and point out to the workers that unemployment is caused by deeper things than this.[6]

McKay never forgot Pankhurst's loyalty to him or her commitment to antiracism. In his autobiography, *A Long Way from Home*, he wrote, "Pankhurst herself had a personality as picturesque and passionate as any radical in London. . . . And in the labour movement she was always jabbing her hat pin into the hides of the smug and slack labour leaders. Her weekly might have been called the Dread Wasp. And where ever imperialism got drunk and went wild among the native peoples, the Pankhurst people would be on the job" (1970, 77).

Her anticolonialist and antiracist perspective further developed politically and intellectually during her involvement in the international communist movement from 1919 to 1924. During July and August 1920, Pankhurst was an official delegate to the Second Congress of the Third Communist International, or Comintern. It was at these international gatherings that the Comintern began discussions on "National and Colonial Questions." The Bolsheviks had distinguished themselves from other radical and socialist tendencies by their concern with the struggles of "oppressed nationalities," and oppressed national minorities. Lenin's analysis that imperialism was the major reason for the persistence of capitalism elevated anticolonial struggles in the underdeveloped world to the level of class struggle in the developed world. The Bolsheviks or Communists called upon oppressed nations, nationalities, and national minorities to struggle for national self-determination and independence. According to Lenin, this applied to African-Americans (and African-Britons, one would assume). In his "Preliminary Draft of Theses on the National and Colonial Question," written for the Second Congress of the Communist International, Lenin explained, "it is necessary for the Communist parties to render direct aid to the revolutionary movements in the dependent and subject nations (for example, in Ireland, the Negroes in America etc.) and in the colonies" (1966, 10:235).

The Russian communists were very critical of their western European and U.S. comrades' inability to understand the centrality of race to socialist revolution. The Report of the Commission on the National and Colonial Question, for example, singled out English socialists:

> I would like to emphasize the importance of revolutionary work by the Communist parties not only in their own but also in the colonial countries, and particularly among the troops employed by the exploiting nations to keep the colonial peoples in subjection.... Comrade Quelch of the British Socialist Party spoke of this in our commission. He said that the rank-and-file British worker would consider it treasonable to help the enslaved nations in their uprisings against British rule. True, the jingoist and chauvinist-minded labour aristocrats of Britain and America present a great danger to socialism. (Lenin 1966, 31:213–63)

James P. Cannon explains how the Russian communists influenced their western comrades:

> After November 1917 this new doctrine—with special emphasis on the Negroes—began to be transmitted to the American communist movement with the authority of the Russian Revolution behind it. The Russians in the Comintern started on the Americans with the harsh insistent demand that they shake off their unspoken prejudices, pay attention to the special problems of the American Negroes, go to work among them, and champion their cause in the white community. (1962, 234)

In this way, the Comintern prioritized and internationalized the struggles of Africans, African-Americans, and Afro-Europeans, and Pankhurst had been involved from the beginning. Her earlier commitment to women's emancipation and Irish independence connected to the international communist position on colonialism and race. From 1919 to 1924, Pankhurst was immersed in radical working-class activities in London's East End and in the debates over international communism.

In 1934, after a ten-year respite from political activism, Pankhurst threw herself into the antifascist movement, in particular, Italian antifascism. This led her to what she considered to be the most important political activity of her life: the defense of Ethiopia. Her reasons for focusing on Italy are understandable. Her son Richard explained that "travel to Italy, as an art student and later as an international minded socialist caused Sylvia to develop an abiding love of that country" (1979, 149). Her long-time companion and Richard's father, Sylvio Corio, was an Italian anarchist who immigrated to England. Pankhurst was one of the first people to understand the danger of fascism. While attending the 1919 conference of the Italian Socialist Party in Bologna, she had witnessed firsthand a demonstration of Mussolini's fascist brownshirts. As early as November 1922, Pankhurst published a series of articles in the *Dreadnought* describing and analyzing the horrors of Italian fascism. The next year the *Dreadnought* called attention to Hitler's activities in Bavaria. In 1930, she joined the pacifist Women's International League for Peace and Freedom and the International Peace Crusade, and became treasurer of the Women's World International Committee Against War and Fascism. In 1932 she organized the Women's International Matteotti Committee, an organization that tried to protect the widow of Giacomo Matteotti, a well-known Italian socialist who was murdered by Mussolini's troops in 1923. By 1934, she was publishing antifascist tracts and speaking at antifascist rallies demonstrating against local fascists. By 1940, Pankhurst would hold very strong pro-war views, declaring that war was the only way to defeat fascism; London's fascists bombed her office and physically threatened her. She received the highest antifascist accolade; she was put on the Nazi list of people to be killed or interned in case of a successful German invasion.

Her most important antifascist campaign was her defense of Ethiopia in the 1930s. That Pankhurst was white, European, middle-aged, and a woman working with a mostly Pan-African milieu in defense of an African nation has no doubt contributed to journalists and historians dismissing this important part of her political life. Pankhurst's long-standing history of opposition to colonialism and racism was as much, if not more, a factor in her involvement in Ethiopian politics than some sort of generalized sympathy for the underdog. Pankhurst was aware of fascism's expansionist nature: of Mussolini's dream of avenging the Italian defeat by the Ethiopians at Adawa in 1896 by Menelik II—the most devastating defeat inflicted on a European power on African soil—as well as his desire to carve out an Italian empire in the Horn of Africa. In addition, she knew first-hand about the attitudes of Italian soldiers toward Africans. In the late 1890s, Corio had been a conscript in the Italian army, had known soldiers returning home after capture by Emperor Menelik II, and no doubt confided to Pankhurst about his countrymen's colonial mentality toward Ethiopians. Thus, according to Giulia Barrera, even before Mussolini's fascist regime imposed racial restrictions in Ethiopia, Italian racial politics toward Africans were characterized by the need to underline European superiority over Africans, to "protect" natives from "unruly Europeans," but most important "to secure government prestige and authority over both natives and Europeans with an iron fist, more firmly than is necessary in Europe." These policies, Barrera continues, made Italy's colonization of Ethiopia similar to the settler states of Zimbabwe (then Rhodesia) and South Africa (2003, 82).

The Italian invasion of Ethiopia in 1935 triggered an international crisis involving the League of Nations. In 1923, Ethiopia had joined the League, which was bound by treaty to defend the territorial integrity of each member state. While England and France officially objected to Italy's aggression, they never cut off vital supplies, especially oil, to Italy. Very few whites knew or cared much about Ethiopia in the 1930s. Black nationalists in Europe and the United States viewed the invasion of Ethiopia in racial terms—the only independent black nation was fighting for its survival against white European fascism and colonialism. "The defense of Ethiopia," writes Robin D. G. Kelley, "did more than any other event in the 1930s to internationalize the struggles of black people in the United States" (1994, 128–29). However, even the Soviet Union, which professed antifascism and anticolonialism, refused to condemn Italy at the 1935 meeting of the League of Nations and continued to sell oil to Italy. George Padmore, an early communist, Pan-Africanist, and later advisor to Kwame Nkrumeh, argued that the Soviets had become a reluctant partner in the "united front of white Europe against Black Africa" (quoted in Naison 1983, 156). During the 1920s, the Garvey movement had generated a great deal of interest among blacks in the idea of a liberated Africa, and particularly Ethiopia. Kelley notes, "Also known as Abyssinia, the particular section of the Horn of Africa held considerable historical, religious, and cultural significance for black communities throughout the world. Not only had the Ethiopians under Menelik II managed to maintain their independence while the rest of Africa was being carved up by Europeans, but their land had developed a reputation as the cradle of civilization" (1994, 128–29). Paul Robeson claimed the Ethiopian invasion was a "watershed" in American politics, since it "exposed the parallel between [black American] interests and those of oppressed people abroad" (quoted in Von Eschen 1997, 11). Pankhurst was familiar with Garveyism by then, having published articles on it in the *Dreadnought*. In England, the crisis galvanized black Britons. George Padmore organized the International African Service Board. He gathered together a remarkable cadre of black intellectuals and activists, among them C. L. R. James, Pan-Africanist, Trotksyist, intellectual, historian, and essayist (who was also kicked out of the U.S. for his socialist sympathies), and Jomo Kenyatta, the future president of Kenya. Also in this circle were a British Guianan, originally named Griffiths, who took the Ethiopian name of T. Ras Makonnen, and Eric Williams, a student at Oxford who later became prime minister of Trinidad and Tobago. In *Race and Empire: Black Americans and Anticolonialism, 1937–1957*, Penny M. Von Eschen explains that "this group of transplants from colonial societies—who still maintained strong ties to their homelands and were aware of the burgeoning trade union and anticolonial activities there—grasped the vulnerability of colonialism and predicted its collapse in the next decade" (1997, 12).

Pankhurst, who was already familiar with some of the people and many of the political arguments, entered this Pan-African and Black Nationalist milieu by throwing herself into the defense of Ethiopia. In 1935, she began writing letters to the *Manchester Guardian*, *Daily Telegraph*, *Times*, *Daily Herald*, and *Daily Express* urging Britain and the rest of Europe to defend Ethiopia from imperialist aggression. Disheartened, and furious at the inaction of the League of Nations, Pankhurst decided to act. As she had done in 1912 as a suffragette in the East End, she established a weekly tabloid newspaper, *The New Times and Ethiopia News (NTEN)*. Its purpose was to keep the issue of Ethiopia alive within the context of antifascism. The first edition went to press May 5, 1936, the day fascist armies marched on Addis Ababa. The editorial page explained the paper's antifascist stance: "*The New Times and Ethiopia News* appears at a moment when the fortunes of Ethiopia appear at their lowest ebb. . . . The cause of Ethiopia cannot be separated from the cause of International justice. . . . As friends of Ethiopia, we most solemnly protest against the attack on her millennial independence; we condemn the atrocious barbarities employed against her. . . . We shall strive to induce measures by the League to resist the Fascist usurpation, and to aid and defend Ethiopia. . . ." Pankhurst was all but alone on the left as she echoed the concerns of black nationalists and Pan-Africanists: "People stood by while Ethiopia was vanquished: this is only Africa; this is not a White Man's Country. They listened to the Italian propaganda; these are primitives, their customs are barbarous" (August 1, *NTEN*, 1936).

Pankhurst was the editor of *NTEN*, as well its most frequent contributor. But as with the *Dreadnought*, which she edited fourteen years earlier, Pankhurst employed a wide range of writers, including Nancy Cunard, descendant of the wealthy Cunard shipping family, whose involvement in radical antiracist movements is discussed in Tory Young's essay in this volume, "Nancy Cunard's *Black Man and White Ladyship* as Surrealist Tract."

Patricia Romero, a hostile biographer of Pankhurst equally unsympathetic to Cunard, has to admit, "From a distance Nancy and Sylvia worked to help the Italian anti-Fascist Brigade. . . . Nancy tackled the French authorities, while Sylvia took the cause to parliament, seeking admission into Britain for anti-Fascist foreigners" (1987, 211). Other contributors included the Ethiopian minister in London, Azaj Warqneh; Helen Napier of the Friends of Abyssinia [Ethiopia] League of Service; Cecil Turner, who had served in the British Red Cross during the invasion; and Harold Moody, founder of the League of Coloured Peoples. At times, Pankhurst was the only European Moody would consult (Romero 1987, 213). The paper participated in and helped organize events in support of Ethiopia. Pankhurst found herself working with international, anticolonial, and antiracist organizations such as the India League, the League of Coloured People, the African Service Bureau, the Negro Welfare Association, and the Kenya Association. According to Richard Pankhurst, the paper had a circulation of ten thousand, although most of its funding came from private donors (2003, 23). The *NTEN* issued a number of Amharic editions that were smuggled into Italian-occupied Ethiopia and circulated in West Africa and the West Indies. It carried a series of articles called "Africa for the Africans," and a number of these articles appeared in the African Press. One West African student in Britain wrote to Pankhurst, "the young people of African descent feel that Italy has invaded our fatherland. If it were not for your paper the young Africans would not know what is happening in Africa today, as the whole of the press in Europe has no room to publish the Ethiopian case" (February 13, 1954). Pankhurst exchanged the *NTEN* with other African and African-American newspapers, such as the *West African Pilot* and the *Chicago Defender*. The paper was widely quoted throughout West Africa, especially in Sierra Leone (Romero 1987, 213).

Her work in defense of Ethiopia led Pankhurst to correspond with international and Pan-African figures such as W. E. B. DuBois and Amy Jacques Garvey. According to Joseph E. Harris, "Pankhurst enhanced the [Ethiopian] cause's international standing. She had been in contact with Ethiopians and African Americans throughout the struggle." Along with such notable African-Americans as Adam Clayton Powell and Mary Church Terrell, Pankhurst served on the non-members' advisory board of the *Voice of Ethiopia*, a journal published by the U.S.-based Ethiopian World Federation. Lij Andargue of Aden, Michael Dei-Anan of the Gold Coast, Richard Rathell of South Africa, and Nyabongo of Uganda were also members of the board (Harris 1994, 140).

In its early years, *NTEN* was a radical anticolonial and antiracist tabloid that often challenged the British and Italian governments, sometimes broke new ground, and on occasion made theoretical inroads. After 1939, the British government, hoping to dissuade Mussolini from entering the European war and attempting to placate El Duce, tried—unsuccessfully—to prevent the *NTEN* from entering Italy. While the paper focused on Ethiopia, it did so from a clear antifascist perspective, in particular linking the fight against fascism in Spain to the victory of Ethiopia over Italy. Until Italy was forced to give up its claims to Ethiopia, the *NTEN* was the primary source for information about guerilla resistance. In spite of the triumphs of fascism, Pankhurst never sought to rejoin the Communist Party. Horrified by Stalinism, she wrote scathing critiques about the Russian invasion of Finland, the USSR's less than noble record in Spain, and finally, the purge trials in which "The Execution of the Old Bolsheviks" was carried out. Pankhurst remained antiracist to her death, speaking out against apartheid in rallies in Trafalgar Square and in columns in the *New Times and Ethiopia Review*. In 1955, when Southern whites attacked Autherine Lucy, an African-American woman, for attempting to integrate the University of Alabama, the pages of the *NTEN* excoriated racism in the U.S. and came to Lucy's defense (February 22, 1956).

Pankhurst first met Haile Selaisse in 1936 when he began his London exile. According to Richard Parkhurst, his mother supported the emperor "clearly as a Republican, not because he was an emperor but because of his cause" (1992, 152). With the fascist collapse in Africa and Britain's growing involvement in the Horn of Africa, the *NTEN* continued to be anticolonialist and pro-Africa. Pankhurst tirelessly opposed British proposals to maintain colonial rule over Ethiopia and to dismember or impose extraterritorial rights over it. She denounced the Anglo-Ethiopian agreements of 1942 and 1944. She bitterly protested when the British government forgot or refused to include Ethiopia as one of the Allied forces fighting fascism. After Mussolini was defeated, Pankhurst campaigned to reunite Eritrea with other "motherland" countries, that is, lands that were historically linked to Ethiopia before European colonization. For the rest of her life, she remained involved in rebuilding the country. After the war, she led a campaign to build the first modern hospital, named after the emperor's youngest daughter, Princess Tsahay. After Corio died in 1956, she shut down the *New Times and Ethiopia News* and moved to Addis Ababa. There she started another newspaper, the *Ethiopia Observer*, which she edited until her death in 1960. She was given a state funeral and buried as a patriot in a special plot reserved for Ethiopia's heroes in front of Trinity Cathedral.

Pankhurst began her involvement in the struggle for Ethiopian independence as a supporter of the "cause," not as a supporter of an emperor. But, especially after 1941, Pankhurst's support for the cause of anti-imperialism and anticolonialism transformed itself into uncritical support of Haile Selaisse. The reasons behind this were as political as they were personal. Pankhurst was never formally or systematically educated or trained in politics, history, economics, or journalism. She was not a political theorist, nor did she join the kind of political organizations that demanded disciplined readings and discussions of political issues as well as reflection and critique of actions. This partially explains both her strengths and her weaknesses. Through her political activism, beginning with women's suffrage and culminating in antiracist and anticolonialist movements, she involved herself with a wide range of conflicting and contrasting theories. Pankhurst also prided herself on her fierce independence and her rigid adherence to principles that she believed to be right, regardless of the cost in terms of both political and personal support. She saw herself as the lone campaigner for Selaisse, whose support and approval she needed more and more in order to give her the credibility needed to establish herself as an authority on Ethiopia. In Pankhurst's own mind, she remained a socialist. She joined the Labour Party in 1948, but never wrote about the contradictions between her socialist principles and her support of an emperor. Toward the end of her life, she wrote to a friend saying that she felt "the victory of Ethiopia has been the most satisfactory achievement I have seen."[7] Ethiopians, on the other hand, worry less about the contradictions. Ras Andargatchew Massai eulogized Pankhurst at her funeral: "Your history will live forever written in blood, with the history of the Ethiopian patriots. Since by his Imperial Majesty's wish you rest in peace in the earth of Ethiopia, we consider you an Ethiopian" (quoted in Romero 1987, 289).

Notes

I wish to thank Jane Marcus for inviting me to present an early version of this paper at Inroads and Outposts, the September 15, 2000, conference on British Women Writers of the 1930s held at the City University of New York Graduate School and University Center, Gay Wachman for asking me to develop the talk into a paper, and Stephanie Golden for her editorial and sisterly support. Thanks also to Murray Armstrong, Mark Naison, John Rose, Richard Pankhurst, and Sheila Rowbotham. I used the manuscripts and books housed at the Robert Hess Collection on Ethiopia and the Horn of Africa and the Robert L. Hess Collection on the Continent of Africa at Brooklyn College of the City University of New York.

1. Patricia Romero, a hostile biographer, dismisses Pankhurst as only a "propagandist for Ethiopia" (1987, 239).

2. In an interview on July 17, 1985, Richard Pankhurst said that his mother "believed in the humanity of man" and supported the downtrodden (quoted in Romero 1987).

3. See Noel Ignative (1996) and/or Sven Lindquist (1999) for more about race, oppression, and the Irish.

4. Letter from Hannah Sheehy Skeffington to Sylvia Pankhurst, 1932, National Library, Dublin.

5. See, for example, Vron Ware (1992).

6. From Sylvia Pankhurst's Appeal in the Pankhurst Papers Collection, 140, pages 16–17.

7. Letter from Pankhurst to Teresa Billington-Greig, n.d., Fawcett Library, London.

Works Cited

Barrera, Giulia. 2003. "The Construction of Race and Hierarchies in Colonial Eritrea." In *A Place in the Sun: Africa in Italian Culture from Post Unification to the Present.* Edited by Patrizia Palumbo, 81–115. Berkeley and Los Angeles, CA: University of California Press.

Cannon, James P. 1962. *The First Ten Years of American Communism.* New York: Pathfinder Press.

DuBois, W. E. B. 1960. *Ethiopia Observer* 5.1 (September): 52. *Ethiopia Observer 1956–1960.*

Harris, Joseph. 1994. *African-American Reactions to War in Ethiopia, 1936–1941.* Baton Rouge: Louisiana State University Press.

Ignative, Noel. 1996. *How the Irish became White.* New York: Routledge.

Kelley, Robin D. G. 1994. *Race Rebels: Culture, Politics and the Black Working Class.* New York: The Free Press.

Lenin, V. I. 1966. *Collected Works.* Vols. 10 and 31. New York: International Publishers.

Lindquist, Sven. 1999. *Exterminate All the Brutes.* New York: The New Press.

McKay, Claude. 1970. *A Long Way from Home.*New York: Harvest Books.

Naison, Mark. 1971. "Marxism and Black Radicalism in America." *Radical America* (May–June).

———. 1983. *Communists in Harlem During the Depression.* Urbana: University of Illinois Press.

New Times and Ethiopia News NTEN 1936–56.

Pankhurst, E. Sylvia. 1932. *The Home Front: A Mirror to Life in England during the World War.* London: Hutchinson.

———. 1951. *Ex-Italian Somaliland.* Foreword by Peter Freeman. London: M. P. Watts.

———. Pankhurst Papers. Amsterdam: International Institute for Social History.

Pankhurst, Richard. 1979. *Sylvia Pankhurst: Artist and Crusader*. New York: Paddington Press.

———. 1992. "Sylvia and New Times and Ethiopia News." *Sylvia Pankhurst: From Artist to Anti Fascist*. Edited by Ian Bullock and Richard Pankhurst, 149–91. New York: St. Martin's Press.

———. "Sylvia and the Emperor." *New Times and Ethiopia News*, 152.

———. 2003. "Sylvia Pankhurst: Counsel for Ethiopia." Hollywood, CA: Tschai.

Romero, Patricia E. 1987. *Sylvia Pankhurst: Portrait of a Radical*. New Haven, CT: Yale University Press.

Von Eschen, Penny M. 1997. *Race Against Empire: Black Americans and Anticolonialism, 1937–1957*. Ithaca, New York: Cornell University Press.

Ware, Vron. 1992. *Beyond the Pale: White Women, Racism and History (Questions of Feminism)*. New York: Verso.

Winslow, Barbara. 1996. *Sylvia Pankhurst: Sexual Politics and Political Activism*. New York: St. Martin's Press.

Woman's Dreadnought, 1914–16.

Workers' Dreadnought, 1917–1924.

Rebecca West: Constructing a Public Intellectual through Letters of the 1930s

BONNIE KIME SCOTT

BY THE 1930S—THE ERA CONCENTRATED UPON IN THIS VOLUME—Rebecca West was at the apex of her long life, and well into her career as a public intellectual. Indeed, no decade of her life would better exemplify her in that role. She had collected the output of a decade of bold critical writing and reviewing for both British and American journals in *The Strange Necessity* (1928) and *Ending in Earnest* (1931). Her marriage to Henry Andrews in late 1930 seemed to promise a personal serenity that had been lacking through the 1920s, as well as someone who faced fascism in accord with her. In 1936, she traveled as a lecturer for the nascent British Council and turned her tour of Yugoslavia into a mission to record a vanishing culture whose vitality and creative expression she valued and wished to preserve, particularly in the face of advancing fascism. Letters help us to assess the scope and politics of her public writings at a critical stage leading up to World War II; they also give insight into the constructed nature of a public self, and the complexities of playing that part for this woman writer.[1]

West puts to the test feminist theories of women's biography, as articulated by Linda Wagner-Martin, who has helped to redirect this previously underanalyzed genre toward the unabashed treatment of private aspects of life. Wagner-Martin asserts on the one hand that "most women's lives are a tightly woven mesh of public and private events" (1994, 6), and on the other that "few women—even women like Eleanor Roosevelt—live public lives" (7). This effort to legitimate and pursue the private, domestic lives of women runs counter to the very deliberate construction of a public life by just such a writer as Rebecca West. This is something that Wagner-Martin does anticipate: "Private events may be the ones purposely kept secret by the subject" (7). West was a unique, forceful, but self-protective, individual.

This essay attends to that mesh of public with private in the lives of women, so as better to understand how women can lead public lives that make a difference—for example, taking into account private necessities, standards, and analogies that carry over into the public realm. This study joins an active discussion of the permeability and variability over time and within gender of public and private spheres.[2] Women at the turn into the twentieth century were not the first to challenge an assignment to the feminine domestic private sphere that denied women public intellectual expression. For example, Anne K. Mellor argues that romantic women writers (1780–1830) "participated in the *same* discursive public sphere and in the *same* formation of public opinion as did their male peers" (2000, 3). She sees further "the values of the private sphere associated primarily with women—moral virtue and an ethic of care—infiltrating and finally dominating the discursive public sphere during the Romantic era" (11). I would not, however, suggest that early twentieth-century women imported the same ethic into the public sphere, nor did they so straightforwardly support "the emancipatory project of enlightened rationality" that Mellor sees as the project of the Romantic women (142). I have argued elsewhere that there was much more overlap of discursive spaces between the genders and genres than the most polemical sketches of the early twentieth century would suggest.[3]

I find it very much in the spirit of the public intellectual that Arthur Schlesinger, Jr., who to me was the quintessential male public intellectual of the late twentieth century, was the first person to respond to my notice in the *New York Review of Books*, to the effect that I was looking for letters by Rebecca West.[4] The fascination of the reading public with her public and private lives has been reasserted in the recent reviews of *Selected Letters of Rebecca West*. Headlines for these reviews are almost equally divided between ones that cast her in the role of public crusader ("A Glorious Cavalry Charge," "Big Thinks," or "Witness to a Century"), and those that conjure up an outlandish statement regarding her private life ("Devil who ruined my life," "I married a zombie," or "Spurned Lover"). A third category also relates to public life, in that she has left very outspoken, quotable quotes assessing well-known writers, performers, and politicians ("Damned by the Dame," "That Stupid Lout Norman Mailer," and "Ingrid, your husband has no talent"). Notably, these assessments, like many of her book reviews and articles, borrow from the images appropriate to domestic life in order to make public judgments on aesthetics or politics.

For example, in a review that drew his attention, she described H. G. Wells's "sex obsession" in terms of "cold white sauce [that] was merely old maids' mania, the reaction towards the flesh of a mind too long absorbed in airships and colloids" (West 1983, 64). It irritated James Joyce that in the free indirect discourse of her important essay on modernism, "The Strange Necessity," her female protagonist mixes the purchase of stylish hats with her evaluation of Joyce's masterpiece, *Ulysses*.

West's attempts to control biographical accounts of her personal life through letters and other means are understandable, given its early notoriety. Because of her ten-year alliance with H. G. Wells (1913–23), West ran the danger of being forever typecast as "the mistress of H. G. Wells" and the mother of his child (Anthony West, born 1914, when West was 21). The Wells connection continued to haunt her even after she left him and attempted to re-launch her career through an extended lecture tour in the United States (1923–1924). She was treated almost like a celebrity when she arrived in New York, where just off the boat she faced two hours with reporters. One of them wrote what she described as an "impertinent interview—'when asked if she were a literary protégé of Mr Wells she quickly changed the subject'" (West 2000, 65). West's reluctance to have her relationship with Wells paraded before the public persisted throughout her life. At the height of her fame in 1947, when *Time* was doing a feature story on her, West insisted that the magazine withdraw a paragraph identifying Wells as the father of her son Anthony. She used both the newspaper magnate Lord Beaverbrook (veteran of another love affair she preferred to keep private) and the journalist Dorothy Thompson (veteran of a failed marriage with Sinclair Lewis) to bring pressure upon them. One suspects that it was at least partially for her own private reasons that she urged that a biography concerning the public life of H. G. Wells be written only after his death.

West had set out for something quite different from this identification with Wells when, in 1907, at the age of fourteen, and already a veteran of the suffrage activities around Edinburgh, she wrote what was probably her first public missive. This was a letter to the editor of *The Scotsman*, responding to a woman whose earlier letter offered a program that would send wives back into the private sphere, where they would heed the imperial politics of their husbands. Already keenly aware of class difference as it affects women's public versus private labor, this youngest Rebecca directs attention to conditions dangerous to the health of factory women engaged in industries such as the making of chains and white lead. She goes on to urge married women's right to a legal share of their husbands' wages.

While she may challenge the previous correspondent's patriarchal nationalism, she has also begun to forge her own form of national construction, a concern of her public writing that would persist throughout her life.

While still a teenager, West sought a series of public positions. She pursued a career in the theater by enrolling in the Academy of Dramatic Art. West joined the summer school run by the Fabians, where she met George Bernard Shaw, and delivered feminist lectures. She found her way onto the staff of *The Freewoman*, and was particularly influential regarding the presentation of the arts in its reincarnation, *The New Freewoman*. She also wrote regularly for George Blatchford's socialist journal, *The Clarion*,[5] and became part of circles associated with both journals, as well as a playful observer of their foibles. On a more literary front, West met Violet Hunt and Ford Madox Hueffer (later Ford), and participated in their gatherings of young writers. Despite this introduction to coterie modernism, she welcomed a chance to write for profit for the women's page of the *Daily Herald*. She confided to Dora Marsden, "They are tired of baby-clothes, they say, and want 'non-Gospel' talks to women. I fear this means trials for sedition, so I may not long be free" (West 2000, 13). This comment is typical of the sort of rapport she established early with her editors. There is a sense of shared politics, in this case a resistance to public regulation—her threatened "free" existence identified ideologically with Marsden's *Freewoman*.

I would hazard the guess that Rebecca West got into her relationship with H. G. Wells because of his appeal as a public intellectual. She reported to a friend after their first meeting, "I found him one of the most interesting men I have ever met. He talked straight on from 1.15 till 6.30 with immense vitality and a kind of hunger for ideas" (West 2000, 17). To Marsden, she disclosed, "It is fun watching his quick mind splashing about in the infinite" (West 2000, 19). Her life as the mother of his child, some 18 months later, was neither public nor in touch with the infinite. She and Anthony were rusticated from London for the sake of secrecy, Wells already having angered his public with his extramarital affairs. West issued her protest against this existence, even with the comforts of mail-ordered consumer products, to another homebound novelist, Sylvia Lynd: "*I hate domesticity*. . . . I can't imagine any circumstances in which it would be really amusing to order 2 ounces of Lady Betty wool for socks for Anthony, or to try to get a fawn-coloured mail-cart. I want to live an unfettered and adventurous life and spend all my money on buying clothes on Bond Street" (West 2000, 26). Her relationship with Anthony became the greatest disaster of a far from smooth life—occasioning battles that entered the public sphere. They argued primarily over Anthony's sense of lost patrimony—whether Wells's paternity of him was her private matter or his public asset, and whether she had deprived him of financial resources that might have come from Wells. A letter written in late 1917 to S. K. Ratcliffe, a journalist whom she had met in Fabian circles, reveals how difficult it was for her to turn out writing while sharing her life with a child:

> Now for my confession—I can't send you any *New Republic* stuff by the 28th. I have the notes by me, notes chiefly of stuff I handed out to the Fabians two summers ago {& some stuff I wrote a fortnight ago} and it only needs what would be a couple of nights' work, a few connecting paragraphs, compression, and a Beccas big bow wow peroration, and I cannot do it. I never now can sleep till 1, and Anthony wakes me up several times in the night and finally starts singing comic songs and doing conjuring tricks and otherwise hymning the dawn at 6.30. The consequence is that when I put him to bed at 6 I cannot do anything except sit and stare at my work. I am dog-tired. Please don't be angry with me. Remember that since I was twenty I have had exactly seven weeks . . . of the working conditions that people of my age & occupation usually have. In those seven weeks I've done [the] end of my novel and worked off my arrears for the *News* and written this stuff for the *New Republic*—I was glad to find I could still work! (West 2000, 34–35)

West was not reluctant to share with her correspondents the depleting effects of domestic life, particularly as experienced by women writers. One senses that letters such as this one are written out of frustration, but also out of the desire to demonstrate that her heart is in the public realm, and that productivity was important to her survival as an intellect. She also generalized from her individual case. Another letter from this era ends with a list of women writers who have had physical and mental breakdowns of various sorts.

> I believe there is something in the art of literature unsuited to women. Evidence:
>
> G.B. Stern — has a nervous breakdown.
> Sheila Kaye Smith — ” ” ” ”.
> Clemence Dane — ” ” ” ”.
> Olive Wadsley — ” ” ” ”.
> I have — ” ” ” ”.
>
> (West 2000, 29)

West's letters also contribute to the growing documentation of a history of sexual harassment of women in the public sphere. One letter to Sylvia Lynd describes a World War I era tour of Coubitt's shell factory with a guide who gained attention "by placing a damp hand on one's breast" (West 2000, 27). A long letter written from New York to her older sister Letitia Fairfield (who seems to have been very concerned about the family image West might project to the public) told of a dangerous brush with an apparently deranged man. This representative of a film company had earlier discussed the possibility of a film version of her story "Magician of Pell St." He returned to her hotel late at night, and on gaining admission, tried to catch and strangle her. West was so conscious of avoiding a story in the papers that she didn't scream and was saved only by the fact that the man fainted in some sort of a fit. The same letter reports that Charlie Chaplin stalked her through much of California. The pattern continued into her middle years; West described to her husband a long series of unwelcome advances by her otherwise invaluable pressburo guide to Yugoslavia in 1936.

West had carefully orchestrated her return to public life in the early 1920s. By 1921, she had started a column, "Notes on Novels," for the *New Statesman*. As a regular columnist in this and other journals and newspapers, she became a real presence on the intellectual scene, and readers came to look forward to having her voice on a regular basis. Her 1923–24 lecture tour in the United States was both an escape from Wells and a major step into the realm of the public intellectual. Back in London in 1924, she went out of her way to set up a positive British reception of Emma Goldman, who had recently come from Russia. In these negotiations we find her manipulating others with a growing tone of authority, laced with humor. When one of Maxwell Beaverbrook's papers printed an unfavorable account of Goldman, West retorted to him, "not only is Emma Goldman worth six of you (or three of me) but she is the most powerful Anti-Bolsh[evik] eyewitness I have yet encountered. Her effect as an Anti–Bolsh speaker ought to be tremendous" (West 2000, 78). West had begun her lifelong defense of the Western World against communism, claiming Goldman as an ally in promoting her views on international affairs, even as she shaped the British press's reception of Goldman. Interestingly (and part of the anticipated tangle of private with public), she still sought to manipulate Beaverbrook's public expressions (and succeeded), even though she had recently failed in private life as his lover. Indeed, she seems to have developed a manner of strategically playing the public against the private self.

By the mid-1920s, West had syndicated columns on both sides of the Atlantic and agents in both London and New York. Her reviews for *Herald Tribune Books* (edited by Irita Van Doren) began in 1926. These formed part of the notable collection, *The Strange Necessity*, published in 1928. This book (both initially, and in its recuperation in the 1990s) establishes West as an important critic of modernism, wrestling against the public power of T. S. Eliot. Her challenge to the carefully orchestrated early 1920s reception of Joyce's *Ulysses* sparked one of her liveliest public debates ever—a situation in which she took on the Joyce establishment of the day. In a similar pattern, her essays written for the American *Bookman*, as collected in the 1931 volume *Ending in Earnest*, culminate in "Regretfully," a criticism of T. S. Eliot and his affiliation with the humanism of Irving Babbitt and Paul Elmer Moore. She continued the theme in a 1932 review of Eliot's *Selected Essays* in which she takes on even the wisdom of Eliot's now highly celebrated essay, "Tradition and the Individual Talent" for one of its most quoted lines: "Someone said: 'The dead writers are remote from us because we know so much more than they did.' Precisely, and they are that which we know." Working along national lines, she argues that, if anything, English people err in the direction of "ancestor worship" and would never have made the sort of "imbecile remark" that provokes Eliot's pronouncement. "But there are people in the Middle West (though mercifully not many, and in diminishing numbers) who do talk like this. . . . To them, and not to us, Mr. Eliot should address his repetitious formulae" ("What Is Mr. T. S. Eliot's Authority as a Critic?" in Scott 1990, 591).[6]

With her marriage to the international banker Henry Maxwell Andrews in November 1930, West seems to have anticipated domestic tranquility that would sustain her for public life. One explanation provided to her New York agent, George Bye, also shows a typical blend of public and private in the intimate note she strikes with Bye. West declares that Henry "seems to be the nicest man I ever met, barring you, of course, sweetheart—So I've acceded to the suggestion. He says he's going to look after me and let me write, so it ought to be grand" (West 2000, 124). I think that West chose Andrews as a form of relief, following the exhausting period of travel, professional establishment on both sides of the Atlantic, and various romantic skirmishes that characterized the 1920s for her. Henry was interested in architecture and art, spoke numerous languages, dressed fashionably, and had polite manners to offer. His early international experiences, particularly in Germany, gave the couple mutual interests and shared attitudes as they began the 1930s together. Both were children of empire, and his was a family deeply involved in commerce. Born in Burma to parents who identified themselves as British, much of his childhood was spent in Hamburg, Germany, where his father worked in an import-export business. Henry was interned as a civilian prisoner of war in Germany for the duration of World War I. West could sympathize with unhappy aspects of his childhood experience, including a father who succumbed early to Graves' disease. The marriage was long-lasting but satisfying only for five or six years. Henry may have had an early stroke that altered his intellectual capacities and his attraction to Rebecca herself. But she started the 1930s with the sense that her life had entered a more steady and sustainable phase.

As the decade advanced, West took on the role of an experienced investigative journalist and world traveler, with political opinions to offer her native country. Part 3 of *Selected Letters of Rebecca West* begins with 1930 and bears the title, "Ric, Rac, and the Fight against Fascism."[7] West was already recording a negative position on Germany during a 1931 visit to Berlin with Henry. As is typical for West's national constructions, domestic habits provided clues to the public attitudes of the Germans.

> I never loathed any place so much as Berlin. The people have all the bad characteristics of the Scotch without any of their virtues. They have that habit which used to madden you in Scotland—and which I think is found nowhere else in the world—of keeping you out in the street at the garden gate until they pull a lever indoors. They are perpetually in a state of inflamed exaltation over their own common sense and other people's lack of it. This, considering that they have got themselves into the worst scrape the world has ever known and are trying to get everybody who comes along to help them out, is faintly irritating. (West 2000, 127)

The rise of fascism in Germany called for some private initiatives. As early as 1932, she wrote to her friend Ruth Lowinsky in a roundabout effort to find out the fate of a Jewish psychoanalyst, Edith Jacobsen, who had been working in Berlin. Jacobsen was arrested after one of her patients was accused of participating in a communist plot. West's remarks show that she has been consulting various sources for the best strategy, and she arrives at one that again mixes private with public action: "I am told by people who ought to know that the Nazis do not care a fig about exposure in the Press, and that the only way to do anything is to get hold of a 'friend of Germany' and put it to them that the matter is causing a good deal of criticism in England." She wants Ruth to go through this strategy with Enid Bagnold, Lady Jones, wife of the head of Reuters. She is hesitant to act too personally because Henry was at that time in Germany, and might be endangered by her direct action. She ends her letter with a casual extension of personal to national identity, "Pray God we—I meant the Andrews, but we could extend the prayer to England—how can we have anything to do with these cannibals?—soon[er] sever all connection with this horrible country" (West 2000, 135).

By late 1933, Henry was at odds with his employers, the banking firm Schroders. He resigned when they replaced a Jewish employee of his choosing with a Nazi. Writing on May 23, 1934, Rebecca lamented the death of her "great surgeon" in Berlin, a man of "a most angelic character" who was "tortured to suicide by the Nazis, being a Jew" (West 2000, 127). Both Henry and Rebecca were wary of the economic and military exploits of the Germans and concerned themselves increasingly with the welfare of Jews and refugees of various affected nations. Their receptivity to foreign nationals in England was not universally shared. As the thirties progressed, many of West's letters, like her other writing, turned toward cultural and political analysis. West's letters interpret the factions of the Spanish Civil War, and Ireland's position during the war; they record the Italianizing of Albania, a long series of accommodations to Hitler, and wartime conditions in Britain. In 1937, West responded to Nancy Cunard's survey of attitudes on the Spanish Civil War with a letter supporting the Republican government of Spain against Franco and fascism. In 1939 she wrote publicly to *Time and Tide* (where she published regularly throughout her career), debating with Naomi Mitchison about the merits of going to war over fascism; she used the letter to challenge inconsistencies in the "Left-wing," who had endorsed war for the Spanish Republicans, but now seemed disinclined to go to war against Hitler. West shared Mitchison's concerns about the power of privileged capitalists, but saw greater evils in the imperial ambitions of Germany. For her, one of the greatest accomplishments of World War I was that it "prevented the Austrian ambition, explicitly stated ten thousand times, of an Empire stretching to the Black Sea, where Serbs and Bulgars would have been reduced to the same state of subjection as the Bosnians of before the war."[8] West was writing about a part of Europe she had come to know intimately, against the tide of rising fascism.

West had launched into a new phase and direction in her career as a public intellectual when she became affiliated with the recently formed British Council, beginning a series of lecture tours for them in 1935. The most notable of these journeys took her to Yugoslavia in 1936. Her detailed travel letters from a total of three visits there anticipate *Black Lamb and Grey Falcon* (1941)—the work considered by many her masterpiece. She writes to Henry at the end of her first trip to Yugoslavia, "I am much more interested in life here than I am in England; and I feel so ashamed of our national policy. If only we were solid with the French we could have filled this part of the world with light. How frightened they are, poor dears! I wish I could have stayed in Macedonia much longer" (West 2000, 145).

West wrote a long, fussy missive to the British Council summarizing her experience, and suggesting ways they could get their new act together. She recommends that they think more carefully about appealing to specific audiences, some of whom had relatively little training in the English language, and were more interested in folk culture than high literature. Of Zagreb, however, she said, "This is a field worth cultivating, as Zagreb is the nursery of Croat intelligence (which is very considerable) it should be well worth while to send them lecturers to give isolated and (let me reiterate) series of lectures." She recognizes familiar and tragic divisions, even among people who run clubs for those who wish to learn English: "Of course the antagonism between the Serbs and Croats and Slovenes is so great that Dr. Popovic could not be trusted to give advice regarding the whole country. I noticed that he showed the greatest jealousy of the Zagreb Club, and quite unfairly mocked at its cultural pretensions. It is significant that the Zagreb Club is so anti-Serb that it refuses the Government subsidy, and that the Belgrade Club bitterly resents this refusal" (West 2000, 162). She is well aware that the British Council is in the business of propaganda, and she presents strategies to extend British national influence: "I found everywhere that there was a substantial residue left of the pro-English feeling that began in the war; and since the French influence is so rapidly fading there is an appetite for culture and liberalism which will be unsatisfied unless we take steps to fill it. It is a field worth cultivating" (162). She is unsparing of personal details concerning the discomforts and fatigue that arose from the poorly constructed itinerary they had arranged for her, and advises them to defer more to local authorities on travel. The sexual harassment she apparently experienced from one of her native guides is only vaguely, and even playfully, hinted at: "But the young women would have to be chaperoned. It is love that makes the Balkans go round" (West 2000, 162). West was putting the Council on notice that public intellectuals have personal needs.

On return visits to Yugoslavia, West tried to fill in what she had appreciated only in passing on the first tour. This included the performance of religious rituals for Easter and St. George's day, rites of transcendent importance to West's reading of human nature in *Black Lamb and Grey Falcon*—a work that manages not to make an exotic Other of Eastern Europeans. West was keenly aware of political economics. For example, she visited Trepca, a site of mines designed by the British, where valuable zinc and lead deposits were to be mined; these still figure in the real estate value of Kosovo, and are a principal reason why it has been so recently contested.

National identification and even stereotyping of specific national habits and types are recurrent motifs in West's fiction as well as in her letters, as shown earlier. West was fascinated by the cultural diversity of Yugoslavia, and wonders in *Black Lamb and Grey Falcon* "whether they can be organized into an orderly state" (West 1941, 662). She cultivates British resistance to the rise of fascism. In a 1938 letter back to Henry, she expresses her dislike for an Austrian priest who had become "a violent pro-Nazi" and ominously reports hearing that Göring and Hitler "are coming here on a triumphal tour in the autumn" (West 2000, 166). In *Black Lamb and Grey Falcon* she records the German cultural invasion in subtle forms, such as the appearance of German hearts and flowers as elements in the embroideries on sale in Zagreb; she is most blatant in her construction of objectionable characters, based on life models. There is nothing subtle about Gerda, the wife of her Serbian-Jewish guide, a woman whose Eurocentric values do not extend to an appreciation of Eastern European native arts, but turn instead to anything German, even the war monuments.[9]

In letters to her editors at Viking Press, West defends her attacks on Germans for their attitudes toward Slavic culture. In May 1941, she shares with them her worries that "the Germans have led out into Roumania very large numbers of Yugoslav soldiers and boys down to the age of ten. These are presumably to be treated as the young Poles have been treated" (West 2000, 129). Her dedication of *Black Lamb and Grey Falcon* would read, "TO MY FRIENDS IN YUGOSLAVIA, WHO ARE NOW ALL DEAD OR ENSLAVED."

West's concern for Yugoslavia continued, extending to its refugees, some of whom she and Henry housed and supported financially after their flight from fascism. She worked through and after the war attempting to reunite the family of Milan Gavrilovitch (a member of the Yugoslavian government in exile), dispersed on both sides of the Atlantic. In 1938, she tried to settle a German-Jewish specialist on tuberculosis, a relative of her Yugoslavian guide and friend Stanislav Vinaver, in the United States. To this end, she solicited help on immigration strategies from her publisher and friend at Viking Press, Ben Huebsch, who knew about the route through Cuba that worked for a time, provided practical advice about the medical profession, and filtered West's money to her beneficiary. She wrote him in appreciation, "Bless you for what you've done. You are an angel. I cannot sufficiently express my gratitude to you, the poor battered thing would have been hideously on my conscience. Here is another cheque for 250 dollars. When it is spent I'll send another. But could I pay say 1000 dollars a year to some institution to employ him, if that would help him to get into the country?" (West 2000, 167).

In letters and articles, West defended the slain Serbian leader Draza Mihailovitch and expressed her disfavor of Churchill's anointed leader of Yugoslavia, Tito, who she feared would be the agent for Russian domination of Yugoslavia.[10] She used events of the International PEN club to place in the public mind exiled Yugoslavians who left with the Nazi onslaught, and would not return to Yugoslavia, once Tito was ensconced. Ironically, considering West's opposition to communism and Tito, it was under his regime that the contentious cultural groups in Yugoslavia did function together after the Nazis came and went.

We would do well to study more carefully West's construction of ideas of the nation, to understand how national identification may be inflected by gender, and how it may serve or be served by a private self. Earlier, we touched briefly on West's response to Naomi Mitchison's form of pacifism, as debated in *Time and Tide* in 1939. There are numerous comparisons and contrasts to be struck with the much better known pacifism of Virginia Woolf, who has become such a centerpiece for feminism of the 1930s.[11] With her 1938 work, *Three Guineas*, Woolf affiliates herself with an "outsider's society," rather than with a nation that denied her "an education or any share in its possessions" (Woolf 1966, 108). Woolf, like West, sees connections between private and public life, and she endorses the importance of importing insights from the private realm into public policy. This she dramatizes by situating her persona in the realm of a private woman writing to public man, "Had you not believed that human nature, the reasons, the emotions of the ordinary man and woman, lead to war, you would not have written asking for our help" (6). She, like West, builds upon feminism to challenge fascism, though here she makes a real challenge of her analogy: "'Feminists' were in fact the advance guard of your own movement. They were fighting the same enemy as you were and for the same reasons. They were fighting the tyranny of the patriarchal state as you are fighting the tyranny of the Fascist state" (102). Playing around the edges of national identification, Woolf's persona avows (now famously) that, "as a woman, I have no country. As a woman I want no country," ending remarkably "as a woman my country is the whole world" (109). There remains a suggestion of Englishness that she classifies as emotional and identifies with early private life: "still some obstinate emotion remains, some love of England dropped into a child's ears by the cawing of rooks in an elm tree, by the splash of waves on a beach, or by English voices murmuring nursery rhymes." But this does not lead her to West's sort of thinking—arguments that would have Britain cultivate a foreign field such as Zagreb, suggested in her reports back from Yugoslavia, or wars of containment that she justified to Mitchison. Woolf's faint nationalism would be expressed "to give to England first what she desires of peace and freedom for the whole world" (109).

West was no more the recipient of a prestigious education than was Woolf, though she trusted in her ability to find things out as an investigative journalist, and blasted educated young men who challenged her facts. Perhaps she realized that the great universities didn't teach what she needed to know for her kind of work. West was no pacifist and publicly allied herself with people in government, including those who worked in war ministries and the diplomatic service. Writing to the American drama critic Alexander Woollcott in May 1940, she comes across as both physically and mentally intense, not the least bit feminine in defining her "we," and dangerous to any invader: "We are all going about our business, with one eye on the map and a certain amount of curious feeling about the bowels. I have never felt so coldly ferocious in my life, and optimistically carry a couple of linoleum knives wherever I go" (West 2000, 172). Debating national issues with Stoyan Pribicevic, who favored Tito, West enters a discussion of what a nation owes to a person, and vice versa. Here West expresses a strong sense of obligation, in both directions: "A nation cannot disown its sons by any theory of international law if it recognizes law at all" (193). Pribicevic's refusal of military service, in her mind, comes close to "disowning your country" (193). Interestingly, West writes selectively, perhaps with her male audience in mind, with the gendered inflection of "sons."

West's politics after World War II have been assigned fairly universally to a conservative category. Over affiliations to nation and law, she was already more conservative than Woolf and Mitchison in the 1930s. After the war, one of West's first assignments was to the Nuremberg trials (1946), journalism now overshadowed in biographical accounts by her last love affair, with the justice Francis Biddle.[12] Margaret Stetz offers one recent exception to this is. She argues that West's public account of the trials, and the ambivalences she felt, had lasting private effects, perhaps even occasioning writer's block. Nuremberg "became part of her intellectual constitution and moral framework," entangling her personal history in the public events she witnessed (Stetz 2001, 230). In the 1950s, West took to writing regularly on treason, spies, and the dangers of communism, ostensibly to uphold the order of nations. Building on the understanding of the United States she had begun to cultivate in the 1920s, and making the most of her contacts with American investigative journalists such as Dorothy Thompson, she began a new phase as a trans-Atlantic public intellectual. Her research on American congressional committees and their investigations of supposed communist activities was initiated to promote better understanding of America among her British readers.

West did not see herself as conservative. When J. B. Priestley, like many others including Arthur Schlesinger, Jr., suspected her of McCarthyism, she objected that "I am afraid I am the last liberal left" (West 2000, 297). If so, her liberalism was as unique as her construction of herself as a public intellectual. One of my favorite reviews of the *Selected Letters* labeled her a "conservative rebel"—a simple statement of her seeming contradictions, in public as well as private pronouncements, and fitting for one who would remake but preserve the concept of nations. West was certainly not a narrow nationalist, but she did believe that orderly, democratic states allowed people a measure of freedom and material resources to flourish spiritually and creatively in private life. She sought to bring these conditions back to people who had lost them.

Notes

1. I have estimated that West wrote 10,000 letters; slightly fewer than 300 could be contained in my edition of West's letters, though in selecting and collecting them I have read and transcribed many more.

2. Starting with Jurgen Habermas's *The Structural Transformation of the Public Sphere*, feminists have challenged his view on women's participation, and have proposed additional configurations, such as Rita Felski's "counter" public sphere, proposed in *Beyond Feminist Aesthetics*. See Mellor (2000, 1–3) for a recent summary.

3. See Scott 1995a, chapter 11, "Becoming Professionals," especially 225–27.

4. Jane Marcus has repeatedly invoked the name of public intellectual for West, Nancy Cunard, Virginia Woolf, and others of their generation, both in the conference where this paper originally appeared and in other venues. Historian, biographer, and upholder of liberal values, Schlesinger was special assistant to President John F. Kennedy and regularly used his capacity as a reviewer for *The New York Review of Books* to write political commentary. If we were concerned with the 1950s, Schlesinger's debates with

West over communism, which began their relationship, would be a more central concern. In the interval between the writing and the publishing of this essay, Schlesinger has passed away, but his good will toward scholarship on West has lasting expression.

5. This era of West's public life is represented in *The Young Rebecca: Writings of Rebecca West, 1911–1917*, collected and edited by Jane Marcus, (1983).

6. West's essay "What Is Mr. T. S. Eliot's Authority as a Critic?" holds a valuable, revisionary place in Scott's *The Gender of Modernism* (1990).

7. Ric and Rac were pet names used by Rebecca (Rac) and Henry (Ric).

8. Regrettably, this letter to *Time and Tide* was one of many left on the cutting room floor when the final draft of *Selected Letters* was cut to specifications. See Lassner (1998) for another summary of West's debates with Mitchison, and a more thorough treatment of Mitchison's views of fascism and war.

9. See Scott 1995b (154–55) for a more extensive discussion of Gerda and other German presences in the text.

10. In 1945, West had a spirited exchange with a Yugoslav exile, Stoyan Pribicevic (West 2000, 192–93), who had written a negative review of *Black Lamb and Grey Falcon*, and in later correspondence sought to gain West's support for Tito's administration of Yugoslavia. She objects to his line, "It is facile to be a friend of Yugoslavia when your personal friends are in power" but more of a challenge "to be a friend of Yugoslavia when your personal enemies are in power." She cannot see Tito as a personal friend or enemy and retorts: "I require no reminder that it is necessary to differentiate between a country and its regime and have often done so in the case of my own." What lies beneath the dispute is a sense that the "personal" can enter into the political, and into political judgments.

11. See Lassner 1998 (4–6) for an analysis of the effect of centering feminist discussion of war on Woolf's now canonical *Three Guineas*.

12. Carl Rollyson does ably summarize West's article (republished as "Greenhouse with Cyclamens" in *A Train of Powder*) as "the story of the German imagination, of its penchant for fairy tales and overbuilding, its Wagnerian dreams of grandeur, which contributed to the excesses of Nazism" (Rollyson 1995, 220). The bulk of his chapter, however, goes to the Biddle affair.

Works Cited

Lassner, Phyllis. 1998. *British Women Writers of World War II: Backgrounds of Their Own*. Basingstoke, UK: Macmillan; New York: St. Martin's Press.

Mellor, Anne K. 2000. *Mothers of the Nation: Women's Political Writing in England, 1780–1830*. Bloomington: Indiana University Press.

Rollyson, Carl. 1995. *Rebecca West: A Saga of the Century*. London: Hodder and Stoughton.

Scott, Bonnie Kime, ed. 1990. *The Gender of Modernism*. Bloomington: Indiana University Press.

———, 1995a. *Refiguring Modernism, Vol. 1: Women of 1928*. Bloomington: Indiana University Press.

———. 1995b. *Refiguring Modernism, Vol. 2: Postmodern, Feminist Readings of Woolf, West, and Barnes*. Bloomington: Indiana University Press.

Stetz, Margaret D. 2001. Rebecca West and the Nuremberg Trials. *Peace Review* 13.2: 229–35.

Wagner-Martin, Linda. 1994. *Telling Women's Lives: The New Biography*. New Brunswick, NJ: Rutgers University Press.

———. 1931. *Ending in Earnest: A Literary Log by Rebecca West*, Garden City, New York: Doubleday.

West, Rebecca. 1939. November 18 Letter. *Time and Tide* 20: 1466–1467.

———. 1941. *Black Lamb and Grey Falcon*. New York: Viking.

———. 1983. *The Young Rebecca: Writings of Rebecca West, 1911–1917*. Edited by Jane Marcus. London: Virago.

———. 1987. *The Strange Necessity: Essays and Reviews*. London: Virago.

———. 2000. *Selected Letters of Rebecca West*. Edited by Bonnie Kime Scott. New Haven, CT: Yale University Press.

Woolf, Virginia. 1966. *Three Guineas*. New York: Harcourt Brace and World.

Modernist Melancholy: Edith Sitwell's Black Sun

JEAN RADFORD

> The English aristocrat, six feet tall, aquiline, haughty, dressed in long robes and wearing barbaric ornaments, was a strange sight in happy-go-lucky Montparnasse.
>
> —Bowen, *Dawn from Life*

EDITH SITWELL MIGHT SEEM AN UNLIKELY FIGURE FOR FEMINIST RE-cuperation. Made a Dame of the British Empire in 1954 and awarded no less than four honorary doctorates, she was extensively photographed by Cecil Beaton and painted by Alvaro Guevara, Nina Hamnett, Roger Fry, Wyndham Lewis, and Pavel Tchelitchew, whose 1927 portrait of her is in the National Portrait Gallery. Although recognized by the Establishment in later life, she was an ambiguous figure for many of her contemporaries: burlesqued by Noël Coward as "the poetess Hernia Whittlebot" of the Swiss Family Whittlebot, satirized by Wyndham Lewis in *The Apes of God*, and made the butt of jokes by the "Auden Generation." She was admired by Yeats, who compared her with Swift, but dismissed by the Cambridge critic F. R. Leavis, who claimed that the Sitwells "belong more to the history of publicity rather than the history of poetry" (1932, 64). Leavis's comment proved prophetic, a self-fulfilling prophecy perhaps, for her work has escaped canonization. Sitwell is absent from most modernist syllabi and only a handful of her poems survive in anthologies—alongside the image of her as "an icon of eccentricity" (Bennett 1996, 95–96).

Without giving ground to Leavisite dichotomies, or to what Sitwell called "the sandy desert of Dr Leavis's mind" (1934, 30), one could argue that Edith Sitwell belongs to both—to the history of poetry and to the history of publicity. What we might now call a "performance artist." Like her brother Osbert, she used the newspapers and journals of the period to conduct elaborate literary feuds, positioning herself as the champion of the avant-garde and/or the victim of philistine reviewers. She was both David and Goliath. Her reactions to the work of her contemporaries could be effusively generous or outrageously dismissive. Flamboyant in print and in person, she believed in keeping up appearances; her "façade" was important to her—one of the things she shared with Nancy Cunard and many other women writers of the twenties and thirties. Her stylized appearance—the turbans, the enormous rings she wore on her hands, and the brocade frocks that she had made up for her from furnishing materials—have become legendary. Yet in her lifetime, she was not just a painted lady nor an English eccentric; she was also a woman of the Left Bank who, as Shari Benstock points out, was one of the first to use the term "modernist" and to insist on the distinctive nature of women's art: "Art is magic, not logic. This craze for the logical spirit in irrational shape is part of the present harmful mania for uniformity—in an age when women try to abolish the differences between their aspects and aims and those of men" (quoted in Benstock 1987, 33–34).

Edith Louisa Sitwell (1887–1964) was a co-founder with Nancy Cunard and Iris Tree of *Wheels*, the anti-Georgian poetry magazine published between 1916 and 1921. Her collection *Façade*, set to music by William Walton, was first performed with her brothers Osbert and Sacheverell Sitwell in 1922, the same year that *The Waste Land* appeared. She published three further volumes of poetry before her radical epic poem *Gold Coast Customs* appeared in 1929. *Gold Coast Customs* is a lengthy attack in drumbeat rhythm on London's postwar society, comparing its fashionable parties to human sacrifice rituals of nineteenth-century Ashantee societies. The treatment of civilization and barbarism links it with Walter Benjamin's claim that "[t]here is no document of civilization which is not at the same time a document of barbarism" (1970, 258). By the end of the twenties, she was widely known for her attack on traditional metrics and her attempt to adapt poetry to the musical rhythms of jazz and modern dance. Throughout the thirties, although producing little new poetry, she continued her role as an energetic polemicist and publicist for the modern arts and editor of several major anthologies. She wrote numerous articles for popular as well as high literary journals—the *Yorkshire Post*, *Vogue*, and *Harper's Bazaar*—in addition to *Time and Tide* and *Life and Letters Today*. She also produced a number of prose works in order to support herself and her companion, Helen Rootham. During and after the Second World War, Sitwell began a new phase of poetic activity, producing some of her best known poems, such as "Still Falls the Rain," "A Song of the Dust," and her *Poems of the Atomic Age*.

Signs of renewed interest in her poetry suggest it may be time to reread her only novel despite the verdict reached by one contemporary reviewer that "Miss Sitwell is a delightful poet, but she is decidedly not a novelist" (Shawe-Taylor 1937).[1] *I Live Under a Black Sun*, which I want to consider in this essay, was published by Victor Gollancz in September 1937, four months after Virginia Woolf's *The Years*—with which it is compared on the original dust jacket. Although there were several subsequent editions, it is currently out of print. Written between her two major poetic periods in the 1920s and 1940s, the novel sheds significant light on the development of a woman poet. As Jack Lindsay suggests, it can be seen as a reworking of *Gold Coast Customs* and a "rough quarry" for her later Post Atomic poems (1968, 78). The novel is therefore of interest to all those concerned with Sitwell as a modernist poet.

There are, however, other reasons to put *I Live Under a Black Sun* back into circulation and into dialogue with novels and poetry about the First World War, as well as with the essays and fiction of the 1930s. The passionate antimilitarism of the *Wheels* poets is here deployed on a broader canvas to address questions about power, authority, and the nature of fascism. For *I Live* is not only a biographical fiction about the life of Jonathan Swift, and a powerful (autobiographical) meditation on mourning and melancholia, it is also a political allegory that, I want to argue, anticipates the arguments on masculinism and war made by Virginia Woolf in *Three Guineas* (1938), and has structural similarities to Djuna Barnes's *Nightwood* (1936). My detailed examination of the similarities and differences between these interwar narratives enables us to reevaluate our orthodoxies about this period. Putting neglected, noncanonical writings back into dialogue with the now familiar texts *Three Guineas* and *Nightwood* also enhances our understanding of the relations between literature and history.

Swift Modernized

"Swift was power gone mad" (Sitwell 1997, 208–9).

Sitwell often recycled her own writings—and sometimes those of others.[2] She had already written a chapter on Jonathan Swift in her biography of Alexander Pope (1930); in *I Live Under a Black Sun* she re-presents some of that material in new form. In the novel, Swift's letters and writings are quoted together with comments by his biographers, notably Johnson in his *Lives of the English Poets.* Johnson's presentation of Swift's love relationships with Esther Johnson and Esther Vanhomrigh (the "Stella" and "Vanessa" of Swift's writings)[3] is sandwiched into an account of Swift's political career—his move from Whig to Tory, his important role in the Irish question—and it ends with a consideration of his literary work. Sitwell, on the other hand, focuses primarily on Swift's relations with women. Moreover, she deletes the politics of eighteenth-century England and replaces them with the politics of twentieth-century Europe. Sitwell's story of Jonathan Swift (renamed Jonathan Hare) and his relationships with Stella (Anna) and Vanessa (Essy) is set in 1914 at the outbreak of World War I and during its aftermath. The two epigraphs to the novel, from *Troilus and Cressida* and Nadezhda Krupskaya's *Memories of Lenin*, suggest Sitwell's double intention: to present an old love story and a new social critique.

The modernized Swift story is cross-cut with the story of a young girl, Susan Daw, whose lover, Jim Noon, is killed in the Great War. On a pilgrimage to his grave in France, Susan meets and falls in love with his killer, the German soldier Hans Orthoven. The plot of this storyline resembles that of Wilfred Owen's poem "Strange Meeting," published in the fourth issue of *Wheels*, with important differences. Owen's strange meeting is between two men, both combatants, and the horror and pity of war evoked in the poem ends with their homoerotic reconciliation in death. In *I Live*, a similar scene takes place:

> He [Orthoven] said: "I was blackened by my hate. But then, in that long night, when the hating men and the men who were mad with fear had retreated, and we were left on the field, the boy who was dying and I with my wound that was less than the wound in my soul, hate died—died as if it had never been born, and love came in its place. I loved and forgave mankind. For this boy whom I had killed, as he lay in my arms, suddenly it was my child that lay there, my child that was murdered by a man as foolish and as blind as me. He had come back to me." (1937, 270–71).

As in Owen's poem, Orthoven's love overcomes hatred, leading to a new recognition of the other as "a man as foolish and as blind as me." But Sitwell adds an element of maternal love, with the "hating men" giving way to a kind of *deposition* that becomes a *pieta.* Sitwell's narrative then takes the story further, allowing the survivors, Orthoven and Susan Daw, to overcome hatred and celebrate their love, for each other and the dead man, in marriage. The story of their marriage is used to contrast with the main plot and Hare/Swift's refusal of marriage and human sexuality: "To love, as human beings love, appeared to him as a form of physical decay, was, as he had said, to 'ruin oneself out of a maggot'" (1937, 56). For in Jonathan Hare's relation to women, love takes the form of domination: "Throughout his life it had been his need to inhabit another being, conquer the will of another, remake the world of another personality, seeing in this victory a symbol of destiny overcome, the universe moulded to his will" (1937, 16). What is overcome is not hatred but the will of the other, "a symbol of destiny" itself. Hatred, for Hare, is not the opposite of love, rather it is another source of power—whether for good or evil—which he is unwilling to relinquish. After the betrayal and death of both women, Hare (like Swift) is left in a state of increasing melancholy, unable to mourn: "He was alone for ever. And in the years that followed, slowly, gradually, his flesh changed into stone, until he became like the eyeless statue of a giant in an immense and tropical forest" (1937, 388). Sitwell uses the story of Swift's final paralysis and madness to stage her own beliefs, already evident in her early poetry: spirit and body are one, and the will to power, unredeemed by human love, will petrify the most gigantic of gifts. The contrasting images of stone and forest used in this passage echo the stone–stream opposition in Yeats's "Easter 1916" and perhaps also recall Blake's poem, "The clod and the pebble." The imagery underlines the contrasts set up in the two plot lines which pose two, very Blakean, kinds of love in a clear-cut opposition.[4] This opposition is complicated, however, by the use of the black sun image to denote not only hatred and domination but also loss, melancholy, and madness.

The "black sun" in the title of the novel is taken from a line in Gerard de Nerval's poem "El Desdichado" ["The Disinherited"] from *Les Chimères*, first published in 1853:

> Je suis le ténébreux,—le veuf,—l'inconsolé,
> Le prince d'Aquitaine à la tour abolie;
> Ma seule étoile est morte,—et mon luth constellé
> Porte le *Soleil noir* de la *Mélancolie*.
>
> [I am the brooding shadow,—the bereaved,—the unconsoled,
> Aquitaine's prince of the doomed tower;
> My only *Star* is dead and my astral lute
> Bears the *black sun* of *melancholy*.][5]

According to Sitwell's biographer, she had considered calling the novel *Black Sun, Dark Sun* or *Nowhere to Go* before settling on the rather cumbrous *I Live Under a Black Sun* (Glendinning 1981, 207). Suns—gold, white, and black—were already part of Sitwell's repertoire of poetic symbols, but the reference to de Nerval serves to emphasize the link to melancholy. Further, I would argue that de Nerval's sonnet provides not only the title but in some sense the structure for Edith Sitwell's novel. As various commentators on de Nerval have noted, the problem with "*El Desdichado*" is not to decide what is being said but to decide where the emphasis lies. The statements made in the poem are plain, but the relations between those statements are not, because the logical connections between the parts are not made clear by grammatical links.[6] This might also be said of Sitwell's novel, which is a collage of quotations taken from Swift (some modernized, some not), poetic descriptions of nature, and imagery drawn from Owen, Eliot, Lawrence, and other contemporaries. The result is a generic mix, a montage of pastoral, letters, romance, war fiction, jeremiad, satire, and social protest. "The final impression left by Edith's novel is one of confusion of intent and execution" according to Victoria Glendinning: "Prophetic utterances, social observation, rustic flights of fancy, psychological insights, modern sensibilities, twentieth-century events, eighteenth-century usages and quotations, have the reader constantly adjusting his viewfinder" (1981, 210). This comment, although accurate enough, implicitly demands a unity and coherence absent from many modernist narratives that employ a shifting viewpoint. Victoria Glendinning also contrasts the reception and reputation of *I Live Under a Black Sun* with that of Djuna Barnes's comparably "confused" work *Nightwood*: "It [*I Live*] achieved a minor *succès d'estime*—but not as great or as lasting a one as that enjoyed, for example, by *Nightwood*, by Charles Henri Ford's friend Djuna Barnes, which had been published the previous year with an introduction by T. S. Eliot" (1981, 207). Glendinning does not say whether Sitwell had read Barnes's novel, but her comment is suggestive. Eliot, whose poetry Sitwell had promoted and whom she knew well, not only introduced but, notoriously, edited *Nightwood* to half its original length, whereas *I Live Under a Black Sun* is a long unwieldy book, published without benefit of T. S. Eliot's editorial interventions.[7] Charles Henri Ford, Barnes's onetime friend and lover, then became the lover of Pavel Tchelitchew, the Russian painter whom Sitwell loved and whom she uses as the model for the Swift figure in *I Live*. Beyond the tangled web of common friends (Eliot, Ford, and Gertrude Stein, among others) and the common theme of melancholy, there are some important parallels between the two novels. Each represents the working through of the failure or loss of love; each can be read as an allegory of Europe between the wars; each exhibits what Joseph Frank called "spatial form," where the structure depends on a juxtaposition of images rather than a sequence of narrative events; and both explore the bestialization of the human, when the specifically human powers of love and knowledge are perverted into what Sitwell called "power gone mad."[8]

Mourning and Melancholia

> A lady asked me why, on most occasions, I wore black.
> "Are you in mourning?"
> "Yes."
> "For whom are you in mourning?"
> "For the world." (Sitwell 1965, 17)

Although Hal Foster in *The Return of the Real* (1996) claims paranoia as the characteristic of the modernist period, similar claims might be made for melancholy or melancholia. Melancholy is no longer just "the Elizabethan malady," as Lawrence Babb called it, left behind by Enlightenment narratives of progress and reason, it is arguably also the malady of Modernity. In his study of the early French modernists Gérard de Nerval and Charles Baudelaire, Ross Chambers argues, for example, that "the identity of the melancholic . . . has become the truth of modernism" (1993, 208).[9] The identity of the melancholic is central to *I Live* and *Nightwood*, both of which, it seems to me, are studies of melancholy that are also attempts to inaugurate mourning. Barnes's friend, John Holms called *Nightwood* "a second *Anatomy of Melancholy*," a compliment since Robert Burton's book (1621) and Sir Thomas Browne's *Religio Medici* (1643) were Barnes's two favorite books (Herring 1996, 204, 219).

Sitwell's restaging of the Swift-Stella-Vanessa story in the midst of the losses and bereavements of the First World War presents a gallery of melancholics—a set of case studies that refuses to privilege a single view of melancholy. Like *Nightwood*, *I Live Under a Black Sun* focuses not on a single, culturally privileged form of melancholia embodied in a creative male subject—as Freud arguably does in his use of Hamlet in *Mourning and Melancholia*. For Dr. Matthew O'Connor in *Nightwood* and Jonathan Hare in *I Live* are presented in relation to a number of female figures: Robin Vote, Nora Flood, and Jenny Petheridge in *Nightwood* and Mrs. Noon, Susan Daw, Anna, and Essy in *I Live*. The cross-cutting of figures and images in these two texts has a number of significant effects, two of which concern me here. First, it poses melancholia not just as an individual pathology but also as a condition that may be experienced, in different ways, by all human subjects. Second, the multiplication of examples is used to characterize the interwar period as one of crisis and loss.

The novel also raises issues about the gendering of melancholy similar to those raised by Julia Kristeva.[10] For her analysis of melancholia, Kristeva takes the same line from Nerval's poem that Sitwell takes for her title. *Black Sun: Depression and Melancholia* is the third of Kristeva's trilogy of 1980s writings: *Powers of Horror* (1980), *Tales of Love* (1983), and *Black Sun* (1989). In the latter, her essays on Holbein, de Nerval, Dostoevsky, and Duras consider the ways in which the work of art may function as a work of mourning. As Kelly Oliver has convincingly argued, Kristeva's *Black Sun* is in some sense an autobiographical work (1993, 143), as, I shall argue, is Sitwell's *I Live Under a Black Sun*. Kristeva's *Black Sun* continues the emphasis on the subject's need for separation from the mother already treated in the theory of abjection in *Powers of Horror*. For the subject to come into being and enter the symbolic involves the repudiation of the mother, of the not-me. This problematic differentiation of the self in *Black Sun* necessarily involves matricide: "For man and for woman the loss of the mother is a biological and psychic necessity, the first step on the way to becoming autonomous. Matricide is our vital necessity, the *sine-qua-non* condition of our individuation" (1989, 27–28). Once separation is accomplished, mourning can take place. However, following Freud, Kristeva argues that should this process not take place, or the mourning be incomplete, "a depressive and melancholic putting to death of the subject is what follows"(28), which may lead to self-hatred, asymbolism, linguistic retardation, and, in extreme cases, suicide. Further, she goes on to claim that this matricidal process is for women "more difficult, if not impossible" (29), leading to the supposition that depression or the melancholic position is essentially the lot of women.[11] In Kristeva's theory, separation or the loss of the love object in adult life may trigger a repetition of the earlier trauma. In Sitwell's representation, the melancholy states experienced by both Anna and Essy do involve self-hatred and, although neither commits suicide, their deaths are precipitated by Hare's rejection/betrayal. Again, according to Kristeva, psychoanalysis, or the work of art that can transport the unnameable, pre-objectal Thing of the lost maternal relation into signification, acts as a counterdepressive. This aspect of her theory is relevant to both Sitwell's and Barnes's novels, which represent, among other things, attempts at mourning a lost object. As Djuna Barnes famously said of *Nightwood*, it was by writing it that she was able to come to terms with the loss of her lover, Thelma Wood: "I love what I have invented as much as that which fate gave me—a great danger for the writer perhaps. . . . I came to love my invention more—so am able—perhaps—only so able—to put Thelma aside—because now she is not Robin" (quoted in Herring 1996, 217).[12] Sitwell's comment on the writing of *I Live* acknowledges a similarly personal imperative. She writes, "I felt as if I had been through an earthquake, after I had written it" (1997, 208). One of her biographers, Geoffrey Elborn, calls the novel "a therapeutic, if painful, look at Edith's private feelings . . . a self-analysis" (1981, 133). (Its autobiographical content is also apparent in the portrait of her father as Sir Henry Rotherham, which is repeated word for word in Sitwell's autobiography *Taken Care Of* [1965, 24].) Sitwell's own experience of rejected love and separation from the loved object is split between the two characters of Anna and Essy: the melancholy self-sacrifice of the one and the violent despair of the other. Their abandonment and desolation is paralleled, through a series of freeze-frames at the end of each section, with that of the mother who loses her son in the First World War and with the final images of Hare's madness.

Sitwell's portrait of Jonathan Swift as Jonathan Hare is at the same time also a portrait of Pavel Tchelitchew the twentieth-century painter, for there were, as Glendinning points out, remarkable similarities between Tchelitchew's relations to women and those of Swift (1981, 209). *I Live* is driven, at least in part, by Sitwell's need to understand and come to terms with Tchelitchew's rejection of her as a woman through the characterization of Hare/Swift:

> How could he know or endure a mortal love, he who knew the odour of mortality arising from the most beautiful breast, as if it were already corrupted, seeing the rankness of all human nature, the terror of Nature, and her monstrous breasts in whose shadow he must lie as he would lie in some vast plain beneath the shadow of two hills, or on whose peaks he must be exposed to the light until the world died.
>
> Womanhood was to him a symbol of Nature, a monstrous creative force that, in order that it might create, was willing to destroy all previous life and forms of creation—a force more terrible when it was overlaid with civilisation than when it was rank and naked. "They would often," he said of these giantesses of Brodingnagia, "lay me at full length to their bosoms; wherewith I was much disgusted, because, to say the truth, a very offensive smell came from their skins." (1937, 55–56)

In standard accounts of Swift, his refusal to commit himself to either Stella or Esther Vanhomrigh is explained by his knowledge that he has hereditary madness. But Sitwell, by quoting Gulliver's disgust in the passage above, suggests another explanation. As Kristeva points out, because the dominant representations of woman are as *mother*, the necessary repudiation of the mother may slide into the repudiation of the feminine—of woman as such. The abjection of the mother ("her monstrous breasts") becomes the abjection of all women ("the most beautiful breast"). And this, I think, is what Sitwell's characterization of the Hare/Swift/Tchelitchew figure is about. Hare's inability to commit himself to either Anna or Essy—his need to retain his autonomy—is presented as a "psychic necessity": "I am what I am . . . I am what I am . . ." he repeats at the end of the novel (1937, 397). His cruelty to others is a defense of self. His fear of human love and his need for power make him a tragic as well as a destructive figure. Thus Sitwell's novel presents not only the horror and pity of war, but the horror and pity involved in men and women's relationships.

Again like *Nightwood*, *I Live Under a Black Sun*, I want to argue next, is not only an acute self-analysis and a working through of personal losses; it can also be read as a social analysis of what Virginia Woolf called "the black night that now covers Europe." For as Jane Marcus points out, too often "Sitwell's class origins, like those of Nancy Cunard and until recently, those of Virginia Woolf, have obscured their social critique" (Marcus, "Outlaws").

A Political Allegory

Although some of her early poetry ("I was always a little outside life") suggests that Sitwell could have become a paid-up member of Virginia Woolf's society of outsiders, she remained outside any particular organization. In general she held the view that art should remain distinct from politics and "felt baffled by what she called the Mechanism of Politics" (Lindsay 1968, 72). Like her friend Stella Bowen, who was described as being "basically apolitical," she was "not unusual in being a pacifist in the First World War nor in wishing to fight the Nazis in the Second" (Bowen 1987, viii). One of her biographers seems to take a similar view of Sitwell as apolitical when she claims, "Edith's only politics were personal politics" (Glendinning 1981, 171). Sitwell may not have been confident about her grasp of politics, and certainly distrusted party politics, but she was not—in my view—apolitical.

Her aristocratic identifications did not prevent her, for example, from making extensive use of Engels' *The Condition of the Working Class in En-*

gland in 1844 to depict Victorian conditions in her *Victoria of England* (1936). Her response to the hunger marches and the homelessness she had seen on the streets of London and Sheffield is written into both *Gold Coast Customs* and *I Live Under a Black Sun*. When Susan Daw sleeps out on the Embankment, Sitwell uses the scene to launch a lamentation on cold, hunger, homelessness, and the "howling contrasts" between England's "two nations," one rich, and one poor. While she may well have learned the politics of race from her early friendship with Nancy Cunard, those politics survived when the friendship foundered; in the McCarthyite fifties, for example, she made strenuous attempts, against the advice of friends, to appear on the same platform with Paul Robeson in the United States (Lindsay 1968, 73–74).

Her prompt opposition to anti-Semitism in Germany is registered in a letter to a Jewish friend, Charlotte Haldane, written in December 1933: "Indeed you are right in speaking of the primal horror of Germany at present. It makes my blood boil. . . . So apart from the rage and horror I feel in the cruelty of the Nazis, I understand the cretinism of it all. . . . But do not fear, dear Charlotte, that such outrages against decency and sense will ever occur in England. We know too well what our Jewish citizens have done for us. But I know the anguish you must feel in contemplating Germany" (quoted in Glendinning 1981, 188, 297, 208). Her "personal politics"—friendship, the desire to comfort, rage and horror at all forms of cruelty—in this letter are explicitly linked with the traditional liberal values of "decency and sense." However inadequate one might find those terms, to hold thosc personal values with any seriousness in the 1930s during the period of the Popular Front was to make a political choice.[13] Unlike Cunard, Sitwell was not a political activist, but she did try to activate her antifascist politics in allegorical form.

For Sitwell repeatedly claimed that *I Live Under a Black Sun* was an allegory. Sending a copy of the novel "with some trepidation" to E. M. Forster in 1939 she wrote: "But I beg you to believe that I don't consider it a novel. It is an allegory." Again in the same year, writing to Raymond Marriott, she claimed: "It is an allegory, in a sense. . . . The reason I put Swift into modern clothes is because the spirit of the modern world is power gone mad. And Swift was power gone mad" (Sitwell 1997, 208–9). The novel can also be read as an allegorical treatment of Sitwell's personal situation, with Swift's need for power standing for Tchelitchew's (and perhaps her own) power-driven search for recognition. Moreover, the comment on the "modern world" as "power gone mad" suggests that she saw it as an allegory in yet another sense—the sense argued by Walter

Benjamin, who links allegory to melancholy by claiming that allegory is an *historical* response to destruction: "Whereas in the symbol destruction is idealized and the transfigured face of nature is fleetingly revealed in the light of redemption, in allegory the observer is confronted with the *facies hyppocratica* of history as a petrified, primordial landscape. Everything about history that has been untimely, sorrowful, unsuccessful, is expressed in a face—or rather in a death's head" (1977, 166).

Kristeva's analysis of mourning and melancholia is a psychoanalytic one and except for references to "Western modernity" largely unhistoricized. But at key points in her *Black Sun,* she cites Walter Benjamin's very different analysis of melancholy. In Benjamin's *Origins of German Tragic Drama* (1928), he develops a theory of allegory and melancholy specifically around his analysis of the German mourning-play (the baroque *Trauerspiel*) where the allegorical impulse arises from a country devastated by decades of war—for Benjamin an obvious analogy with Weimar, but which is also relevant to Sitwell's treatment of the First World War. For Benjamin, it is allegory that best achieves melancholy tensions (1977, 232–33); melancholia is always related to a "crisis in values," a crisis of meaning brought about by war and modernity. Starting from the fragments and ruins which history provides, allegory assembles them, gives them new meaning, and so by thus constructing these as an object of "knowledge," brings the possibility of redeeming them.

One of Benjamin's key moves in *The Origin of German Tragic Drama* is to take the opposition between symbol and allegory as set up in Romantic criticism (notably by Goethe and Coleridge), and reverse their values. In Romantic criticism, the symbol is organic and poetic (and for Coleridge, unconscious), whereas allegory is arbitrary, a series of imposed equivalences. Benjamin's preference for allegory over symbol in the *Trauerspiel* relates precisely to this "arbitrariness," to the fact that in post-Saussurean terms the relation between the signifier and signified is NOT organic, but humanly, linguistically constructed, so that "any person, any object, any relationship can mean absolutely anything else" (1977, 175). The "arbitrariness" allows one to see that war—or any other event in human history—is not inevitable but is humanly constructed and that, to cut a long and intricate argument short, things might be otherwise.[14]

I Live seems to me a kind of baroque mourning-play, a series of dramatic scenes whose relation is arbitrary in Benjamin's terms, or "confused," as her biographer puts it. (It might almost be called her *Guernica* in the way it assembles images of violence and suffering.) Sitwell's allegory gives a new meaning to the fragments of Swift's life and writings by relating his horror of nature and the feminine to the horrors of the First World War and "the primal horror of Germany at present." Sitwell uses a "death-mask" description of the eighteenth-century writer to represent precisely what she saw as untimely, sorrowful, and unsuccessful in modern civilization:

> His face, which had been furrowed with thought, was now without a single line to speak of the life within; it was placid and mindless.
>
> So he sat, day after day; and all day long, beneath his window, the footsteps sounded. Sometimes it seemed as if a nation of horses was galloping in a universe of dust; at other moments they were the enormous clatter of a race of paralytics, dancing over the world of the betrayed dead, or the footsteps of the blind—one blind man after another, one blind man after another, finding their way in an unending straight line through a cosmos of gigantic and of universal night, their sticks tapping with a hollow noise upon the slippery ball of the earth. (1937, 398–99)

Similarly, in the figures of Anna, who mourns the child she never had, and of the English mother, who loses her son on the battlefield, *I Live Under a Black Sun* reflects a point made by Kristeva: that the narrative of modernity, or progress as the increased mastery of nature, generates as its dialectical counterpart the compensatory figure of the *mater dolorosa*. The mourning mother persists as the negative face of "civilization," registering the cost of human suffering, which its triumphs have brought (Britzolakis 1999, 179). The notion of two nations, referred to in the epigraph to the novel, is thus given gender as well as class applications. The closing image of the allegory, both apocalyptic and bathetic, is of mice and men:

> Rather than share the piece of bread that had fallen from the giant's hand, they were willing to be wiped out. Squealing and shrieking among the dust, they rushed to destroy each other.
>
> And outside, his paw outstretched, the cat was waiting, watching.
>
> Let them fight. Let them destroy each other.
>
> Then will come Darkness.
>
> Darkness. (1937, 400)

Sitwell's anti-war novel is lyrical, incantatory, and often biblical in its language, whereas Woolf's essay *Three Guineas* is closely argued, well researched, and footnoted. Woolf's "photographs of dead bodies and ruined houses" (2000, 210), a reference to newspaper reports of the bombings and atrocities of the Spanish Civil War, operate as a significant absence within Woolf's essay, whereas Sitwell's allegory, like a newsreel, returns repeatedly to images of dead bodies and ruined buildings. Woolf links religion, in the institutionalized form of the church and its ministers, with other patriarchal and oppressive social institutions. (A photograph of an archbishop is included with those of a general, a judge, and male academics, for example.) Sitwell, on the other hand, uses the religious ideals represented in the Old and New Testaments (justice, compassion, and peace) as a source of alternative values against which to test and judge the modern world she portrays: war, poverty, and man's inhumanity to man — a move that with hindsight one might say anticipates her later conversion to Catholicism. (She was received in 1955 by Father Martin d'Arcy with Evelyn Waugh as her godfather.) Although both women writers use biography as a form of history, one of the most interesting differences between these two texts is the fact that Woolf's examples of "masculinism" are men in positions of power—patriots and heads of families—and it is their investment in warfare that she sets out to investigate (Barrrett 2000, ix). Sitwell, on the other hand, stages the drive for power and authority and the repudiation of the feminine in the figure of Swift, a creative writer whose work she admired, a less polarized target subject, which allows the female author (and reader) to identify and acknowledge her own will to power.

There are, of course, other obvious differences of form, style, and argument between the two texts. Woolf's projected new literary form, the "Novel-Essay," which, as described by Barrett, "would interleave fictional scenes and social interpretation" (2000, lix), might have been much closer in form to Sitwell's "allegory." Nevertheless, *I Live Under a Black Sun* is clearly concerned with the same problem addressed by Woolf in her essay, namely: "how to prevent war?" (2000, 121). The question of prevention leads each to questions about causality and this, it seems to me, is the real point of connection between the two texts. For both writers link war with power and masculinity and, in doing so, challenge conventional notions of where power resides. Power and "the political" are not simply enshrined in the state or nation that goes to war, but dispersed throughout a range of institutions—the judiciary and the education system as well as the army. Writers as well as generals may seek and exercise power. Thus each seeks an explanation for war in the connections between the military and the cultural, the public and the private, the masculine and the feminine. Virginia Woolf's point, that the public and private worlds are inseparably connected and that the tyrannies and servilities of the one are the tyrannies and servilities of the other (2000, 270), is illustrated in her portraits of patriarchs who require an angel in the house—and in Sitwell's portrayal of Stella/Anna who sacrifices her life to the man of genius. It is this analysis, one that charts the flow of power throughout state and civil society and enlarges the notion of what is "political," that underpins Woolf's patriotic patriarchs and Sitwell's abjected mothers.[15]

Woolf, as a feminist, was severely criticized for her attempt to make these connections (Lee 1996, 692), whereas with Sitwell, an icon of eccentricity, the same themes escaped largely unnoticed. Both essay and allegory were written in response to debates in the 1930s over peace and war, debates discussed by Hermione Lee in her biography of Woolf (1996, 684–91). For the rise of dictatorships in Europe, the wars in Abyssinia and Spain, the refugees and homelessness caused by mass migration, and, above all, the threat of a second world war created for these writers, as for so many others,[16] what Benjamin calls a "crisis in values," a crisis that challenged their pacifism, their liberalism, and their views on the separation of art from politics. Both responded by breaking form: Sitwell, the poet, by writing an allegorical novel; Woolf, the modernist novelist, by producing an uncharacteristic chronicle-novel, *The Years,* and an antagonistic sociological essay called *Three Guineas*. The example underlines the point that changes in form, at the level of the individual writer or within modernism more generally, are driven by historical factors. Or as Woolf says to her correspondent at the end of *Three Guineas*, "we can best help you to prevent war not by repeating your words and following your methods but by finding new words and creating new methods" (2000, 272).

One of the reasons to re-read *I Live Under a Black Sun* is not to acclaim it as a "forgotten masterpiece," although as Evelyn Waugh commented, "it is a terrifying book" (quoted in Glendinning 1981, 211), but to remind ourselves of the complexities of another period and what Alison Light calls its "traumatised relation to modernity" (1991, 11). Examining the similarities and differences between interwar narratives thus operates as a check on our narrativization of them, a reality-testing of our present projections. Putting neglected, non-canonical writings back into dialogue with now familiar texts, like *Three Guineas* or *Nightwood*, not only contextualizes these but also enhances our understanding of the relations between literature and history.

Notes

1. For examples of renewed interest in Sitwell's poetry see Celeste Schenck (1989) and Deborah Tyler Bennett (1996).

2. Sitwell was accused of plagiarizing F. R. Leavis and Herbert Read in her 1934 book *Aspects of Modern Poetry.* The accusations led to a long-running controversy. She was defended by "a young lawyer," John Sparrow, who became a friend and to whom *I Live Under a Black Sun* is dedicated. For an account see Geoffrey Elborn, who claims, "There is little doubt that Edith *did* plagiarize" (1981, 114). (The dialogue on wearing black cited on page 3 of the novel bears a close resemblance to the opening of Chekhov's *The Seagull.*)

3. For Swift's relationship with "Stella" (Esther Johnson, d. 1728) see Swift's "Journal to Stella." Esther Johnson was one of the lasting attachments of Swift's life. They may have married in secret, but their relationship was not physical. The story of Swift's love affair with "Vanessa" (Esther Vanhomrigh, 1690–1723) is related in Swift's poem "Cadenus and Vanessa." After initially encouraging her, Swift did not return Vanessa's passion for him. His rupture with her c. 1723 over a letter she wrote to Stella led to Vanessa's early death.

4. The opposition in Blake's poem is between the love which "seeketh not Itself to please" and that which "seeketh only Self to please, / To bind another to Its delight, / Joys in another's loss of ease, / And builds a Hell in Heaven's despite." Sitwell claimed in a letter to L. P. Hartley that "Blake [comes] nearest to being my ideal poet" (1997, 244). For an account of Sitwell's relation to Tchelitchew see Parker Tyler's *The Divine Comedy of Pavel Tchelitchew* (1967).

5. Gérard de Nerval 1999, 28–29. Sitwell's interest in nineteenth-century French poetry is well documented; she was introduced to Baudelaire, Verlaine, and Rimbaud by her companion Helen Rootham and wrote an introduction to the latter's translation of *Les Illuminations* (1932). She quotes the first quatrain of Rimbaud's "Ma Boheme" on page 161 of the novel. De Nerval's "El Desdichado" is also quoted in Canto I of *The Waste Land.* The Black Sun Press, established in Paris in 1924 by Harry and Caresse Crosby, also drew on the poem for its name (see Benstock 1987, 391–92).

6. See Rinsler's analysis of "El Desdichado" (de Nerval 1999, 117).

7. T. S. Eliot's editing role is detailed in Herring 1996, 226 ff.

8. Sitwell's comment on Swift (cited in full in the next section) is from a 1939 letter to Raymond Marriott (1997, 208). The strongest reading of *Nightwood* as an allegory of Europe between the wars is Jane Marcus's "Laughing at Leviticus." Joseph Frank uses the term "spatial form" in his reading of *Nightwood,* in which he claims that it "combines the simple majesty of a medieval morality play with the verbal subtlety and refinement of a symbolist poem" and that "*Nightwood* carries the evolution of spatial form in the novel forward to a point where it is practically indistinguishable from modern poetry" (1963, 48). Both these comments are relevant to *I Live Under a Black Sun.*

9. See also Harvie Ferguson, who locates a shift in the differentiation/periodization of melancholy which he links to the work of Søren Kierkegaard, the nineteenth-century philosopher whose *Sickness unto Death* claimed melancholy as a characteristic way of existing in the modern world: "That our age is an age of mental depression, there is no doubt" (cited in Ferguson 1995, 31). Nietzsche's claim that the death of God, because unmourned, has left a similar legacy is also invoked.

10. See also Kaja Silverman (1998) and Juliana Schiesari (1992) for detailed discussions of Kristeva's—and Luce Irigaray's— theories of melancholy.

11. Judith Butler challenges the logic of this argument in relation to women's position as "melancholy heterosexuals" in *Gender Trouble* (1990, 57–70).

12. From Barnes's letter to E. Coleman, July 22, 1936.

13. The Popular Front, particularly in France and Spain, was an attempt to form a united alliance of left and bourgeois democratic movements against fascism. The Marxist writer Jack Lindsay was in no doubt about Sitwell's left political sympathies and reports a later comment by Harry Pollitt, general secretary of the British Communist Party: "Aye, the lass's heart is in the right place" (1968, 126).

14. For a full discussion of Benjamin's views on allegory see Pensky 1993, chapter 3, and Wolin (1982, 63–77).

15. The terms "state" and "civil society" were used in this way by Antonio Gramsci, writing in prison in the 1930s (though not yet published at the time). Sitwell's and Woolf's notion of the dispersed nature of power might also be called Foucauldian, insofar as their emphasis is on structures of power rather than on class and since they see power as embodied in networks of institutions and their associated discourses.

16. For a discussion of other antifascist fiction of the period see Joannou 1995, Chapter 6.

Works Cited

Barnes, Djuna. 1936. *Nightwood.* London: Faber and Faber.

Barrett, Michele. 2000. Introduction to *A Room of One's Own and Three Guineas,* Virginia Woolf. Harmondsworth, UK: Penguin.

Benjamin, Walter. 1970. *Illuminations*. Edited and translated by Harry Zohn. London: Jonathan Cape.

———. 1977. *The Origin of German Tragic Drama.* Trans. John Osborne. London: Verso.

Bennett, Deborah Tyler. 1996. *Edith Sitwell: The Forgotten Modernist*. Sheffield, UK: PAVIC Publications.

Benstock, Shari. 1987. *Women of the Left Bank: Paris, 1900–1940.* London: Virago.

Bowen, Stella. 1987. *Drawn from Life*. London: Virago.

Britzolakis, Christina. 1999. *Sylvia Plath and the Theatre of Mourning*. Oxford: Clarendon Press.

Butler, Judith. 1990. *Gender Trouble: Feminism and the Subversion of Identity*. New York: Routledge.

Chambers, Ross. 1993. *The Writing of Melancholy: Modes of Opposition in Early French Modernism.* Trans. Mary Seidman Trouille. Chicago: University of Chicago Press.

Elborn, Geoffrey. 1981. *Edith Sitwell: A Biography*. London: Sheldon Press.

Ferguson, Harvie. 1995. *Melancholy and the Critique of Modernity: Sören Kierkegaard's Religious Psychology*. London: Routledge.

Foster, Hal. 1996. *The Return of the Real: the Avant-garde at the Turn of the Century*. Cambridge, MA: MIT Press.

Frank, Joseph. 1963. *The Widening Gyre: Crisis and Mastery in Modern Literature*. New Brunswick, NJ: Rutgers University Press.

Glendinning, Victoria. 1981. *Edith Sitwell: A Unicorn Among Lions*. Oxford: Oxford University Press.

Herring, Phillip. 1996. *Djuna: The Life and Work of Djuna Barnes*. New York: Penguin.

Joannou, Maroula. 1995. *"Ladies, Please Don't Smash These Windows."* Oxford: Berg.

Kristeva, Julia. 1989. *Black Sun: Depression and Melancholia*. Trans. Leon Roudiez. New York: Columbia University Press.

Leavis, F. R. 1932. *New Bearings in English Poetry*. London: Chatto and Windus.

Lee, Hermione. 1996. *Virginia Woolf*. London: Chatto and Windus.

Light, Alison. 1991. *Forever England: Femininity, Literature and Conservatism between the Wars*. London: Routledge.

Lindsay, Jack. 1968. *Meetings with Poets*. London: Frederic Muller.

Marcus, Jane. 1991. "Laughing at Leviticus: *Nightwood* as Woman's Circus Epic." In *Silence and Power: A Reevaluation of Djuna Barnes*. Edited by Mary Lynn Broe and Catharine Stimpson, 221–50. Carbondale: Southern Illinois University Press.

———. Forthcoming. "Outlaws: The Making of the Woman Poet as a Perfect Stranger." In *White Looks, Black Books: The Making of Modernist Primitivism*.

Nerval, Gérard de. 1999. *Les Chimères*. Trans. William Stone. London: Menard Press.

Oliver, Kelly. 1993. *Reading Kristeva: Unravelling the Double-bind*. Bloomington: Indiana University Press.

Pensky, Max. 1993. *Melancholy Dialectics: Walter Benjamin and the Play of Mourning*. Amherst: University of Massachusetts Press.

Schenck, Celeste M. 1989. "Exiled by Genre." In *Women's Writing in Exile*. Edited by Mary Lynn Broe and Angela Ingram. Chapel Hill: University of North Carolina Press.

Schiesari, Juliana. 1992. *The Gendering of Melancholia: Feminism, Psychoanalysis and the Symbolics of Loss in Renaissance Literature*. Ithaca, NY: Cornell University Press.

Shawe-Taylor, Desmond. 1937. "Recent Fiction." *New Statesman and Nation* 2 (October).

Silverman, Kaja. 1988. *The Acoustic Mirror: The Female Voice in Psychoanalysis and Cinema*. Bloomington: Indiana University Press.

Sitwell, Edith. 1932. Introduction to *Les Illuminations* by Rimbaud. Trans. Helen Rootham. London: Faber and Faber.

———. 1934. *Aspects of Modern Poetry*. London: Duckworth.

———. 1937. *I Live Under a Black Sun*. London: Gollancz.

———. 1957. *Collected Poems*. London: Macmillan.

———. 1965. *Taken Care Of*. London: Macmillan.

———. 1997. *Selected Letters of Edith Sitwell*. Edited by Richard Greene. London: Virago.

Swift, Jonathan. 1948. *Journal to Stella* 2 vols. Edited by Harold Williams. Oxford: Clarendon Press.

———. 1958. "Cadenus and Vanessa." *Collected Poems*, vol. 2 Edited by Harold Williams. Oxford: Clarendon Press.

Tyler, Parker. 1967. *The Divine Comedy of Pavel Tchelitchew*. London: Weidenfeld and Nicolson.

Wolin, Richard. 1982. *Walter Benjamin: An Aesthetic of Redemption*. New York: Columbia University Press.

Woolf, Virginia. 2000. *A Room of One's Own and Three Guineas*. 1929, 1938. Edited and Introduction by Michele Barrett. Harmondsworth, UK: Penguin.

The Mysterious Politics of Dorothy Sayers

LILLIAN S. ROBINSON

WHAT YOU ARE ABOUT TO READ IS A MYSTERY DISGUISED AS A CRITICAL article. In a sense, of course, any title addressing "the politics of" something promises exposure. Although the revelations may not always be as exciting as the final-scene gathering of the suspects where the murderer is tricked into a confession, the "politics of" formula does uncover *a* politics, on either the world-historic or the personal register or both, in sites that are usually assumed to be politically neutral. In the present case, I am attempting to work through a highly personal and political mystery, namely: Why do I, and so many of my *cosoeurs*—academics, feminists, socialists, all of us women whose research and activism situates gender in the context of class, race, nation, and sexual orientation—consider Dorothy L. Sayers to be a foremother, and her masterpiece, *Gaudy Night* (1935), a book that belongs peculiarly to us? Why does the novel's evocation of an Oxford women's college in the 1930s seem to us to evoke, as well, our own spiritual home?

I first embraced Sayers's invented Shrewsbury College as my true belong-place when I was a doctoral student in the mid-1960s. Even then, however, I glimpsed the contradiction—which only became more salient as my academic and political work acquired increasing definition—between my militancy and what amounted to my nostalgia for Shrewsbury. And the issue came to a head in 1998, when my own detective novel, *Murder Most Puzzling*, was published.

One reviewer remarked that my book resembled a "thinner, less disciplined *Gaudy Night*." The friend who was with me when I read this review proffered loyal if misplaced consolation: "Well, if they'd said, 'This first novel of a young man's development is a thinner, less disciplined *Sorrows of the Young Werther*,' the author would consider it high praise." I assured him I recognized a compliment when I received one, adding, "After all, *Gaudy Night* is Sayers's master work. *Her* first novel was a piece of anti-Semitic claptrap!" Why then did the comparison to Sayers delight me? In fact, it is the continuity between the racism of this early novel and the peculiar brand of feminism espoused in Sayers's work that makes an uncritical embrace of Shrewsbury College so problematic.

Sayers's first novel, *Whose Body?*, was published in 1923, more than a decade before *Gaudy Night*. It thus dates from a moment when the Great War was recent enough that Lord Peter Wimsey's nervousness can be credibly attributed to his experiences in battle. Contemporaries were learning the hard way that "shell shock" might recede and yet continue to resonate in veterans' postwar sensibility for many years. Nevertheless, Lord Peter's initial attitude toward the corpse the police are having trouble identifying is notably lighthearted: "We've both got a body in the bath," he sings, as he and Inspector Parker attempt to connect this new murder with the crime that Parker is investigating, the disappearance of a prominent Jewish financier (1968, 23).

Although writing in the postwar moment, Sayers does not explore Lord Peter's posttraumatic stress disorder, as Virginia Woolf and Rebecca West used shell shock in their work, in order to say something about England, war, or masculinity. Indeed, it is never the sight of violence or its gruesome aftermath that provokes one of Lord Peter's devastating flashbacks, but rather the moment of confronting the moral consequences of his deductions—for example, the culpability of a brilliant and successful aristocrat in *Whose Body?* or the hanging of the murderer he'd helped to convict in *Busman's Honeymoon*.

Writing *Whose Body?* just as Mussolini was seizing power in Italy and years before Hitler and Mosley became actors on the world scene, Sayers could still permit amiable characters to echo in milder form her villain's murderous anti-Semitism. The body in the bath is that of a vagrant who, despite having been hastily barbered and groomed after death, could not be long mistaken for the missing Jewish magnate. His dirty toenails, flea-bites, and odor of hard carbolic soap, as well as his uncircumcised organ, make it abundantly clear that he is not Sir Reuben Levy. The corpse of a deceased street person makes headlines only because of the spectacular circumstances of its discovery, naked except for a pair of pince-nez, in the tub of a respectable Bayswater architect, whereas Sir Reuben's disappearance, even before his death is discovered, has a serious impact on the stock exchange. As Lord Peter's clubman friend Freddy Arbuthnot puts it, "Old Levy bunkin' off like that's knocked the bolts out of the market!" (1968, 61).

Whenever the financier's disappearance is discussed, his Jewishness invariably leads to a certain levity. Inspector Parker explains that the peculiar circumstances force one "to suppose that a respectable middle-aged Hebrew financier . . . went mad between midnight and six a.m. and walked quietly out of the house in his birthday suit on a November night" (1968, 26). That the financier in question is not only respectable and middle-aged but also "Hebrew" apparently adds to the absurdity of his suppositious public nakedness.

In a similar vein, the Dowager Duchess of Denver recalls that Lady Levy had been of good (thus, needless to specify, gentile) family, and had faced strong parental opposition to her marriage. In one inconsequential speech, the Dowager delivers herself of the following observations:

> That was before he made his money, of course. . . . He was very handsome, then, you know, dear, in a foreign-looking way, but he hadn't any means, and the Fords didn't like his religion. Of course, we're all Jews nowadays, and they wouldn't have minded so much if he'd pretended to be something else. . . and I'm sure some Jews are very good people and personally I'd much rather they believe something, though of course it must be very inconvenient . . . . Still. . . ." (1968, 45–46).

As her character evolves through the series, Lord Peter's mother is uniformly understood to be a "delightful" lady, in both substance and style, and these remarks of hers are meant to show off her charm. By contrast, Sir Reuben's valet says he "doesn't hold with Jews as a rule," but admits that "no one could call Sir Reuben vulgar" (1968, 53).

Of course, it is the murderer, Sir Julian Freke, who is the true anti-Semite, reducing his old rival in love, who has for years been married to the woman both courted in youth, to the most abject of conditions. The anonymous corpse in the bath was simply a homeless man who needed to be disposed of, once Freke, a distinguished "nerve specialist," had relegated Sir Reuben's body to the dissecting slab for which the anonymous carcass had been slated. In the anatomy lab, the body parts were distributed among the medical students for dissection. Lord Peter asks his informant whether his classmates "made all the usual jokes about it," and learns that the "local funny man, so to speak," had referred to the subject as "the old Sheeny" when the part he was allotted turned out to be circumcised. But, the young man continues, Freke had "bagged the head himself." It is subsequently discovered that the notable nerve man has had the nerve to visit upon that head all the indignities he can imagine, rendering it, in the process, both grotesque and unrecognizable (1968, 153).

So, prior to burial in a pauper's grave, Sir Reuben had been transformed into a set of anonymous naked parts and organs, marked dead, marked male, marked Jew, a dissected cadaver despoiled of its brain and individual identity—all for the crime of committing consensual marital sex with an Englishwoman. Sensing Parker's skepticism about whether "people keep up old jealousies for twenty years," Wimsey explains," Sex is every man's loco spot . . . he'll take a disappointment, but not a humiliation. . . . It isn't the girl Freke would bother about—it's having his aristocratic nose put out of joint by a little Jewish nobody" (1968, 158). Sayers certainly considers Freke, who has enacted this revenge on the Jew, to be a madman, even assigning him a surname suggestive of abnormality and appropriate to his inhuman actions. She thereby leaves room for the reader to recognize in the murder and its motive the logical consequences of the sexual nightmares that racism breeds. But the author herself never loses the light touch with which she portrays the grotesqueries she conjures up for us.

The problem is that what has been visited upon the body of the Jew, acts that are pruriently dwelt upon through the process of showing Lady Levy only selected portions of the exhumed body, is not represented as grotesque *enough*. It is not, at any rate, powerful enough to bring on Lord Peter's psychological relapse. This reaction comes only with the realization that the perpetrator is one of his own race and class. Wimsey even puts his own life in jeopardy by confronting Freke under pretext of consulting the specialist about his nervous condition. And, even after he has succeeded in aborting both his own murder and Freke's suicide, we learn from the first pages of the next volume in the series, *Clouds of Witness*, that Lord Peter actually followed the demented alienist's advice and took a rest cure in the Mediterranean once the case was concluded (1966, 7).

In *Gaudy Night*, by contrast, the Jewish Question enters the narrative only obliquely and momentarily. One such moment occurs when Harriet Vane contemplates the name-cards affixed to the doors of student rooms in Shrewsbury College, Oxford: "Miss H. Brown, Miss Jones, Miss Colburn, Miss Szleposky, Miss Isaacson" (1970, 104). With these last two, as Jane Marcus points out, we are meant to notice that "[Virginia] Woolf's Angelas and Marys here have Eastern European and Jewish roommates." Jane Marcus speculates that there may be a polluting significance in the fact that "instead of bowls of milk, Sayers sees shoes and 'little heaps of soiled crockery' outside the women's rooms" (1987, 158). Do Szelposky and Isaacson, one wonders, bring exceptionally smelly shoes and unimaginably dirty dishes into the crisp single-sex world of the women's college?

Generally speaking, the politics of *Gaudy Night* center more on matters of gender and class than of race and ethnicity. Indeed, even when nazism is mentioned, Sayers has nothing to say about anti-Semitism and its possible connection with anti-feminism. Commenting on college girls' apparent propensity for pranks, Shrewsbury's genial porter remarks, "Wot this country wants is a 'Itler," to which the painter's foreman, called in to repair the results of vandalism that is, of course, the villain's handiwork and not that of the women undergraduates, replies, "That's right—keep the girls at 'ome" (1970, 114).

More to the point, the "poison pen," by which name the villain is designated until she is unmasked, not only mutilates books in which male scholars are attacked or in which scientific integrity is defended, but one in which a female scholar attacks the status of women under the Nazis. For the woman academic, as for the working-class men who comment on Hitler's Germany, the repression of women is noteworthy, that of the Jews invisible—or at least unmentionable. Combined with the vicious class assumptions at the heart of Sayers's narrative, the refusal to connect the radical misogyny of fascism with its rabid anti-Semitism creates the feminism of *Gaudy Night.* The novel asserts the priorities of late nineteenth- and early twentieth-century British feminism, with the struggle for higher education and professions at its heart. Dorothy Sayers, a member of the first generation of women to receive degrees from Oxford, shows us a women's college that continually has to re-earn and rejustify its place in the university world, perpetually demonstrating its *gravitas* and avoiding not merely the occasions of academic transgression but their very appearance. Only a man as enlightened as Lord Peter Wimsey can state that the question of women's higher education has already been satisfactorily answered and that, in any event, it would be no business of his to pontificate on the rights and wrongs of the matter. "You should not imply" says he to the Warden of Shrewsbury, "that I have a right either to oppose or disapprove."

"I assure you," she replies, "that even in Oxford we still encounter a certain number of people who maintain their right to disapprove."

"And I had hoped I was returning to civilization" (1970, 314). Lord Peter, I need hardly remind us all, is a fictional character.

Sayers herself, when asked whether she thought "women" ought to study Aristotle, rejected the corporate noun, maintaining, "The answer is NOT that all women would be the better for knowing about Aristotle . . . but simply: What women want as a class is irrelevant. *I* want to know about Aristotle . . . and there is nothing in my shape and bodily functions which need prevent me knowing about him" (1947, "Are Women Human?" 121). It was Sayers's eccentric custom to go about the streets and even the street*cars* of London dressed in her Oxford M.A. gown. We may recall that, in Lord Peter's final, successful marriage proposal to Harriet Vane, he addresses her as "magistra," meaning, of course, both mistress and Master—of Arts (1970, 440).

In their posters, pageants, and parades, both the British and the American women's suffrage movements made use of the image of the woman graduate sporting her academic regalia, the point being to contrast that icon's unfranchised status with that of less worthy, uneducated males. However class-biased such representation may have been, the suffragists were at least making a statement about the civil rights of educated women as a body. By contrast, popping about London in her robes, Sayers was making a laughingstock of herself and perhaps the notion of women's higher education, even as her get-up proclaimed that, whatever women in general might do, *she* indeed "knew Aristotle."

In *A Room of One's Own* (1929), one of the most important feminist books to appear in the twentieth century, Virginia Woolf also bases her arguments about the condition of women in general upon their status in Britain's two oldest universities which, despite the volume's origin in Woolf's Cambridge lectures, she deliberately calls "Oxbridge." Woolf's discursive universe is one in which the metaphors reflect and ricochet off one another, so that the famous 500 pounds and a room of one's own are a metaphor for the life of leisurely intellectual privilege that "Oxbridge" provides its male—but not its female—students, at the same time that university education in the masculine register is a metaphor for the intellectual independence essential to the writing that is to be subsidized by the 500 pounds and carried out in that room of one's own.

It is Jane Marcus's contention in two breathtaking pages of her essay "Taking the Bull by the Udders" that "it is unclear if *Gaudy Night* was meant as a deliberate reply to" *A Room of One's Own*, but she characterizes Sayers's novel as an intentional slap at feminism in general and at academic feminism in particular (1987, 158). Before examining this argument, however, we should recall that *A Room of One's Own* was not Woolf's last word on feminism or even on women and higher education. Rather, nearly a decade after *A Room of One's Own* and two years after *Gaudy Night*, Woolf published *Three Guineas*, a document that roots *its* feminism in its immediate historic moment, the 1930s, connecting the situation of women to rising fascism, international economic turmoil, and the adumbrations of war. Here, instead of mooning after her brother's elite education, the Woolfian "daughter of an educated man" is exhorted to make common cause with the other groups excluded from privilege, the working classes of both sexes and the dark-skinned victims of imperialism, all of them constituting a defiant Outsiders' Society and creating a Poor College that will meet new and hitherto unimagined educational needs, one of which is the need to empower the disempowered (1938, 33–36).

By contrast, *Gaudy Night* is a novel of the 1930s chiefly in its relation to the history of women and higher education. Sayers's Shrewsbury College has reached a certain stage in its development, established if not yet secure, a stage at which alumna Harriet Vane rails, "*We* haven't got room for women who aren't and never will be scholars. It's all right for the men's colleges to have hearty passmen" (1970, 153). Sayers seems initially to be almost unaware of the larger history being made in the thirties. The threat of a second world war, she has Lord Peter far from presciently remark, has "made a noise like a hoop and rolled away"(1970, 268). She does, however, mention the Nazis' antifeminism, which makes it (just) possible to interpret the villain's casting of vituperation and excrement on women's search for knowledge as something like the backlash of the "little men" who rallied to Hitler's clarion-call. Only in this case, it's even more tellingly the "little woman," woman as traditional wife under patriarchy, who strikes back against Shrewsbury's new-style women in language not so far from what Hitler and his propagandists used against the Jews.

So Sayers really *is* on the side of the angels, isn't she? Jane Marcus thinks not, seeing in what others read as an ideal community of women "a nightmare of repressed sexuality, jealousy, and hatred." (After all, Sayers did not *have* to choose Bess of Hardwick for her college's tutelary spirit, so that the establishment's very name tells us it's a town of shrews.) Marcus adds, "Sayers's most telling response to Woolf is her bitter argument that women cannot cross class in sisterhood. Sayers's villain, the passionate hater of all intellectual women, is the very charwoman Woolf idealizes in all of her writing. To Woolf, the women's college is a dairy or nunnery, to Sayers it is a toilet or madhouse. The cleaning woman dirties the woman's library. Nothing could be further from Woolf's vision of their common cause" (1987, 158–59).

The problem for Sayers is that she could not be against higher education for women generally or their progress in the professions without opposing her own opportunities. Whatever her feelings about other women, *she* can't "know about Aristotle"—at least in an institutional setting—unless some other women are permitted to know about him, as well. Sayers could, however, create Harriet Vane as a principled feminist and proceed to imagine for her the only man who always knows better than she does. Not only does Lord Peter complete and cleverly cap her verses for her, he comes up with a more feminist explanation for the "poison pen" mystery than she has been able to devise. Having determined on a "spot of celibacy" for herself, he tells her, she has allowed her imagination to people the academic cloister with obscene, "unnatural" monsters, whereas the obscenity and monstrosity actually come from a working-class, heterosexual woman loyal beyond death to a man emasculated by women scholars.

If the Woolf of *Three Guineas* and the Sayers of *Gaudy Night* see their respective colleges as offering women an alternative to the patriarchal family—"the private house, with its nullity, its immorality, its hypocrisy, its servility" (Woolf 1938, 74)—Sayers makes it only a temporary haven for a select few. For it is from Shrewsbury College, rather than from her father's house (both of her parents being, as it happens, conveniently deceased), that in *Busman's Honeymoon* (1937), Harriet Vane is married to Peter Wimsey, entering thereby a clan that is not only patriarchal in structure but also the wealthiest ducal family in England, a household where assimilation comes to mean acceptance by the (of course male) ghost who benignly haunts Dukes Denver, Woolf's "private house" writ very large indeed. And we must not ask what he is the ghost *of* or the fun is spoiled.

Meanwhile, for most women, Sayers sees the choice—if it is a choice—between mind and body as absolute and definitive. Either you are part of the academic cloister or you have a heterosexual life. Only Sayers herself, albeit with a sometimes disabling sense of culpability, could "have it all" in her own life and allow Harriet Vane, at the height of her author's professional achievement to "dwindle," in Millament's deathless phrase, "into a wife."

I think—I hope—I have been suggesting up to this point that there is more than one kind of feminism, and that, if Sayers's ideal is more limited than we might wish, we should not use the vantage point of the twenty-first century to read her more idiosyncratic and individualistic politics out of feminism itself. Yet the critique only becomes harsher if we refocus the argument on the issue that is central to *Gaudy Night*, *A Room of One's Own*, and, far modestly, my own novel: the question of whether feminism needs to redefine the ethical and political bases of truth-seeking itself and of the institutions within which the quest is carried out.

The reason Shrewsbury College's "scout" or cleaner is so bitter is that her late husband, a historian aspiring to a Chair, committed suicide after being detected in an act of academic dishonesty. It was Miss Helen De-

Vine, recently appointed a Fellow at Shrewsbury College, who, several years back, caught him tampering with historical evidence—that is, ignoring and even concealing a document that would call his premature conclusions into question. In the name of intellectual purity, Miss DeVine alerted the other members of the jury or thesis committee of his malfeasance, thus effectively ending his academic career. (Note how this discourse of evidence-tampering, juries, and malfeasance echoes that of criminal courts.) Since the young scholar's breach of integrity was inspired by his need to support his wife and children, that wife, now a widow, considers Miss DeVine no better than a murderess and attributes the Fellow's professional stance to her unwomanly nature, her violation of the correct, divinely mandated order of things, in which the entire women's college, which shelters her and her like and has singled DeVine out for special honor, is also complicit.

Not only does the college necessarily contain a library for the use of women, but that library contains a novel, *The Search* (1935), in which C. P. Snow asserts the importance of intellectual honesty in the pursuit of science. This is the book that has had black ink spilled over its pages some time after the library itself was attacked and fouled. When Miss DeVine herself finally recalls the story of the young man whose dishonesty she'd uncovered, all the other female dons, as well as their guests, Harriet Vane and Peter Wimsey, agree that hers had been the only possible response, that she'd done the only right thing (1970, 326–31). But even they add that most women, inferentially "normal" women, would never put principle above human needs and relationships. (We are in Carol Gilligan country here, only the terms are reversed, so that, whereas Gilligan valorizes a female relationship-based ethics over abstractions, the most advanced women in Sayers's novel fully identify with "masculine" academic values.) This proves to poor addled Annie that the whole kit and boiling of them are indeed and by their own admission contemptible freaks. What Sayers is telling us here is that women—at least those few who make it their life—do belong in the academy, for these chosen ones nobly uphold the highest standards of scholarly integrity. I submit that this is why we love *Gaudy Night*—because it validates us as academics and the principles by which we conduct our own search for the truth. Unfortunately, in so doing, we are inevitably forced to affirm that that pure, disinterested search is indeed what the university is about.

But ought we to encourage for one minute the belief that the male-dominated academy is the site of a pure, disinterested search for truth? Isn't that akin to accepting the view that it is we, as feminist scholars, who are engaged in politicizing (and hence polluting) this pristine institution? Don't we know that it was always already highly political—Sayers's Oxford as much as, say, Amanda Cross's Harvard and Columbia, Jane Langton's Harvard, Susan Kenney's Canterbury, or Clare Munnings's Sanderson—all of these being the venues of academic mysteries written by American women in the late twentieth century, in which it turns out that it was the dean, the president, or the university itself that committed the murder? If we take the time to rehearse the Seven Deadly Sins—Pride, Anger, Envy, Avarice, Gluttony, Sloth, and Lust—don't we see them daily exhibited by our colleagues, especially those who most ardently protest feminist politicization of what used to be *their* campus? And isn't this observation, informed by the politics of the 1930s, the measure of the distance from *A Room of One's Own* to *Three Guineas*?

When I wrote *Murder Most Puzzling*, I deliberately inserted two *hommages* to Dorothy Sayers into my text. One is the use of the cryptic or British-style crossword puzzle as the source of a clue that solves the murder; this is a device that appears in a couple of Sayers's short stories featuring Lord Peter. The other, more complex tribute entailed focusing my plot on a question of integrity in the conduct and publication of academic research. It is only belatedly that I have come to realize the extent to which my novel, whose working title was *Publish or Perish*, offers a critique of Sayers's central argument, as well as a respectful bow to it.

The problem with which my characters wrestle is whether it is right for feminist scholars to publish the findings of their historical research if those findings could have damaging social consequences for present-day women. Two feminist academics go back and forth on this question, eventually deciding that the truth must be told at all costs, that the struggle cannot be carried on any other way. I then proceed to let them off the hook by having a pair of intrepid undergraduate research assistants, one of them an Italian-American student on full scholarship, discover that the potentially damaging information is not the truth, after all.

In a sense, what enchants us about *Gaudy Night* is its evocation of the beloved community of women functioning within masculine university tradition. It is hard to admit that that community does not, cannot exist unless we build it. But, after the 1930s, Dorothy Sayers increasingly turned her own attention to building another ideal city, that Celestial one for which Bunyan's pilgrims are bound, centered on the only truth she considered absolute, the revealed truth of Christianity. Her feminism, too, changed with this new direction, exchanging Peter Wimsey, constructed as the ideal feminist man for the life of the mind and the flesh, for One she considered the greatest male feminist of all time, the ideal Husband for the life of the spirit:

> Perhaps it is no wonder that women were first at the Cradle and last at the Cross. They had never known a man like this Man—there has never been such another. A prophet and teacher who never nagged at them, never flattered or coaxed or patronized; who never made jokes about them . . . who rebuked without querulousness and praised without condescension; who took their questions and arguments seriously; who never mapped out their sphere for them, never urged them to be feminine or jeered at them for being female; who had no axe to grind and no uneasy male dignity to defend; who took them as he found them and was completely unselfconscious. There is no act, no sermon, no parable in the whole Gospel that borrows its pungency from female perversity; nobody could possibly guess from the words and deeds of Jesus that there was anything "funny" about women's nature. (1947, "The Human-Not-Quite-Human," 148).

Or was Sayers not so much replacing one Lord with another, but *translating* Wimsey to a higher realm? From the 1940s on, Dorothy Sayers translated and wrote essays about Dante and also wrote a number of religious dramas for performance on stage and over the airwaves. Well, weren't these once known as Mystery Plays? And isn't Dostoevsky's Grand Inquisitor warned by Christ himself about the true believer's entangled shibboleths of Mystery, Miracle, and Authority? Feminist scholars may have deliberately abandoned those mighty majuscules, but we still cling to the small-m mysteries, don't we?

Works Cited

Cross, Amanda (pseudonym of Carolyn Heilbrun). 1981. *Death in a Tenured Position.* New York: Dutton.

———. 1989. *A Trap for Fools.* New York: Dutton.

Gilligan, Carol. 1982. *In a Different Voice: Psychological Theory and Women's Development.* Cambridge, MA: Harvard University Press.

Kenney, Susan. 1985. *Graves in Academe.* New York: Viking Penguin.

Langton, Jane. 1979. *The Memorial Hall Murder.* New York: Viking Penguin.

Marcus, Jane. 1987. "Taking the Bull by the Udders: Sexual Difference in Virginia Woolf—A Conspiracy Theory." In *Virginia Woolf and the Languages of Patriarchy.* 136–62. Bloomington: Indiana University Press.

Munnings, Clare (pseudonym of Jill Ker Conway and Elizabeth Kennan). 2000. *Overnight Float.* New York: Norton.

Robinson, Lillian S. 1998. *Murder Most Puzzling: A Literary Mystery*. Westport, CT: Wildcat Publishing.

Sayers, Dorothy. 1947. "Are Women Human?" 1938. In *Unpopular Opinions: Twenty-One Essays*. New York: Harcourt, Brace.

———. 1947. "The Human-Not-Quite-Human." In *Unpopular Opinions: Twenty-One Essays*. 142–149 New York: Harcourt, Brace.

———. 1960. *Busman's Honeymoon*. 1937. New York: Harper.

———. 1966 *Clouds of Witness*. 1926. New York: Avon.

———. 1968. *Whose Body?* 1923. London: New English Library.

———. 1970. *Gaudy Night*. 1935. London: New English Library.

West, Rebecca. 1918. *The Return of the Soldier*. New York: The Century.

Woolf, Virginia. 1925. *Mrs Dalloway*. New York: Harcourt, Brace.

———. 1929. *A Room of One's Own*. NY: Harcourt, Brace.

———. 1938. *Three Guineas*. New York: Harcourt, Brace.

Contributors

GENEVIÈVE BRASSARD is an Assistant Professor of English at the University of Portland, where she teaches Modern British Literature. Her essays and reviews have appeared in *Women's Studies*, *Tulsa Studies in Women's Literature*, *Modernism/Modernity*, and *English Literature in Transition 1880–1920*. Her current research examines literary and cultural representations of female sexuality in the modern city.

JULIA BRIGGS (1943–2007) was a pioneering scholar of women's writing and children's literature. She served as Professor of English Literature at De Montfort University, Leicester, and as Emeritus Fellow of Hertford College, Oxford. She is the author of a history of the ghost story, *Night Visitors* (1977), an account of renaissance literature, *This Stage-Play World* (1983, revised 1997), a biography of the children's writer E. Nesbit (1987), a major study, *Virginia Woolf: An Inner Life* (2005), and a book of essays on *Reading Virginia Woolf* (2006). She has edited Hope Mirrlees's poem *Paris* (for *Gender in Modernism*, ed. Bonnie Kime Scott, 2006), and Shakespeare's *Measure for Measure* (2005).

LINDA CAMARASANA completed her dissertation, "The Bed and the Battlefield: Gender, Sex and Nation in the Trans-Modernist Novel," in summer 2007. She has presented her work at MLA and at the annual conferences of the International Virginia Woolf Society and the Modernist Studies Association. Her current projects include a study of the correspondence between Nancy Cunard and Claude McKay, the elucidation of the concept of trans-modernism, and, building on her dissertation, a book-length consideration of the erotics and heroics of modernist fiction. She has taught at Baruch College, Hunter College, and Queens College and is currently Assistant Professor of English at the State University of New York (SUNY) College at Old Westbury.

MARIANNE GUÉNOT-HOVNANIAN is a translator who has translated many American novels into French, including *Brothers and Keepers* (1991) and

Reuben (1994) by John Edgar Wideman and *The Emperor of Ocean Park* (2004) by Stephen Carter. She now works as translator and interpreter at the Organization for the Prohibition of Chemical Weapons in The Hague, Netherlands.

ROBIN HACKETT is an Associate Professor of English at the University of New Hampshire. She is author of *Sapphic Primitivism: Productions of Race, Class, and Sexuality in Key Works of Modern Fiction* (2004) as well as articles on Virginia Woolf's fiction.

FREDA S. HAUSER is an independent scholar and editor who also works as an adjunct professor, substitute high school teacher, and gardener in Downeast Maine. She recently completed her dissertation, "Pictorial Maneuvers: Women's Great War Stories as Conscientious Objection," on the pacifist literary activism of Olive Schreiner, Charlotte Perkins Gilman, Vernon Lee, and Sylvia Townsend Warner through the University of New Hampshire. Her other publications include an essay on the figure of Anon in Virginia Woolf's writing and several short stories.

PHYLLIS LASSNER teaches Gender Studies, Holocaust Studies, and Writing at Northwestern University. She is the author of two books on Elizabeth Bowen, *British Women Writers of World War II*, many articles on interwar and World War II women writers, and most recently *Colonial Strangers: Women Writing the End of the British Empire*. She is currently writing a book about Anglo-Jewish women writing the Holocaust.

JEAN RADFORD, formerly of Goldsmiths College, University of London, is now a freelance writer/researcher. Editor of *The Progress of Romance*, she is the author of books on Norman Mailer and Dorothy Richardson, and articles on Elizabeth Bowen, Bryher, Amy Lowell, and May Sinclair. She is currently working on a book on women, modernism, and religious belief.

LILLIAN S. ROBINSON (1941–2006) was a pioneer in women's studies and, within it, of feminist literary and cultural criticism. She is the author or co-author of six academic books, including *Sex, Class, and Culture* (1978, reissued 1986), *Night Market: Sexual Cultures and the Thai Economic Miracle* (with Ryan Bishop, 1998), and *Wonder Women: Feminisms and Superheroes* (2004). She also compiled and edited the four-volume reference collection *Modern Women Writers* (1996), and published two chapbooks of poetry and the mystery novel, *Murder Most Puzzling,* mentioned in her contribution to this collection. After holding positions at the University of Paris and in American institutions from MIT to the University of Hawai'i and from the University of Texas to SUNY/Buffalo, Robinson headed the Simone de Beauvoir Institute, the women's studies program at Concordia University, Montreal.

BONNIE KIME SCOTT is Professor and Chair of Women's Studies at San Diego State University. In addition to her edition of the *Selected Letters of Rebecca West* (2000), her books include *Joyce and Feminism* (1984), *Refiguring Modernism* (1995), and the critical anthology *The Gender of Modernism* (1990) and its sequel, *Gender in Modernism: New Geographies, Complex Intersections* (2006). She is working on a study of Virginia Woolf's uses of nature.

CLAIRE M. TYLEE is Senior Lecturer in English at Brunel University, West London, following posts at the Universities of Leicester and Malaga, and an AAUW fellowship at the HHRC, University of Texas. She is best-known for her book *The Great War and Women's Consciousness*, as well as for having edited War Plays by Women and *Women, the First World War and the Dramatic Imagination*. She is at present researching for a book on Jewish writing in Britain and has recently published articles on holocaust memoirs, novels, and plays by Jewish women writers.

GAY WACHMAN was an associate professor in the English Language Studies Department at the State University of New York at Old Westbury until 2007, when she retired. Her book, *Lesbian Empire: Radical Crosswriting in the Twenties* (2001) contextualizes lesbian fiction within and against imperialist sexual ideology.

BARBARA WINSLOW is an Associate Professor in the School of Education and the Coordinator of the Women's Studies Program at Brooklyn College of the City University of New York. She is the author of *Sylvia Pankhurst: Sexual Politics and Political Activism*, 1996. She has been published in *The Feminist Memoir Project: Voices from the Women's Liberation Movement* (eds. Snitow and Duplessis, 1998) and *Voices of Women Historians: The Personal, the Political, and the Professional* (eds. Boris and Chudharri, 1999), and has written many other articles on contemporary feminism. She is working on a book about the women's liberation movement of the 1960s.

TORY YOUNG is a Senior Lecturer in English at Anglia Ruskin University, Cambridge. Her teaching and research specialisms are in Modernism, Contemporary Fiction, and Writing in the Disciplines. She has published several articles on Nancy Cunard, as well as a guide to Michael Cunningham's *The Hours* (Continuum 2003), and is currently completing the Cambridge Guide to Studying Literature for Students (2007). Her next project on Modernist Journeys includes a study of Cunard's long poem "Parallax" as well as an examination of the trope as a narrative device in more well known fictions. She is the main organizer of the London Modernism Seminar Series (www2.sas.ac.uk/ies).

Index